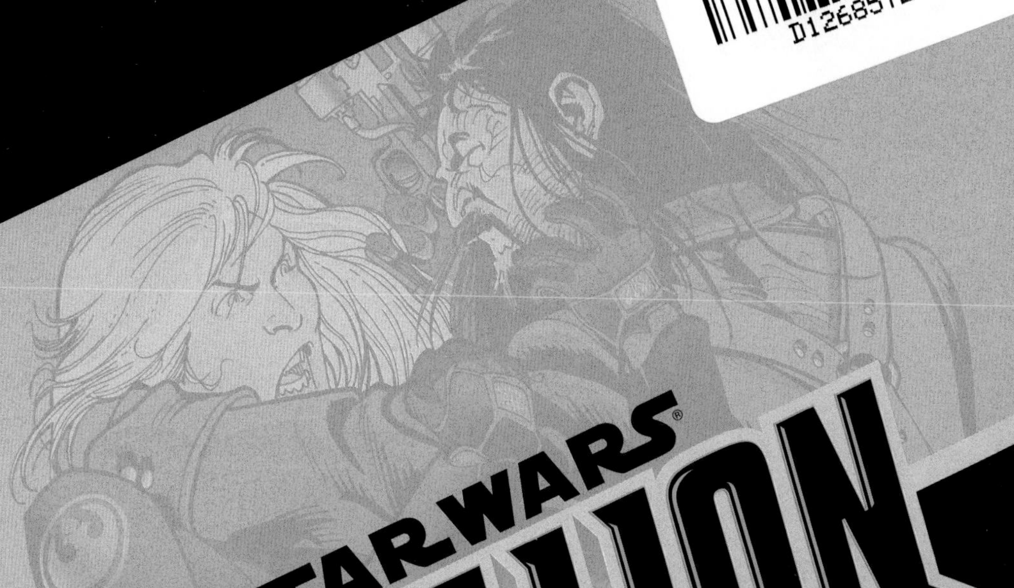

STAR WARS®

REBELLION

volume 3 SMALL VICTORIES

tyranny. Rebel groups unite, and the Galactic Civil War begins. This era begins with the Rebel victory that secured the Death Star plans, and ends a year after the death of the Emperor high over the forest moon of Endor. This is the era in which the events in *A New Hope, The Empire Strikes Back,* and *Return of the Jedi* take place. The events in this story take place approximately nine months after the Battle of Yavin.

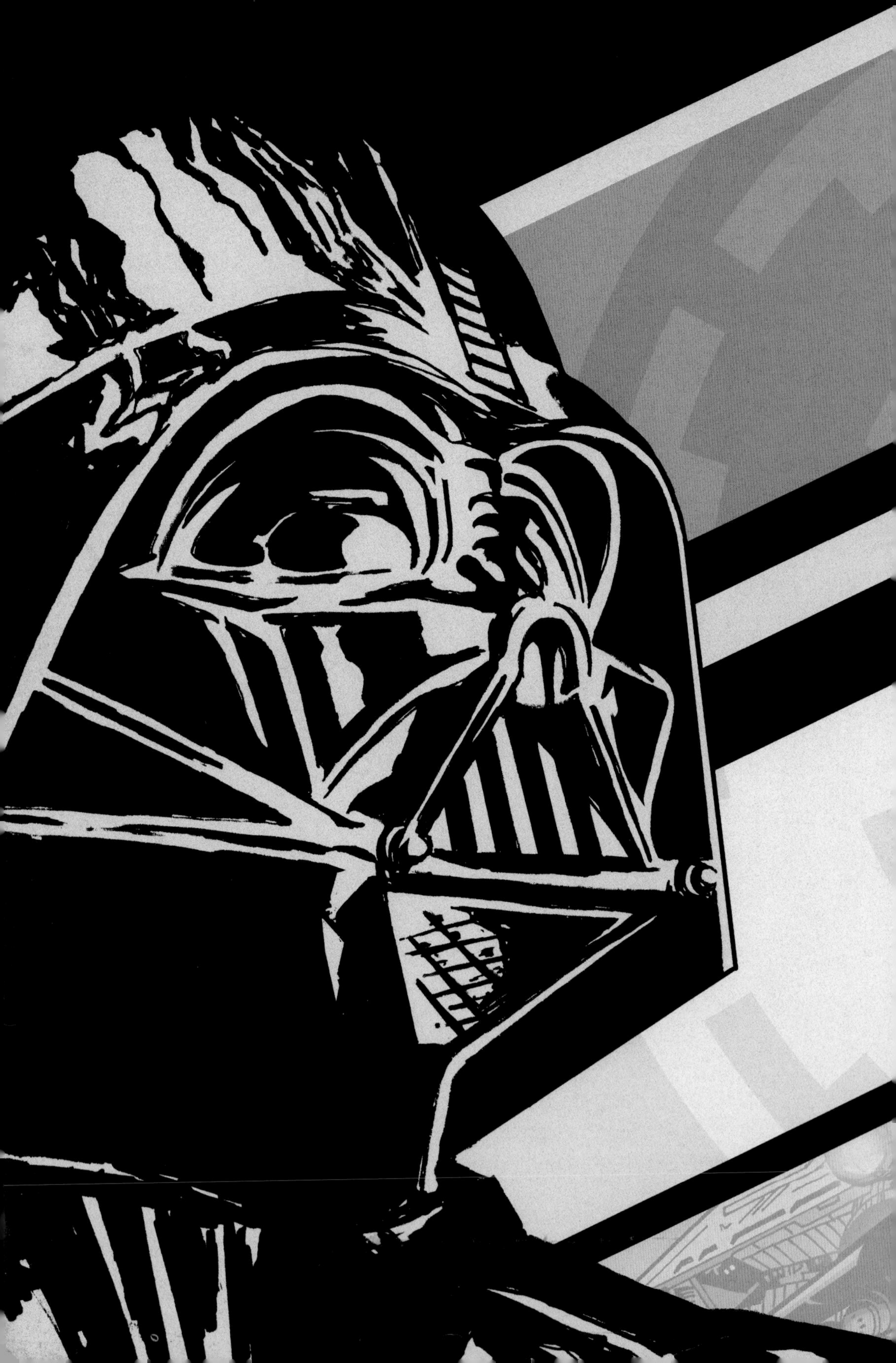

STAR WARS®

REBELLION

volume 3

SMALL VICTORIES

script JEREMY BARLOW
art COLIN WILSON
colors WIL GLASS
lettering MICHAEL HEISLER
front cover art COLIN WILSON
back cover art COLIN WILSON

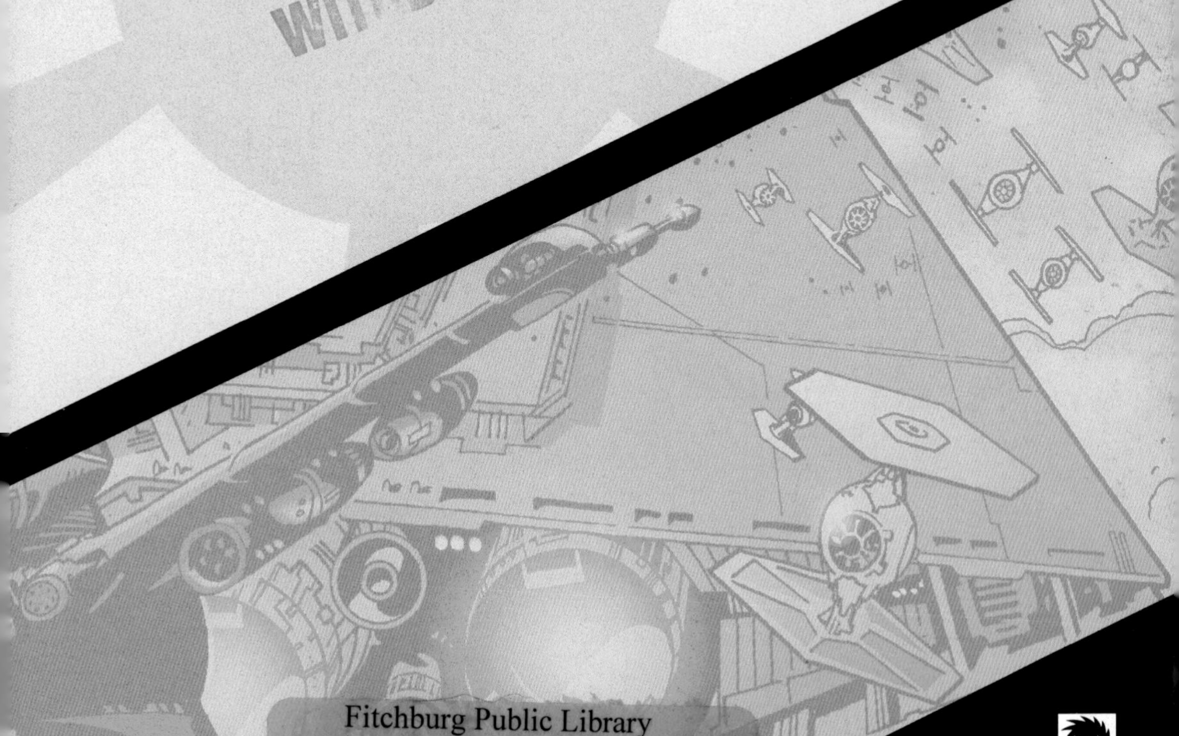

Dark Horse Books®

publisher MIKE RICHARDSON

collection designer JOSHUA ELLIOTT

art director LIA RIBACCHI

associate editor DAVE MARSHALL

assistant editor FREDDYE LINS

editor RANDY STRADLEY

Special thanks to Elaine Mederer, Jann Moorhead, David Anderman, Leland Chee, Sue Rostoni, and Carol Roeder at Lucas Licensing

STAR WARS: REBELLION volume three

This volume collects issues eleven through fourteen of the Dark Horse comic-book series Star Wars: Rebellion.

Published by
Dark Horse Books
A division of Dark Horse Comics, Inc.
10956 SE Main Street
Milwaukie, OR 97222

darkhorse.com
starwars.com

To find a comics shop in your area, call the Comic Shop Locator Service toll-free at 1-888-266-4226

First edition: November 2008
ISBN 978-1-59582-166-9

10 9 8 7 6 5 4 3 2 1

Printed in China

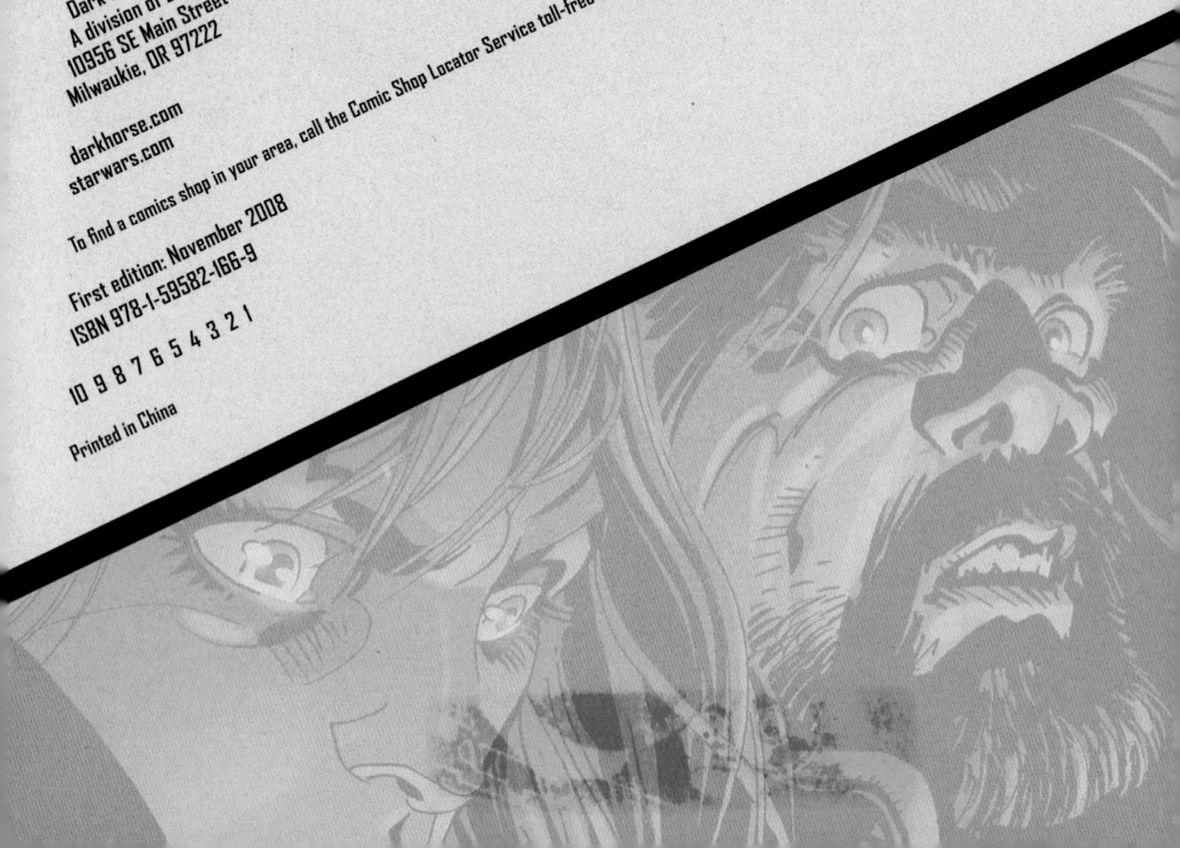

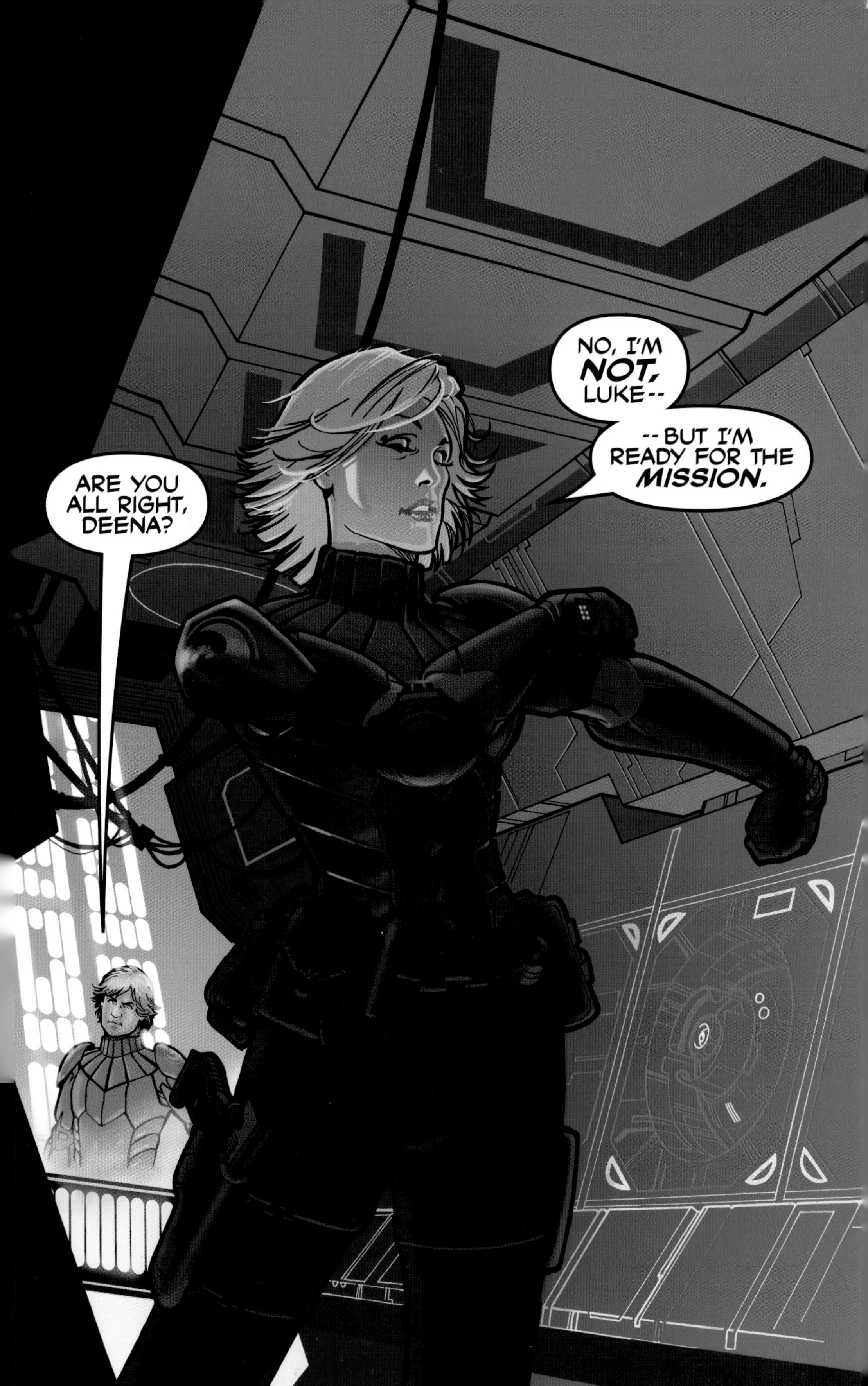
ARE YOU ALL RIGHT, DEENA?
NO, I'M NOT, LUKE--
--BUT I'M READY FOR THE MISSION.

illustration by Colin Wilson

SMALL VICTORIES

Having narrowly escaped destruction at the hands of **DARTH VADER** and the Imperial armada, the Rebel fleet scatters across the galaxy, each ship hurtling through hyperspace toward a different destination.

Badly damaged in the firefight, the Alliance flagship *Rebel One* fretfully carries its valuable cargo to safety—hero **LUKE SKYWALKER**, spymaster **TUNGO LI**, and leader **PRINCESS LEIA.**

Yet these figureheads of the Rebellion are not the only passengers aboard the struggling ship. For **DEENA SHAN**, the trials and tragedies of galactic civil war are not so easily weathered or reconciled . . .

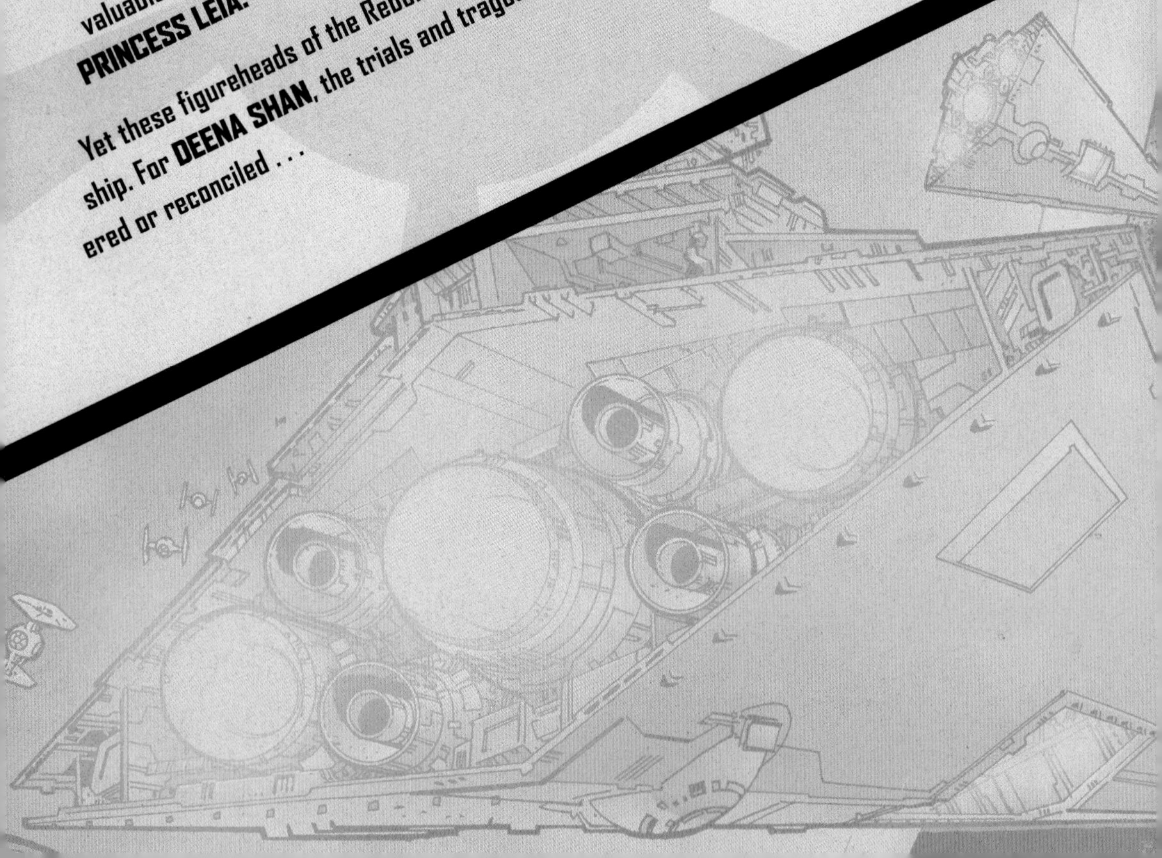

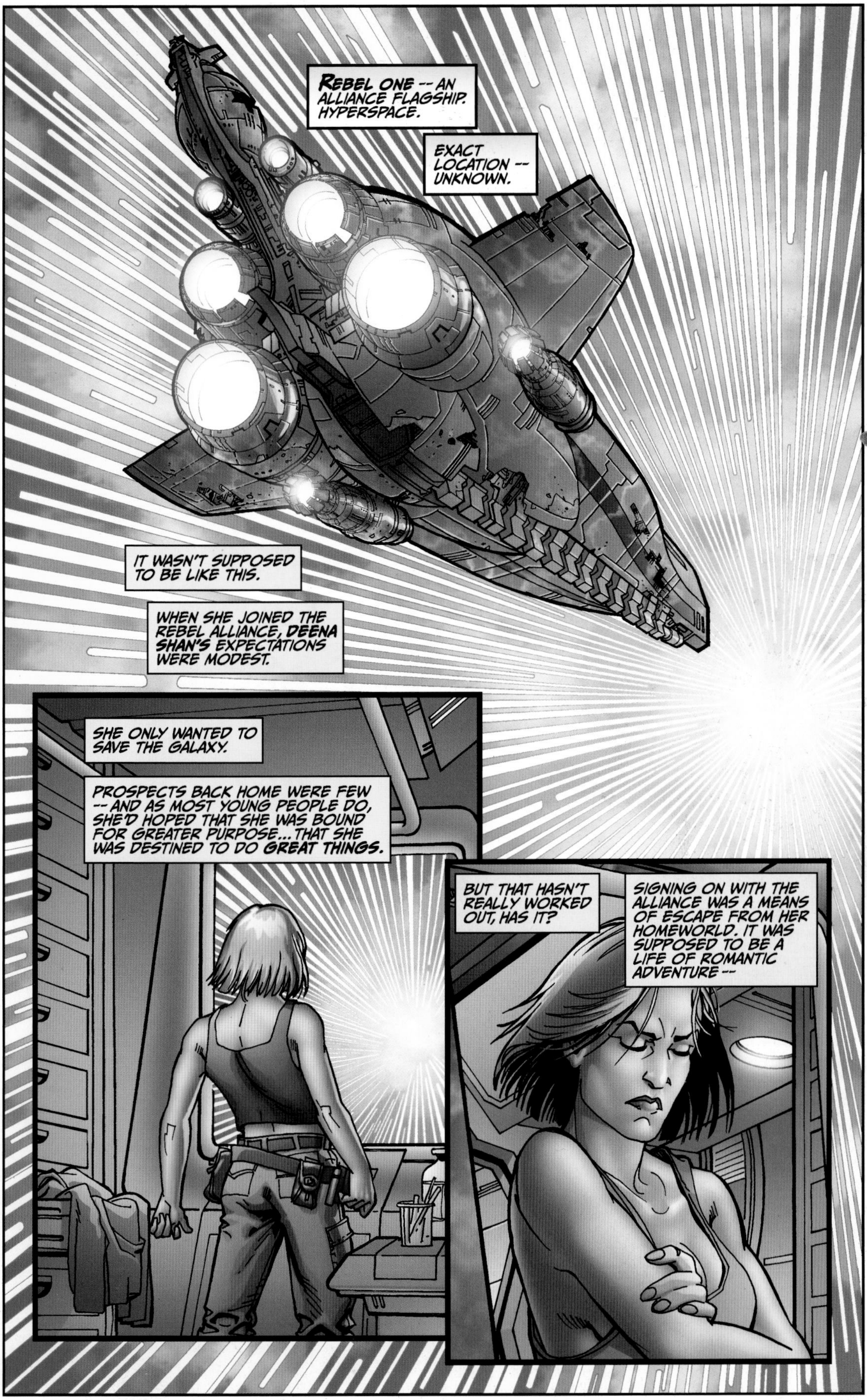
REBEL ONE -- AN ALLIANCE FLAGSHIP. HYPERSPACE.
EXACT LOCATION -- UNKNOWN.
IT WASN'T SUPPOSED TO BE LIKE THIS.
WHEN SHE JOINED THE REBEL ALLIANCE, DEENA SHAN'S EXPECTATIONS WERE MODEST.
SHE ONLY WANTED TO SAVE THE GALAXY.
PROSPECTS BACK HOME WERE FEW -- AND AS MOST YOUNG PEOPLE DO, SHE'D HOPED THAT SHE WAS BOUND FOR GREATER PURPOSE... THAT SHE WAS DESTINED TO DO GREAT THINGS.
BUT THAT HASN'T REALLY WORKED OUT, HAS IT?
SIGNING ON WITH THE ALLIANCE WAS A MEANS OF ESCAPE FROM HER HOMEWORLD. IT WAS SUPPOSED TO BE A LIFE OF ROMANTIC ADVENTURE --

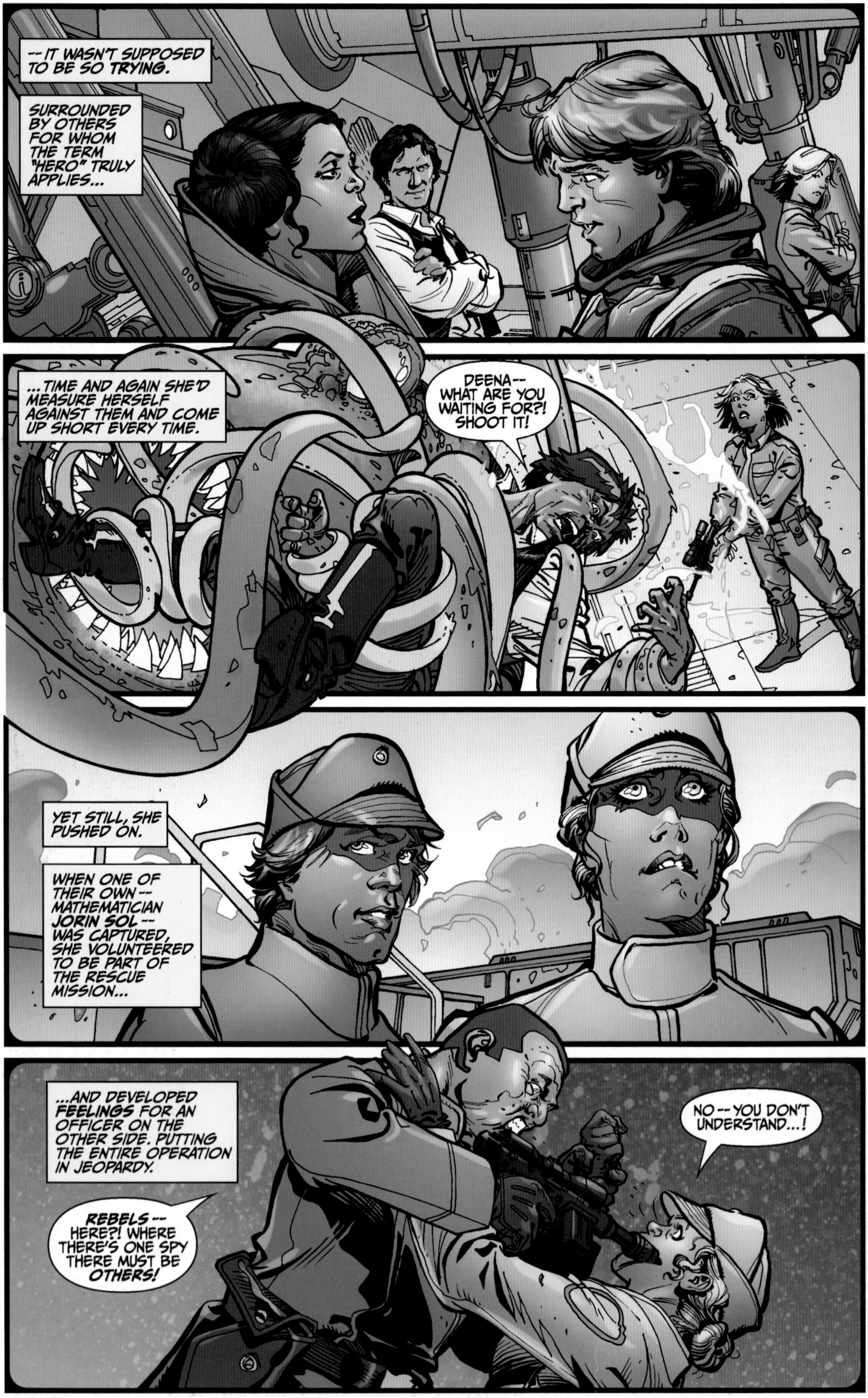

--IT WASN'T SUPPOSED TO BE SO TRYING.
SURROUNDED BY OTHERS FOR WHOM THE TERM "HERO" TRULY APPLIES...
...TIME AND AGAIN SHE'D MEASURE HERSELF AGAINST THEM AND COME UP SHORT EVERY TIME.
DEENA-- WHAT ARE YOU WAITING FOR?! SHOOT IT!
YET STILL, SHE PUSHED ON.
WHEN ONE OF THEIR OWN-- MATHEMATICIAN JORIN SOL-- WAS CAPTURED, SHE VOLUNTEERED TO BE PART OF THE RESCUE MISSION...
...AND DEVELOPED FEELINGS FOR AN OFFICER ON THE OTHER SIDE. PUTTING THE ENTIRE OPERATION IN JEOPARDY.
NO--YOU DON'T UNDERSTAND...!
REBELS-- HERE?! WHERE THERE'S ONE SPY THERE MUST BE OTHERS!

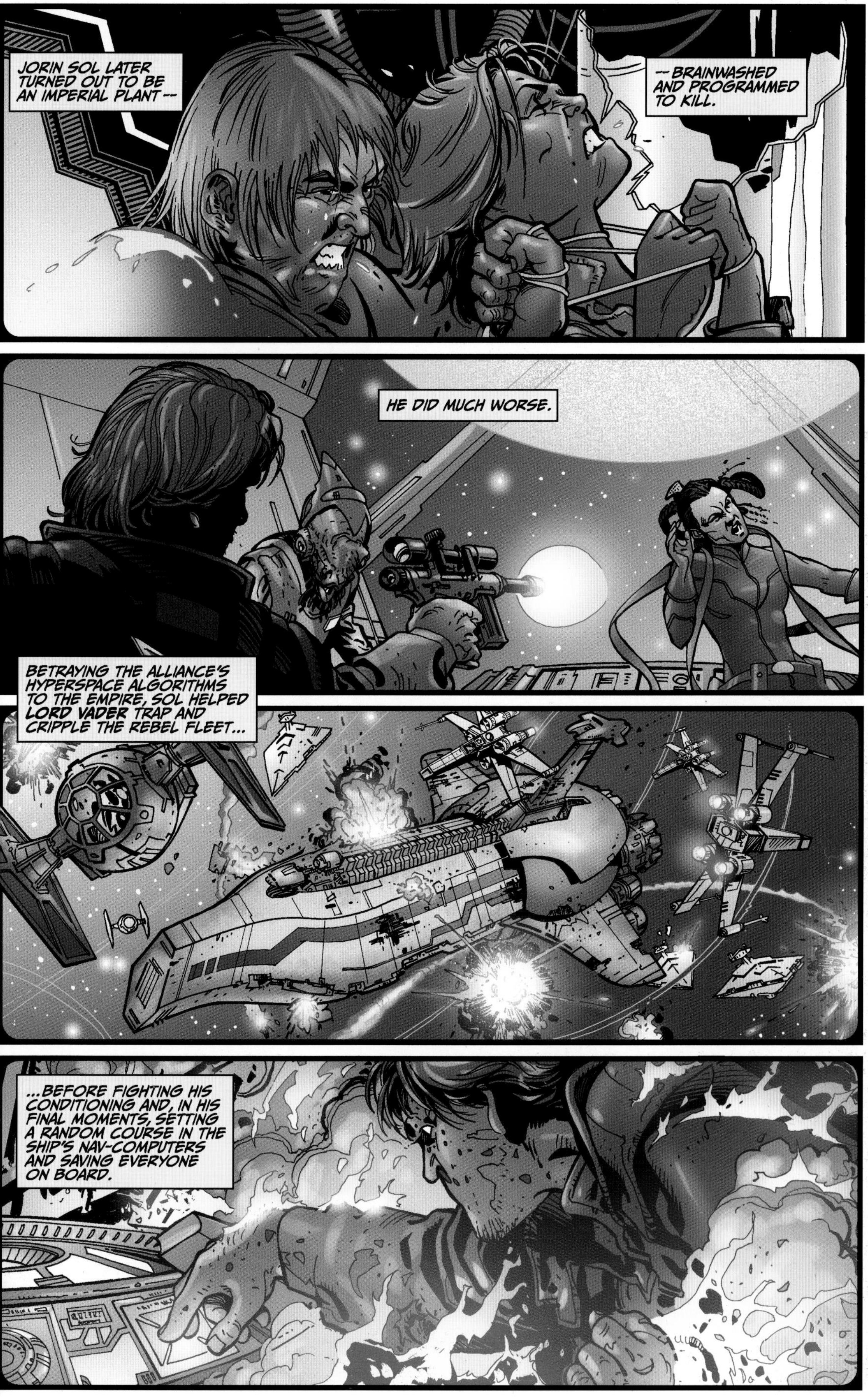
JORIN SOL LATER TURNED OUT TO BE AN IMPERIAL PLANT --
-- BRAINWASHED AND PROGRAMMED TO KILL.
HE DID MUCH WORSE.
BETRAYING THE ALLIANCE'S HYPERSPACE ALGORITHMS TO THE EMPIRE, SOL HELPED LORD VADER TRAP AND CRIPPLE THE REBEL FLEET...
...BEFORE FIGHTING HIS CONDITIONING AND, IN HIS FINAL MOMENTS, SETTING A RANDOM COURSE IN THE SHIP'S NAV-COMPUTERS AND SAVING EVERYONE ON BOARD.

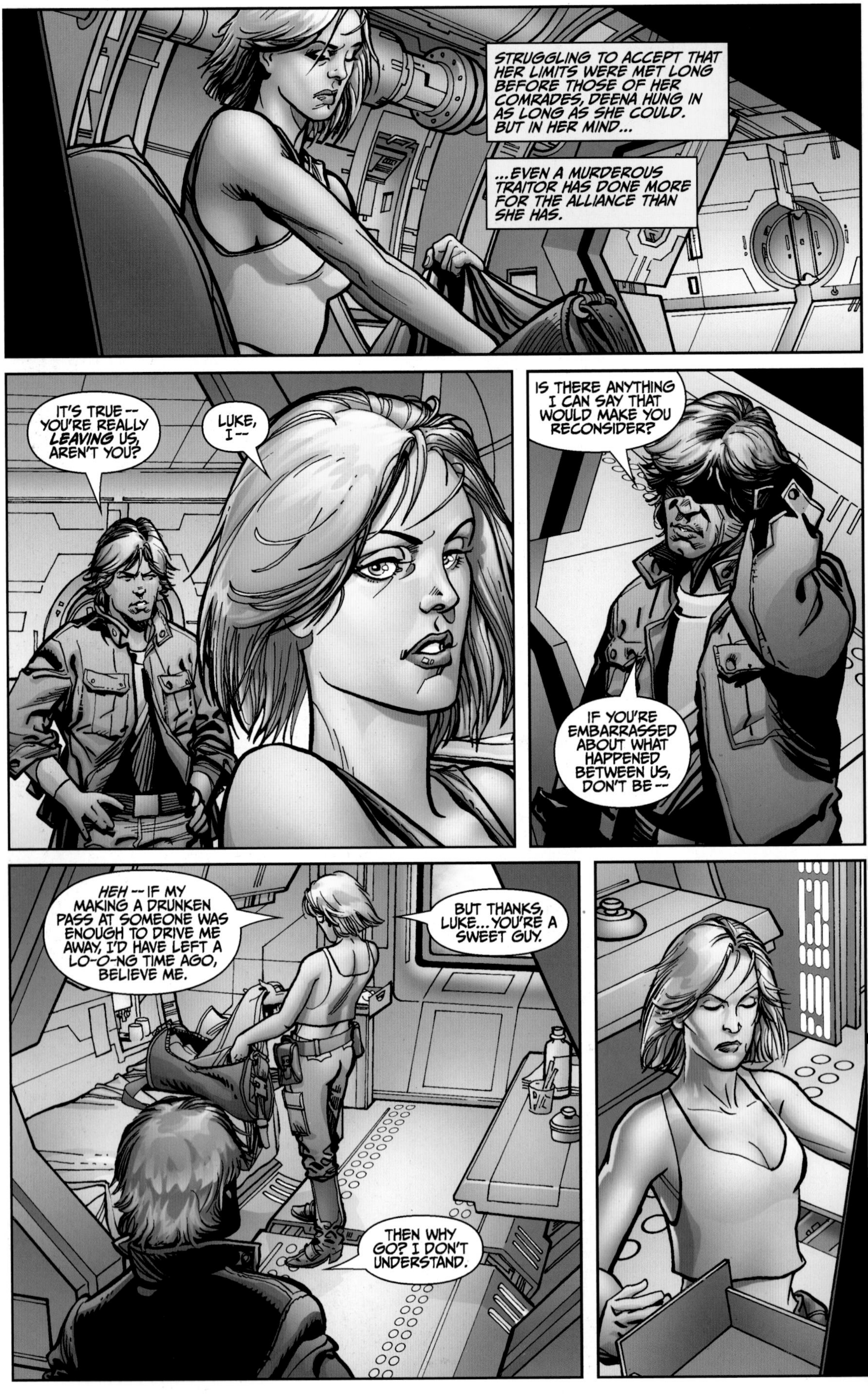
STRUGGLING TO ACCEPT THAT HER LIMITS WERE MET LONG BEFORE THOSE OF HER COMRADES, DEENA HUNG IN AS LONG AS SHE COULD. BUT IN HER MIND...
...EVEN A MURDEROUS TRAITOR HAS DONE MORE FOR THE ALLIANCE THAN SHE HAS.
IT'S TRUE -- YOU'RE REALLY LEAVING US, AREN'T YOU?
LUKE, I --
IS THERE ANYTHING I CAN SAY THAT WOULD MAKE YOU RECONSIDER?
IF YOU'RE EMBARRASSED ABOUT WHAT HAPPENED BETWEEN US, DON'T BE --
HEH -- IF MY MAKING A DRUNKEN PASS AT SOMEONE WAS ENOUGH TO DRIVE ME AWAY, I'D HAVE LEFT A LO-O-NG TIME AGO, BELIEVE ME.
BUT THANKS, LUKE... YOU'RE A SWEET GUY.
THEN WHY GO? I DON'T UNDERSTAND.

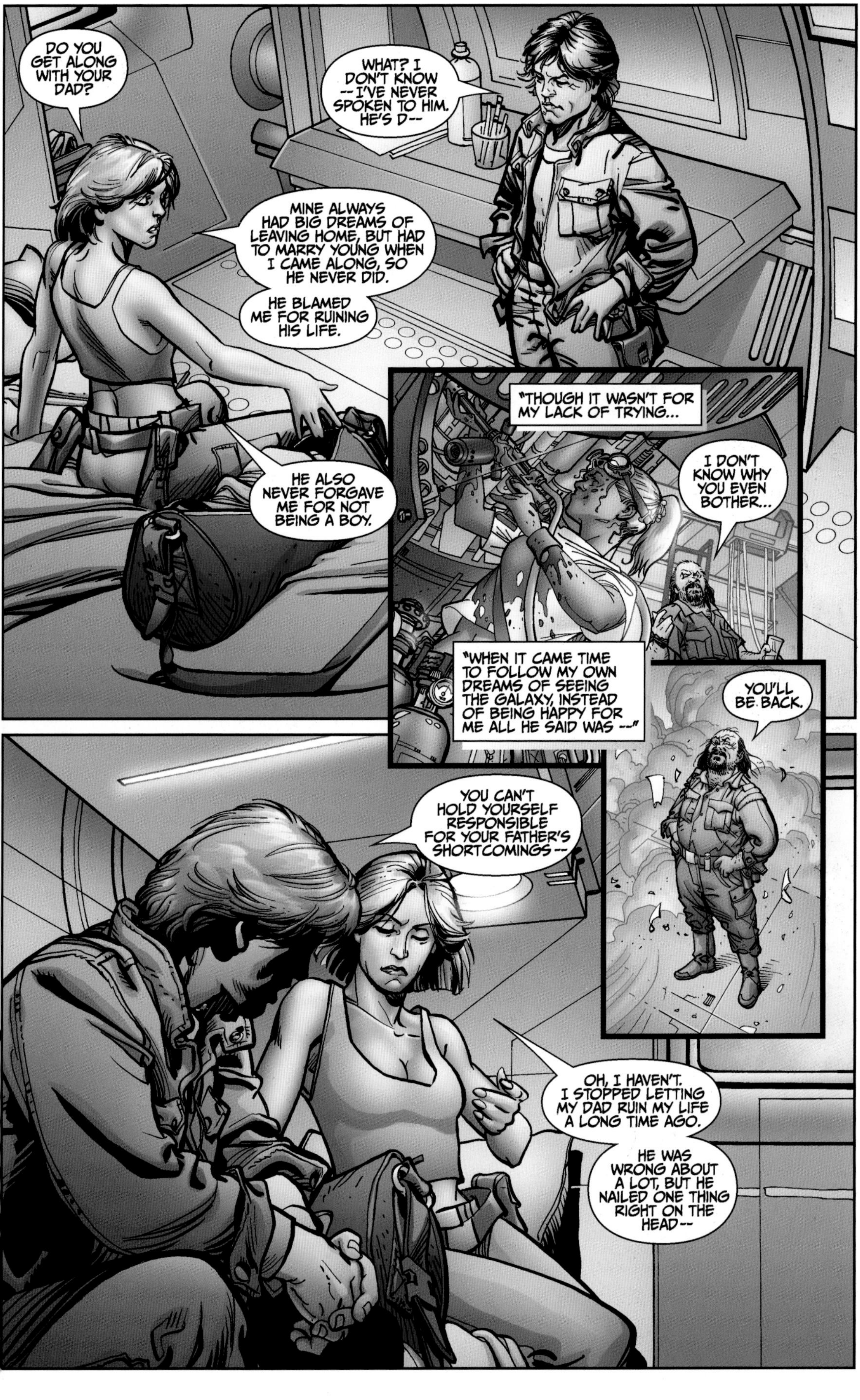
DO YOU GET ALONG WITH YOUR DAD?
WHAT? I DON'T KNOW --I'VE NEVER SPOKEN TO HIM. HE'S D--
MINE ALWAYS HAD BIG DREAMS OF LEAVING HOME, BUT HAD TO MARRY YOUNG WHEN I CAME ALONG, SO HE NEVER DID.
HE BLAMED ME FOR RUINING HIS LIFE.
HE ALSO NEVER FORGAVE ME FOR NOT BEING A BOY.
"THOUGH IT WASN'T FOR MY LACK OF TRYING...
I DON'T KNOW WHY YOU EVEN BOTHER...
"WHEN IT CAME TIME TO FOLLOW MY OWN DREAMS OF SEEING THE GALAXY, INSTEAD OF BEING HAPPY FOR ME ALL HE SAID WAS --"
YOU'LL BE BACK.
YOU CAN'T HOLD YOURSELF RESPONSIBLE FOR YOUR FATHER'S SHORTCOMINGS --
OH, I HAVEN'T. I STOPPED LETTING MY DAD RUIN MY LIFE A LONG TIME AGO.
HE WAS WRONG ABOUT A LOT, BUT HE NAILED ONE THING RIGHT ON THE HEAD--

-- I'M *NOT* A *HERO*. AND I'M NOT CUT OUT FOR THIS -- THE BETRAYALS AND DOUBLE-CROSSES, LIFE ON THE FRONT LINES --

DEENA --

-- ANY OF IT. SOONER OR LATER I'M GOING TO GET SOMEONE KILLED AND I CAN'T HANDLE THAT.

IT'S OKAY, LUKE --

NO, IT'S *NOT*. YOU'RE NOT ALONE -- THESE LAST FEW WEEKS HAVE BEEN TRYING FOR *EVERYONE*.

THE EMPIRE *HURT* US. SPIRITS ARE BROKEN, I KNOW, BUT YOU HAVE TO PUSH THROUGH IT. WE *ALL* DO.

SAYS THE KID WHO BLEW UP THE *DEATH STAR*. IT'S DIFFERENT FOR YOU.

NOT *THAT* AGAIN. PEOPLE NEED TO LET THAT GO, NO ONE'S KEEPING SCORE --

NO, BUT WHATEVER YOU HAVE INSIDE YOU THAT KEPT YOU COOL IN THAT TRENCH --

-- WHATEVER IT WAS THAT TOLD YOU EXACTLY *WHEN* TO DROP THAT TORPEDO... I *DON'T HAVE IT.*

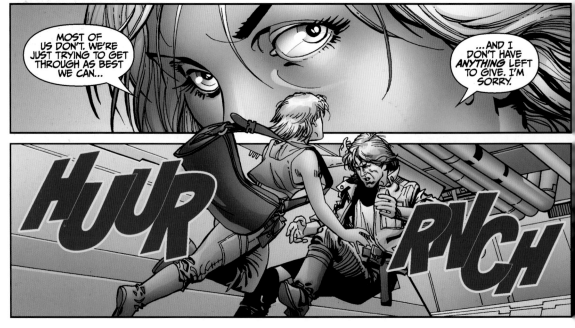

MOST OF US DON'T. WE'RE JUST TRYING TO GET THROUGH AS BEST WE CAN...

...AND I *DON'T HAVE* *ANYTHING* LEFT TO GIVE. I'M SORRY.

HJUR

RNCH

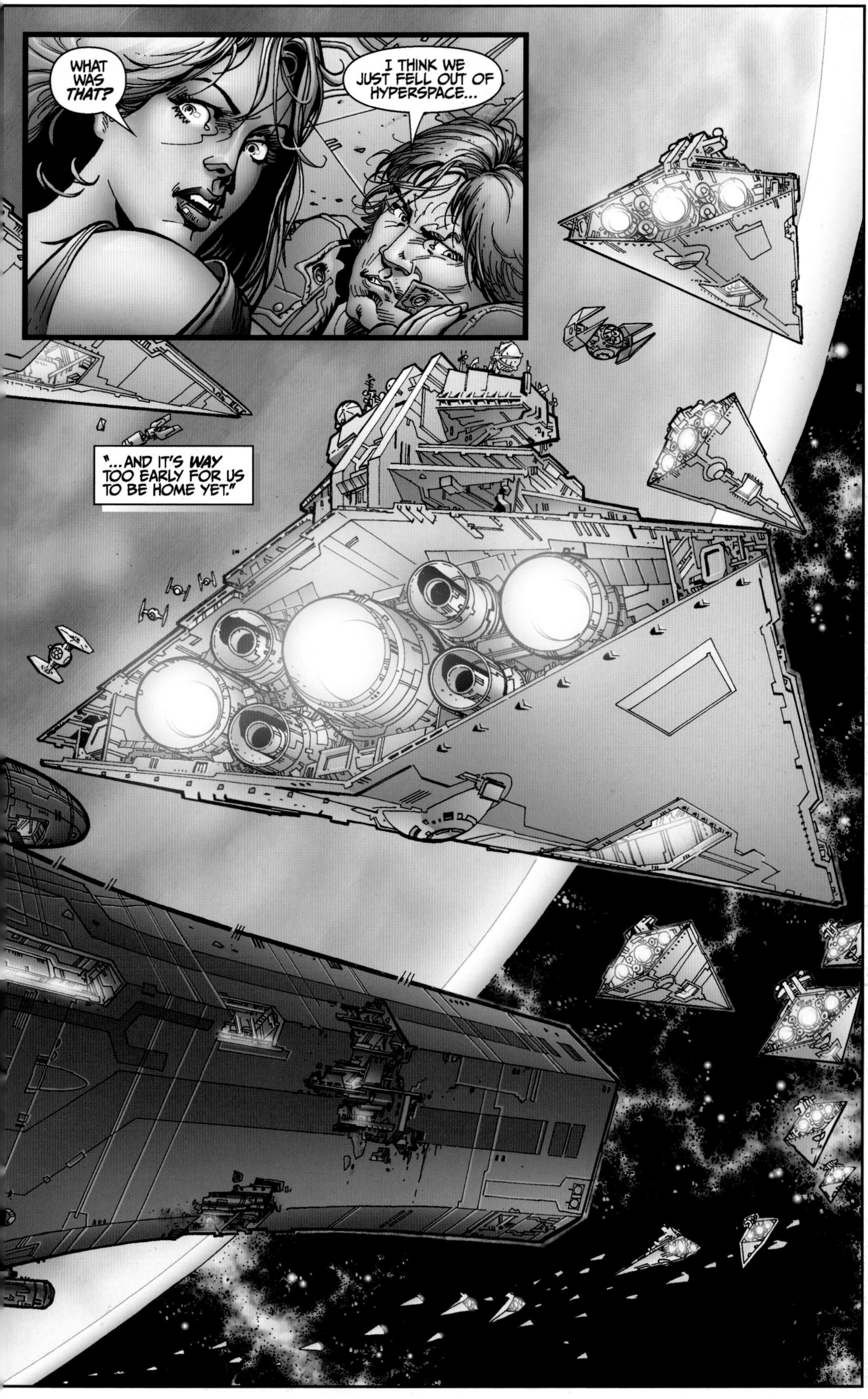
WHAT WAS THAT?
I THINK WE JUST FELL OUT OF HYPERSPACE...
"...AND IT'S WAY TOO EARLY FOR US TO BE HOME YET."

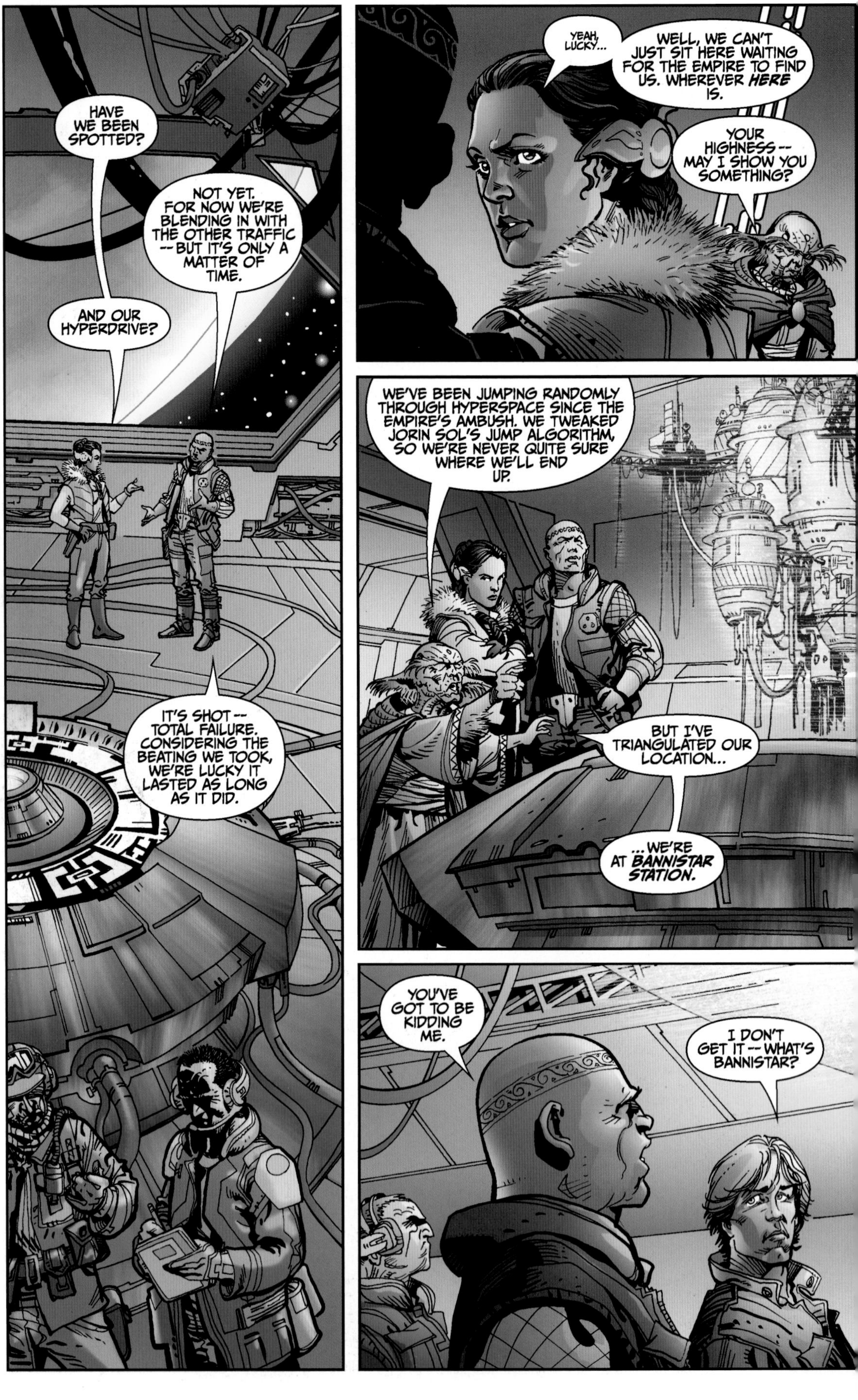
HAVE WE BEEN SPOTTED?
NOT YET. FOR NOW WE'RE BLENDING IN WITH THE OTHER TRAFFIC -- BUT IT'S ONLY A MATTER OF TIME.
AND OUR HYPERDRIVE?
IT'S SHOT -- TOTAL FAILURE. CONSIDERING THE BEATING WE TOOK, WE'RE LUCKY IT LASTED AS LONG AS IT DID.
YEAH, LUCKY...
WELL, WE CAN'T JUST SIT HERE WAITING FOR THE EMPIRE TO FIND US. WHEREVER *HERE* IS.
YOUR HIGHNESS -- MAY I SHOW YOU SOMETHING?
WE'VE BEEN JUMPING RANDOMLY THROUGH HYPERSPACE SINCE THE EMPIRE'S AMBUSH. WE TWEAKED JORIN SOL'S JUMP ALGORITHM, SO WE'RE NEVER QUITE SURE WHERE WE'LL END UP.
BUT I'VE TRIANGULATED OUR LOCATION...
...WE'RE AT *BANNISTAR STATION.*
YOU'VE GOT TO BE KIDDING ME.
I DON'T GET IT -- WHAT'S BANNISTAR?

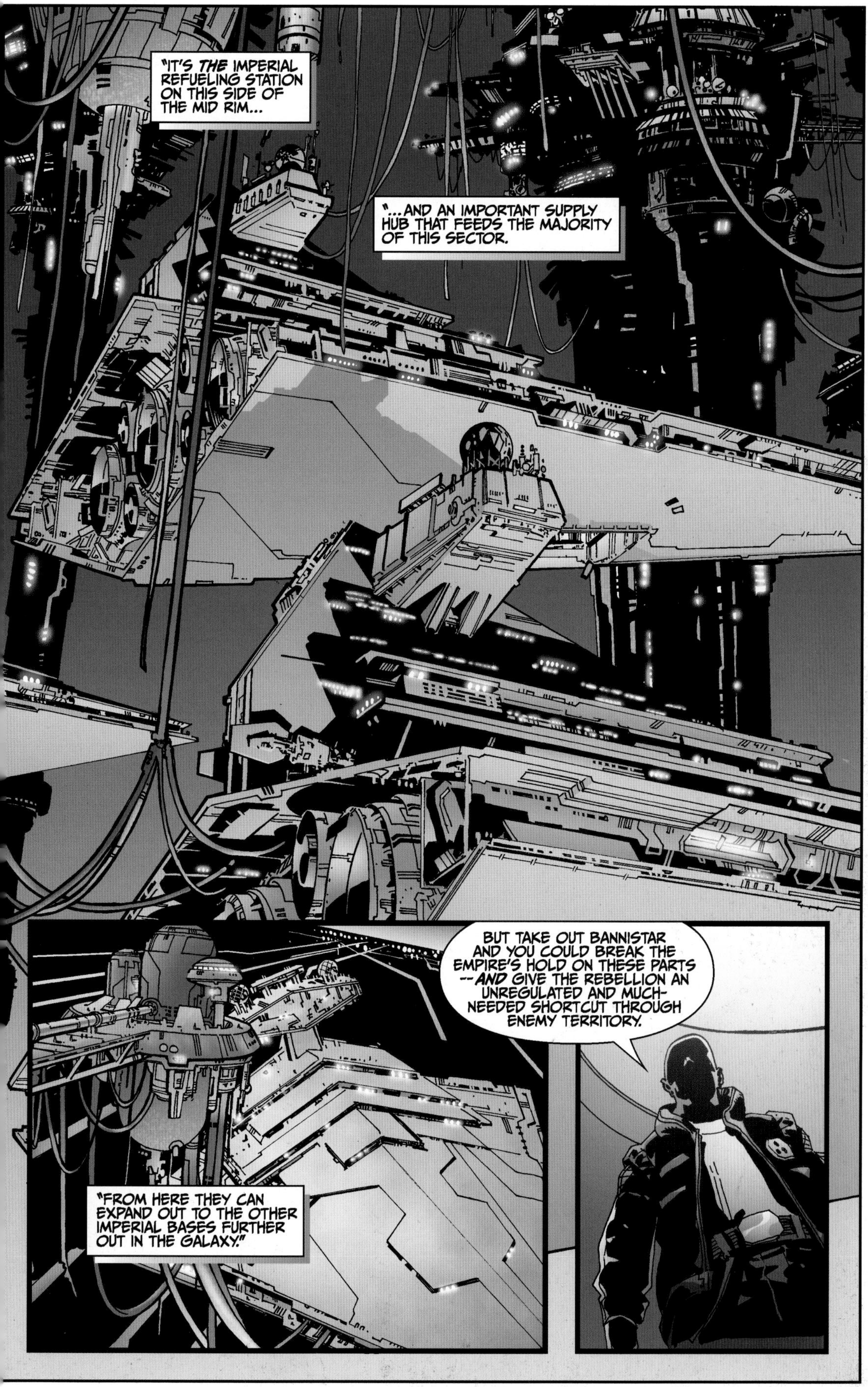
"IT'S THE IMPERIAL REFUELING STATION ON THIS SIDE OF THE MID RIM...
"...AND AN IMPORTANT SUPPLY HUB THAT FEEDS THE MAJORITY OF THIS SECTOR.
"FROM HERE THEY CAN EXPAND OUT TO THE OTHER IMPERIAL BASES FURTHER OUT IN THE GALAXY."
BUT TAKE OUT BANNISTAR AND YOU COULD BREAK THE EMPIRE'S HOLD ON THESE PARTS --AND GIVE THE REBELLION AN UNREGULATED AND MUCH-NEEDED SHORTCUT THROUGH ENEMY TERRITORY.

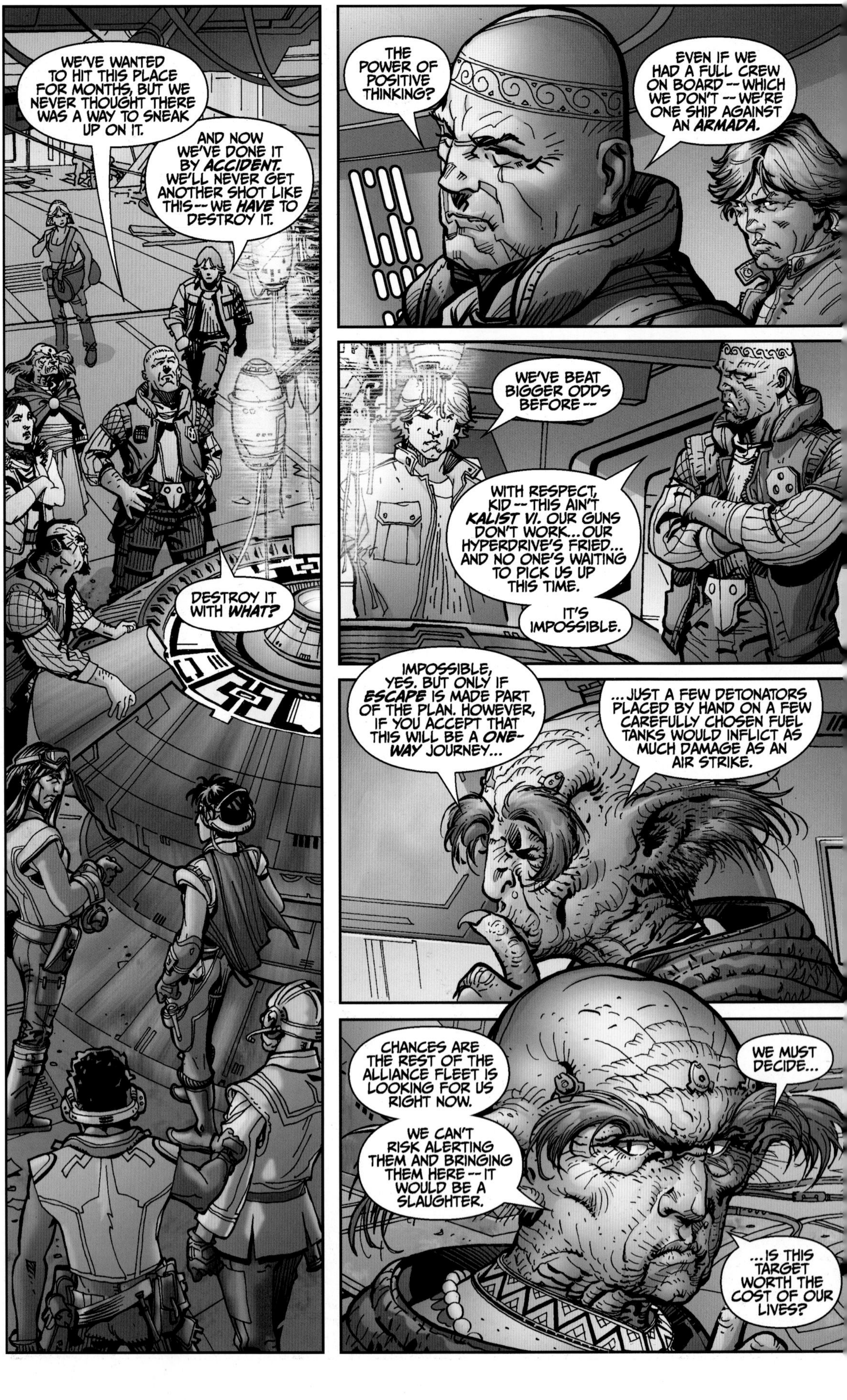
WE'VE WANTED TO HIT THIS PLACE FOR MONTHS, BUT WE NEVER THOUGHT THERE WAS A WAY TO SNEAK UP ON IT.
AND NOW WE'VE DONE IT BY ACCIDENT. WE'LL NEVER GET ANOTHER SHOT LIKE THIS -- WE HAVE TO DESTROY IT.
DESTROY IT WITH WHAT?
THE POWER OF POSITIVE THINKING?
EVEN IF WE HAD A FULL CREW ON BOARD -- WHICH WE DON'T -- WE'RE ONE SHIP AGAINST AN ARMADA.
WE'VE BEAT BIGGER ODDS BEFORE --
WITH RESPECT, KID -- THIS AIN'T KALIST VI. OUR GUNS DON'T WORK... OUR HYPERDRIVE'S FRIED... AND NO ONE'S WAITING TO PICK US UP THIS TIME.
IT'S IMPOSSIBLE.
IMPOSSIBLE, YES. BUT ONLY IF ESCAPE IS MADE PART OF THE PLAN. HOWEVER, IF YOU ACCEPT THAT THIS WILL BE A ONE-WAY JOURNEY...
...JUST A FEW DETONATORS PLACED BY HAND ON A FEW CAREFULLY CHOSEN FUEL TANKS WOULD INFLICT AS MUCH DAMAGE AS AN AIR STRIKE.
CHANCES ARE THE REST OF THE ALLIANCE FLEET IS LOOKING FOR US RIGHT NOW.
WE CAN'T RISK ALERTING THEM AND BRINGING THEM HERE -- IT WOULD BE A SLAUGHTER.
WE MUST DECIDE...
...IS THIS TARGET WORTH THE COST OF OUR LIVES?

THIS IS A DIFFICULT SITUATION, NO QUESTION.

WITH OUR FLEET AS BROKEN AND SCATTERED AS IT IS NOW, THE REBELLION'S FUTURE HANGS ON OUR NEXT COURSE OF ACTION.

AS IMPORTANT TO THE CAUSE AS WE ALL ARE INDIVIDUALLY, THE REBELLION IS BIGGER THAN ANY ONE OF US.

WE MUST DO WHATEVER IT TAKES TO ENSURE ITS SURVIVAL, NO MATTER THE COST.

AND RIGHT NOW, OUR FLEET -- OUR FRIENDS -- ARE BEING HUNTED DOWN AND DESTROYED BY THE IMPERIAL NAVY.

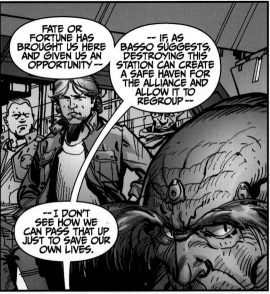

FATE OR FORTUNE HAS BROUGHT US HERE AND GIVEN US AN OPPORTUNITY --

-- IF, AS BASSO SUGGESTS, DESTROYING THIS STATION CAN CREATE A SAFE HAVEN FOR THE ALLIANCE AND ALLOW IT TO REGROUP --

-- I DON'T SEE HOW WE CAN PASS THAT UP JUST TO SAVE OUR OWN LIVES.

THE REMAINING CIVILIANS ONBOARD WILL ABANDON SHIP, WHETHER YOU GO WITH THEM IS UP TO YOU...

THIS CAN'T BE HAPPENING.

...BUT I'M MAKING A STAND HERE.

LET'S HIT THE EMPIRE WHERE IT HURTS.

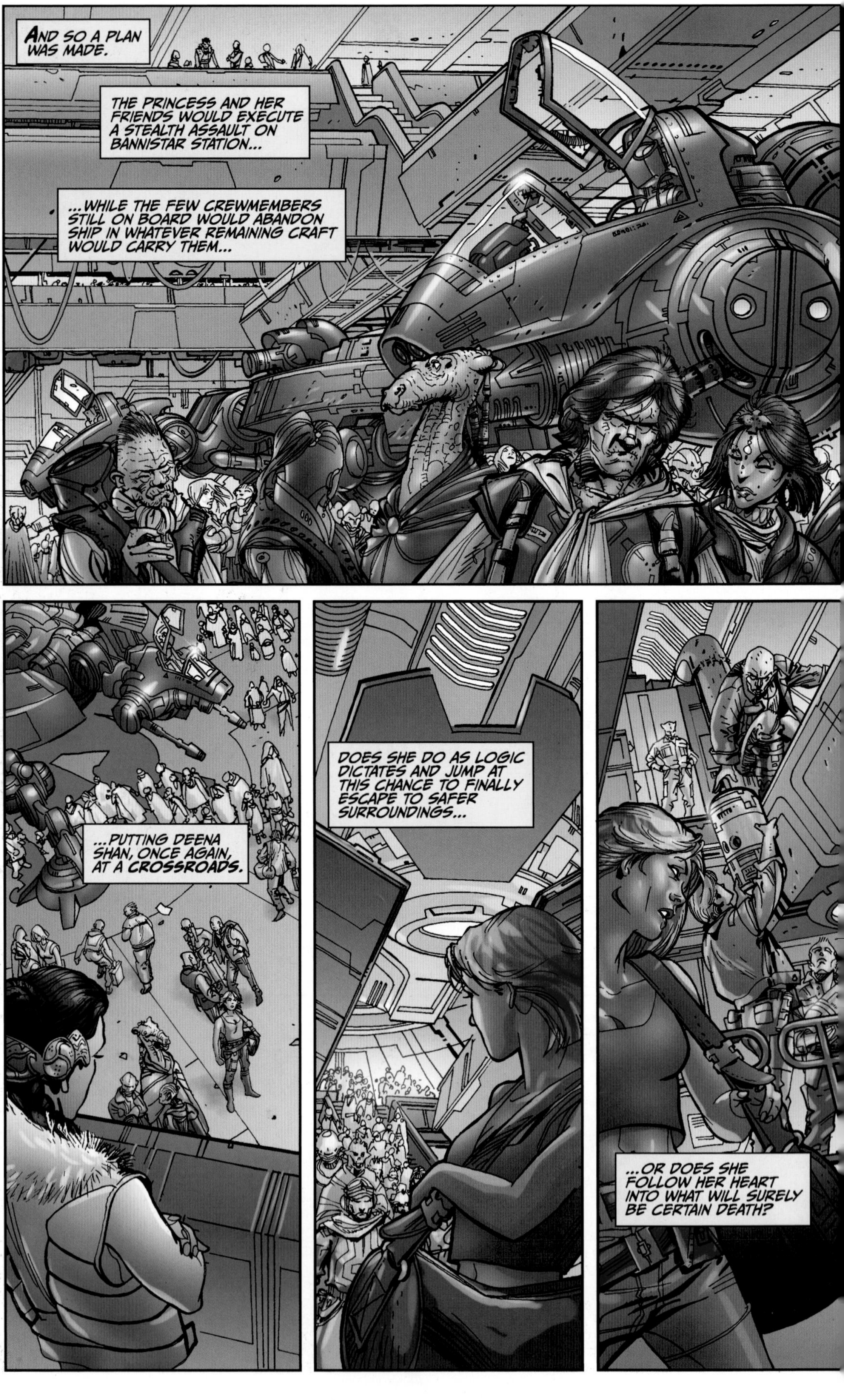
AND SO A PLAN WAS MADE.
THE PRINCESS AND HER FRIENDS WOULD EXECUTE A STEALTH ASSAULT ON BANNISTAR STATION...
...WHILE THE FEW CREWMEMBERS STILL ON BOARD WOULD ABANDON SHIP IN WHATEVER REMAINING CRAFT WOULD CARRY THEM...
...PUTTING DEENA SHAN, ONCE AGAIN, AT A CROSSROADS.
DOES SHE DO AS LOGIC DICTATES AND JUMP AT THIS CHANCE TO FINALLY ESCAPE TO SAFER SURROUNDINGS...
...OR DOES SHE FOLLOW HER HEART INTO WHAT WILL SURELY BE CERTAIN DEATH?

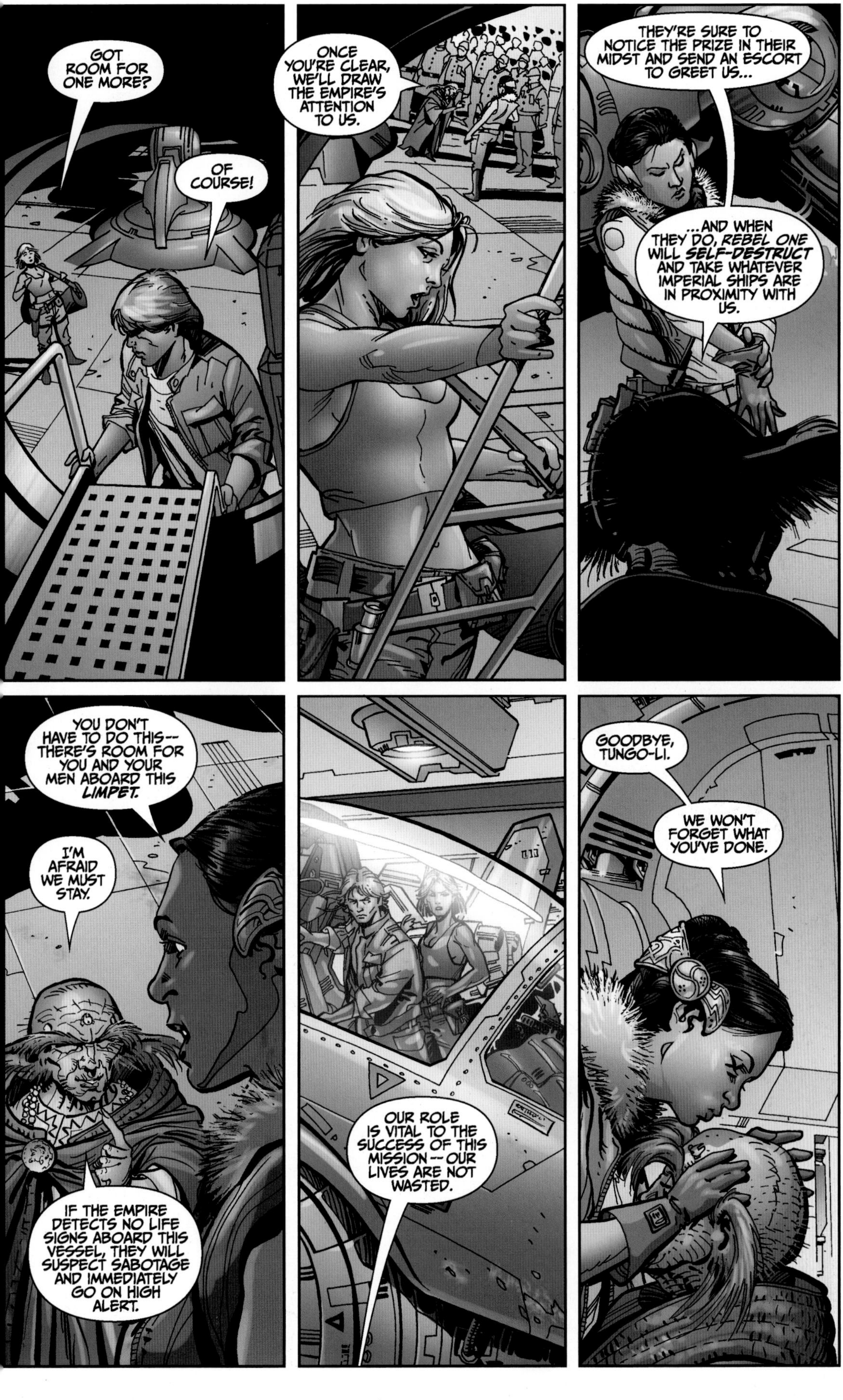
GOT ROOM FOR ONE MORE?
OF COURSE!
ONCE YOU'RE CLEAR, WE'LL DRAW THE EMPIRE'S ATTENTION TO US.
THEY'RE SURE TO NOTICE THE PRIZE IN THEIR MIDST AND SEND AN ESCORT TO GREET US...
...AND WHEN THEY DO, *REBEL ONE* WILL ***SELF-DESTRUCT*** AND TAKE WHATEVER IMPERIAL SHIPS ARE IN PROXIMITY WITH US.
YOU DON'T HAVE TO DO THIS-- THERE'S ROOM FOR YOU AND YOUR MEN ABOARD THIS ***LIMPET.***
I'M AFRAID WE MUST STAY.
IF THE EMPIRE DETECTS NO LIFE SIGNS ABOARD THIS VESSEL, THEY WILL SUSPECT SABOTAGE AND IMMEDIATELY GO ON HIGH ALERT.
OUR ROLE IS VITAL TO THE SUCCESS OF THIS MISSION -- OUR LIVES ARE NOT WASTED.
GOODBYE, TUNGO-LI.
WE WON'T FORGET WHAT YOU'VE DONE.

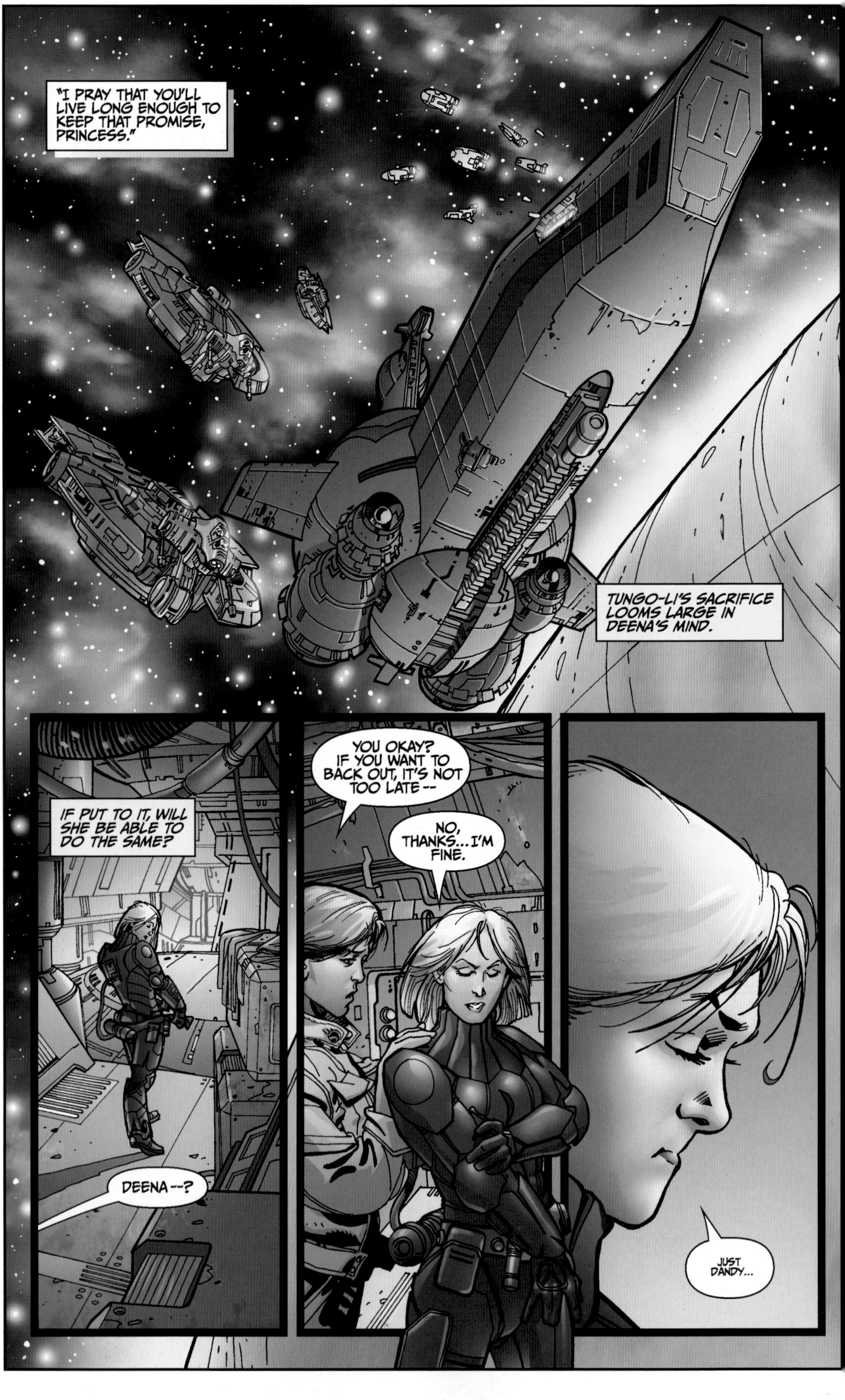
"I PRAY THAT YOU'LL LIVE LONG ENOUGH TO KEEP THAT PROMISE, PRINCESS."
TUNGO-LI'S SACRIFICE LOOMS LARGE IN DEENA'S MIND.
IF PUT TO IT, WILL SHE BE ABLE TO DO THE SAME?
DEENA--?
YOU OKAY? IF YOU WANT TO BACK OUT, IT'S NOT TOO LATE--
NO, THANKS... I'M FINE.
JUST DANDY...

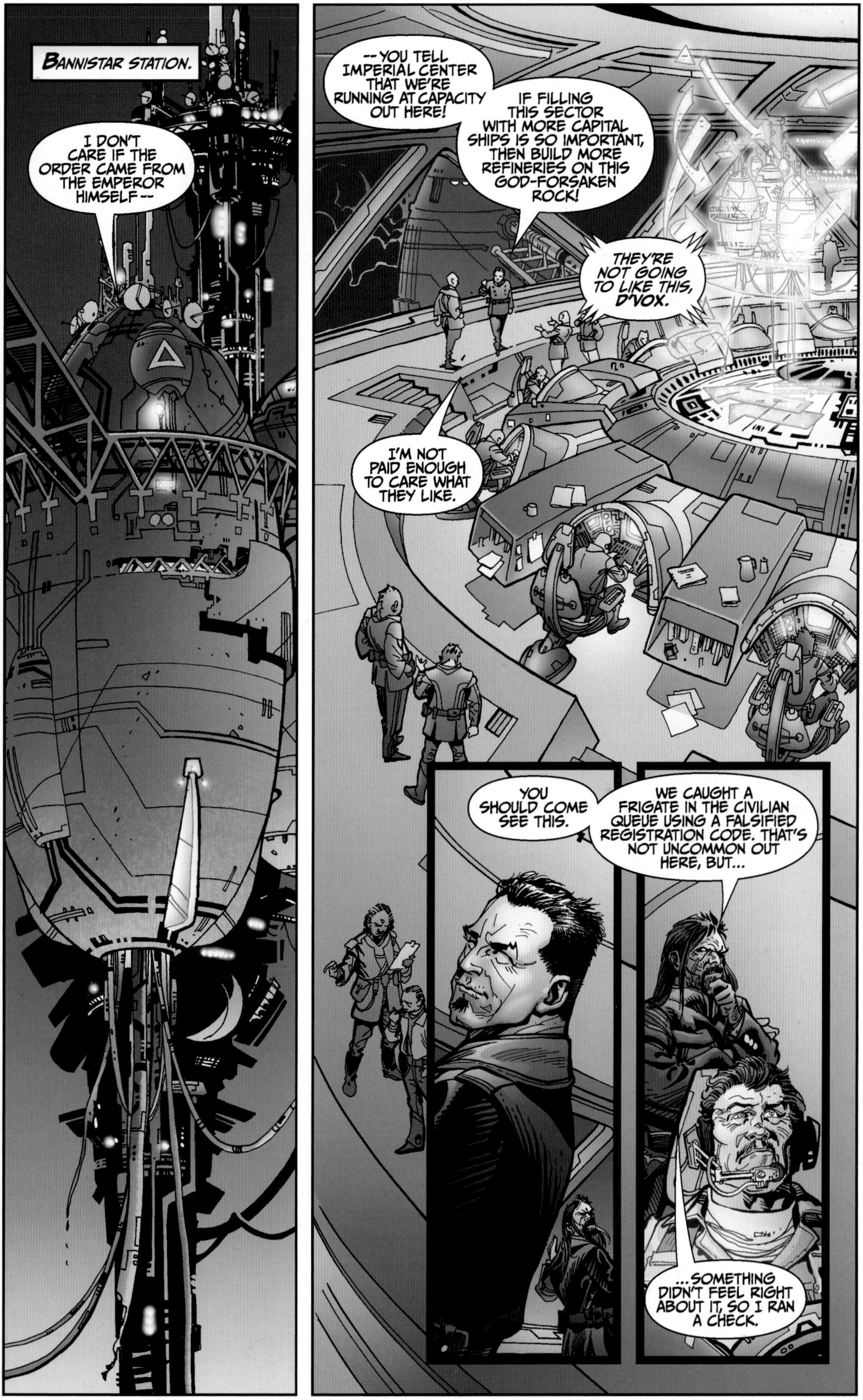
BANNISTAR STATION.
I DON'T CARE IF THE ORDER CAME FROM THE EMPEROR HIMSELF--
--YOU TELL IMPERIAL CENTER THAT WE'RE RUNNING AT CAPACITY OUT HERE!
IF FILLING THIS SECTOR WITH MORE CAPITAL SHIPS IS SO IMPORTANT, THEN BUILD MORE REFINERIES ON THIS GOD-FORSAKEN ROCK!
THEY'RE NOT GOING TO LIKE THIS, D'VOX.
I'M NOT PAID ENOUGH TO CARE WHAT THEY LIKE.
YOU SHOULD COME SEE THIS.
WE CAUGHT A FRIGATE IN THE CIVILIAN QUEUE USING A FALSIFIED REGISTRATION CODE. THAT'S NOT UNCOMMON OUT HERE, BUT...
...SOMETHING DIDN'T FEEL RIGHT ABOUT IT, SO I RAN A CHECK.

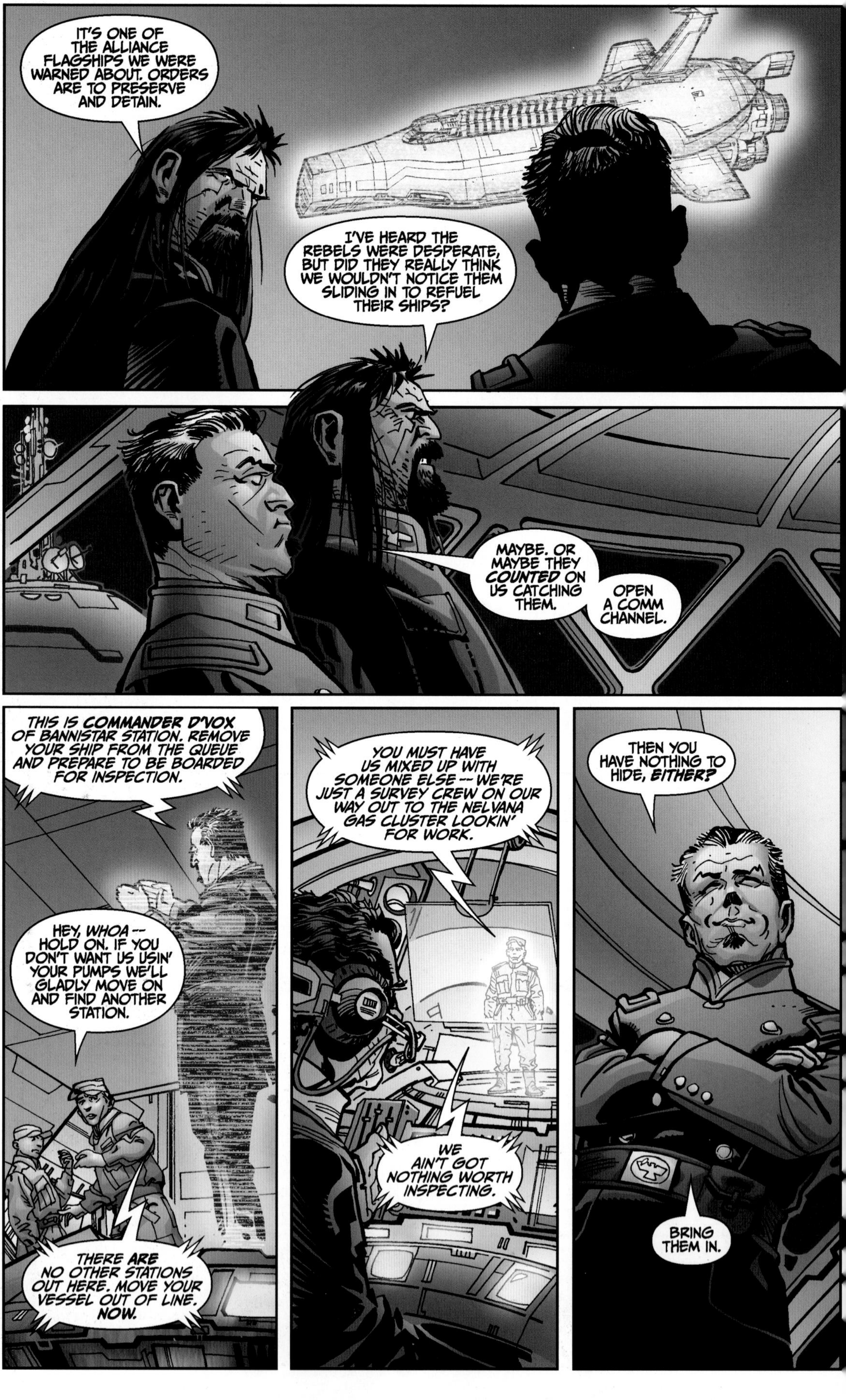
IT'S ONE OF THE ALLIANCE FLAGSHIPS WE WERE WARNED ABOUT. ORDERS ARE TO PRESERVE AND DETAIN.
I'VE HEARD THE REBELS WERE DESPERATE, BUT DID THEY REALLY THINK WE WOULDN'T NOTICE THEM SLIDING IN TO REFUEL THEIR SHIPS?
MAYBE. OR MAYBE THEY COUNTED ON US CATCHING THEM.
OPEN A COMM CHANNEL.
THIS IS COMMANDER D'VOX OF BANNISTAR STATION. REMOVE YOUR SHIP FROM THE QUEUE AND PREPARE TO BE BOARDED FOR INSPECTION.
HEY, WHOA -- HOLD ON. IF YOU DON'T WANT US USIN' YOUR PUMPS WE'LL GLADLY MOVE ON AND FIND ANOTHER STATION.
THERE ARE NO OTHER STATIONS OUT HERE. MOVE YOUR VESSEL OUT OF LINE. NOW.
YOU MUST HAVE US MIXED UP WITH SOMEONE ELSE -- WE'RE JUST A SURVEY CREW ON OUR WAY OUT TO THE NELVANA GAS CLUSTER LOOKIN' FOR WORK.
WE AIN'T GOT NOTHING WORTH INSPECTING.
THEN YOU HAVE NOTHING TO HIDE, EITHER?
BRING THEM IN.

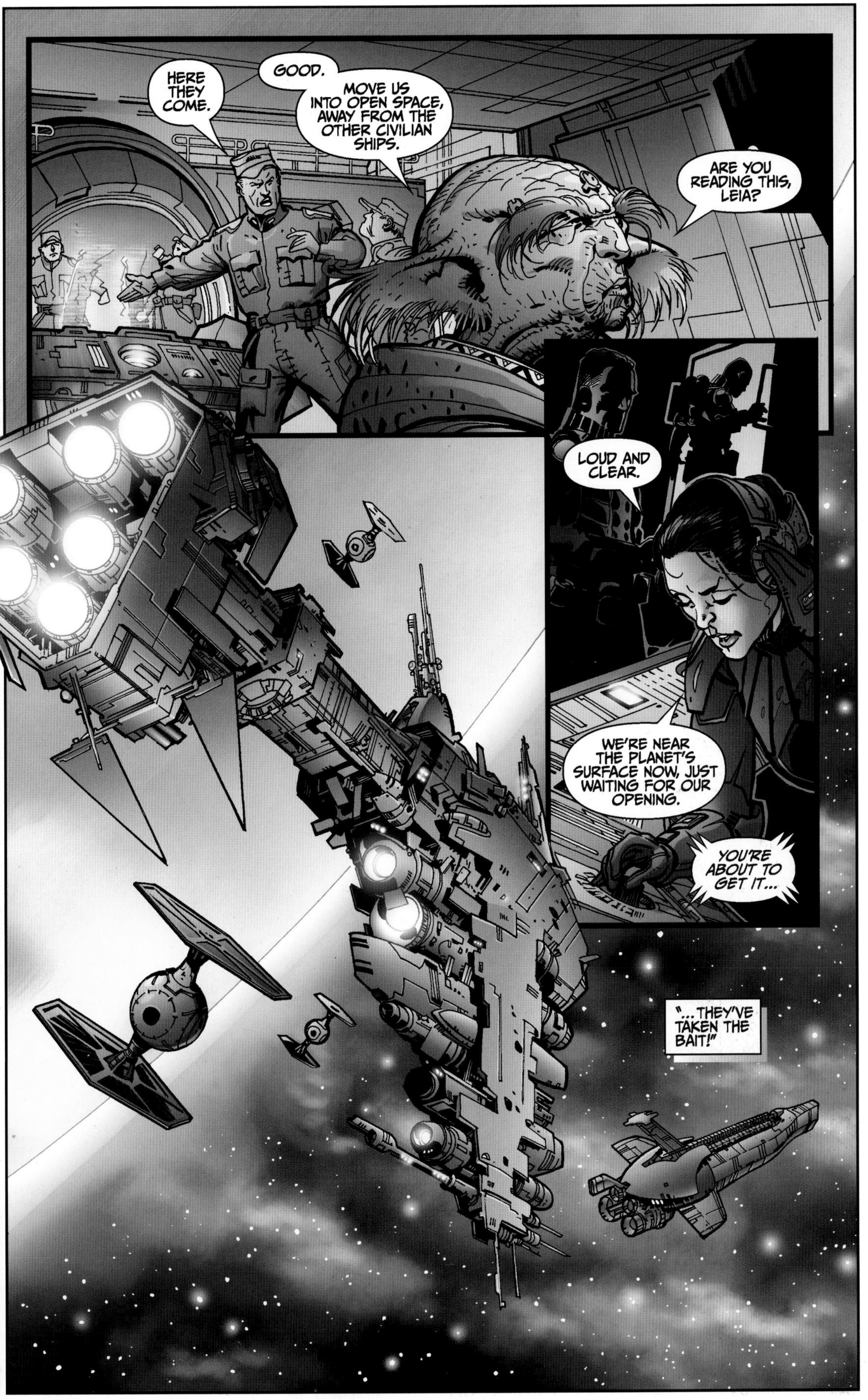
HERE THEY COME.
GOOD.
MOVE US INTO OPEN SPACE, AWAY FROM THE OTHER CIVILIAN SHIPS.
ARE YOU READING THIS, LEIA?
LOUD AND CLEAR.
WE'RE NEAR THE PLANET'S SURFACE NOW, JUST WAITING FOR OUR OPENING.
YOU'RE ABOUT TO GET IT...
"...THEY'VE TAKEN THE BAIT!"

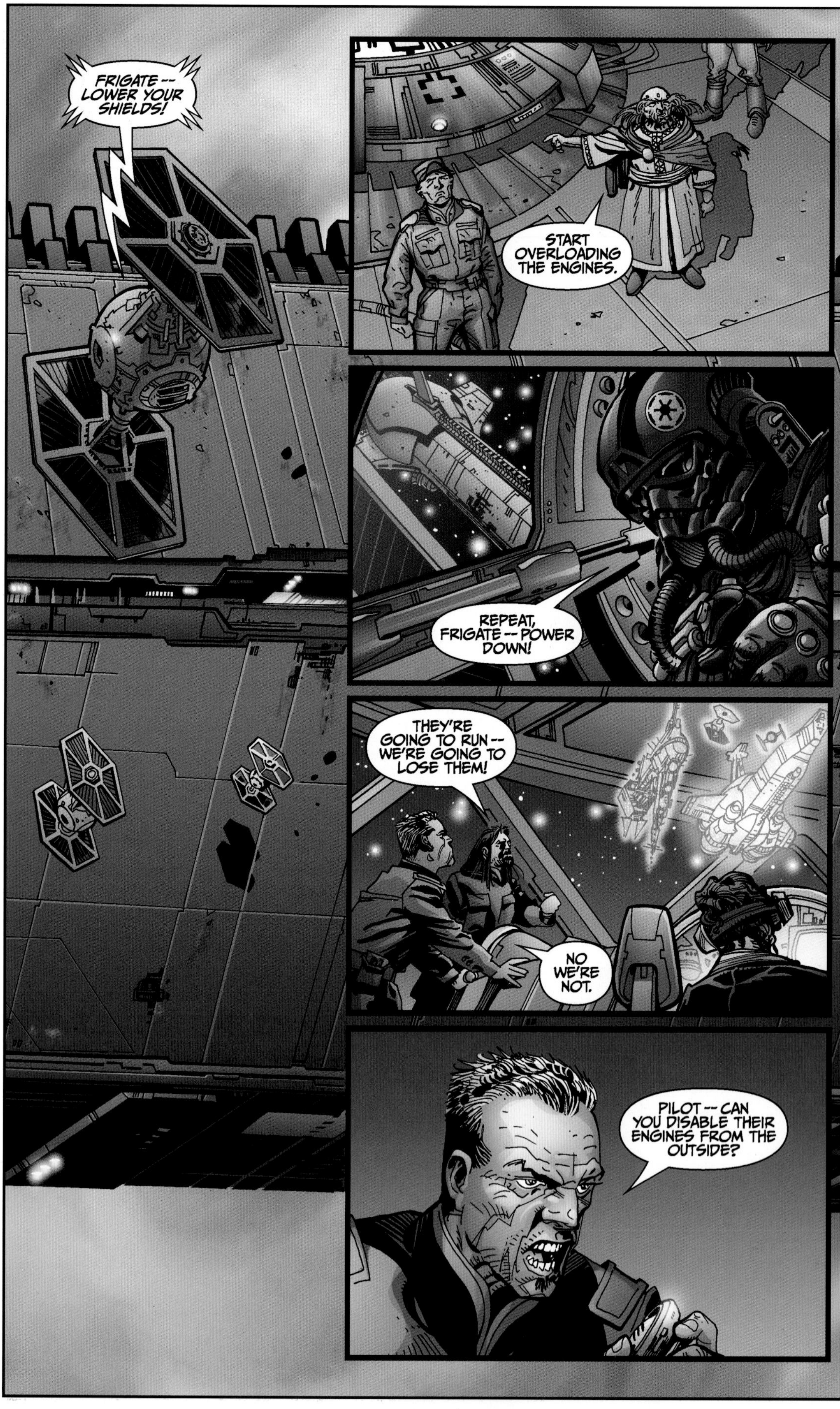
FRIGATE -- LOWER YOUR SHIELDS!
START OVERLOADING THE ENGINES.
REPEAT, FRIGATE -- POWER DOWN!
THEY'RE GOING TO RUN -- WE'RE GOING TO LOSE THEM!
NO WE'RE NOT.
PILOT -- CAN YOU DISABLE THEIR ENGINES FROM THE OUTSIDE?

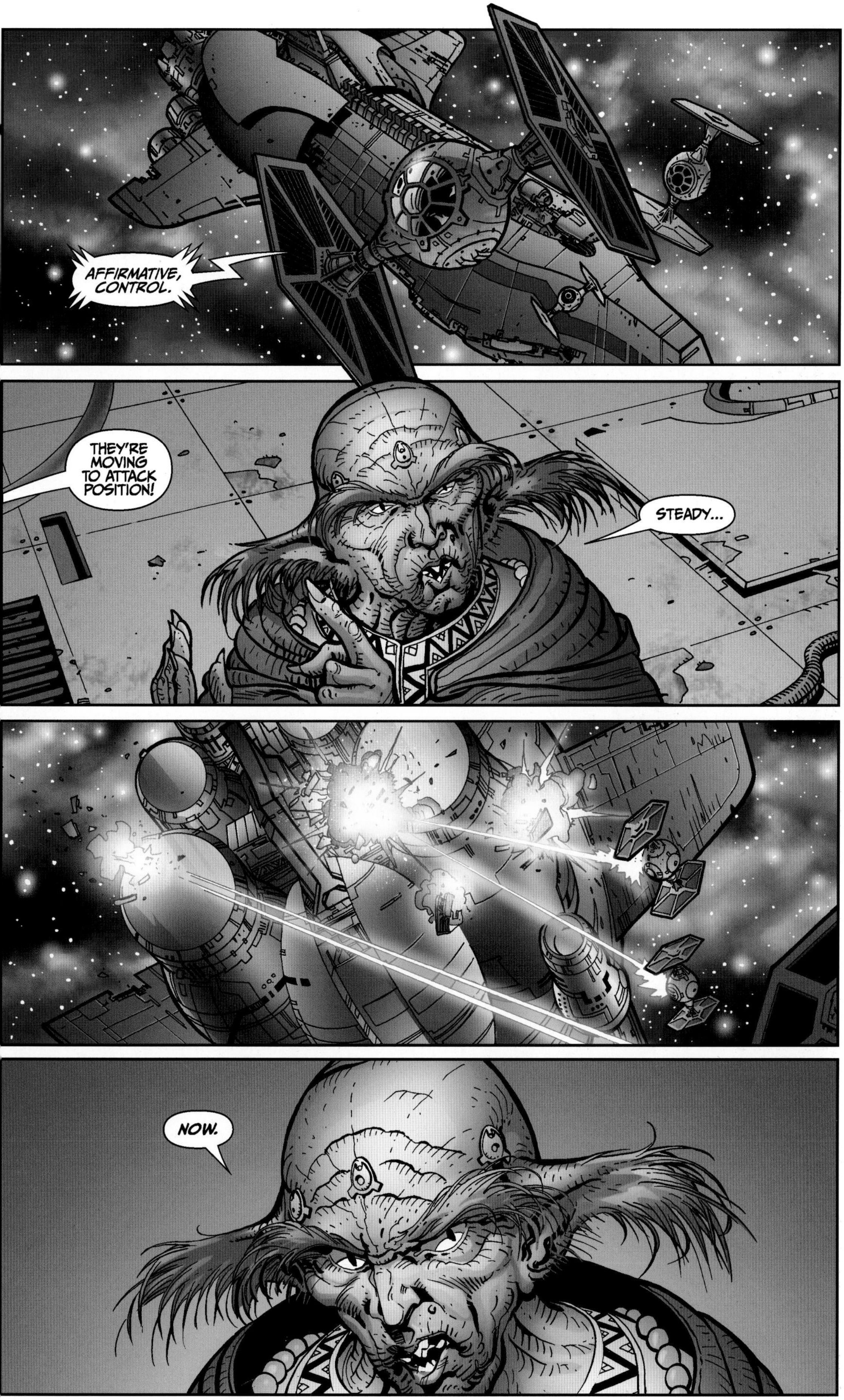
AFFIRMATIVE, CONTROL.
THEY'RE MOVING TO ATTACK POSITION!
STEADY...
NOW.

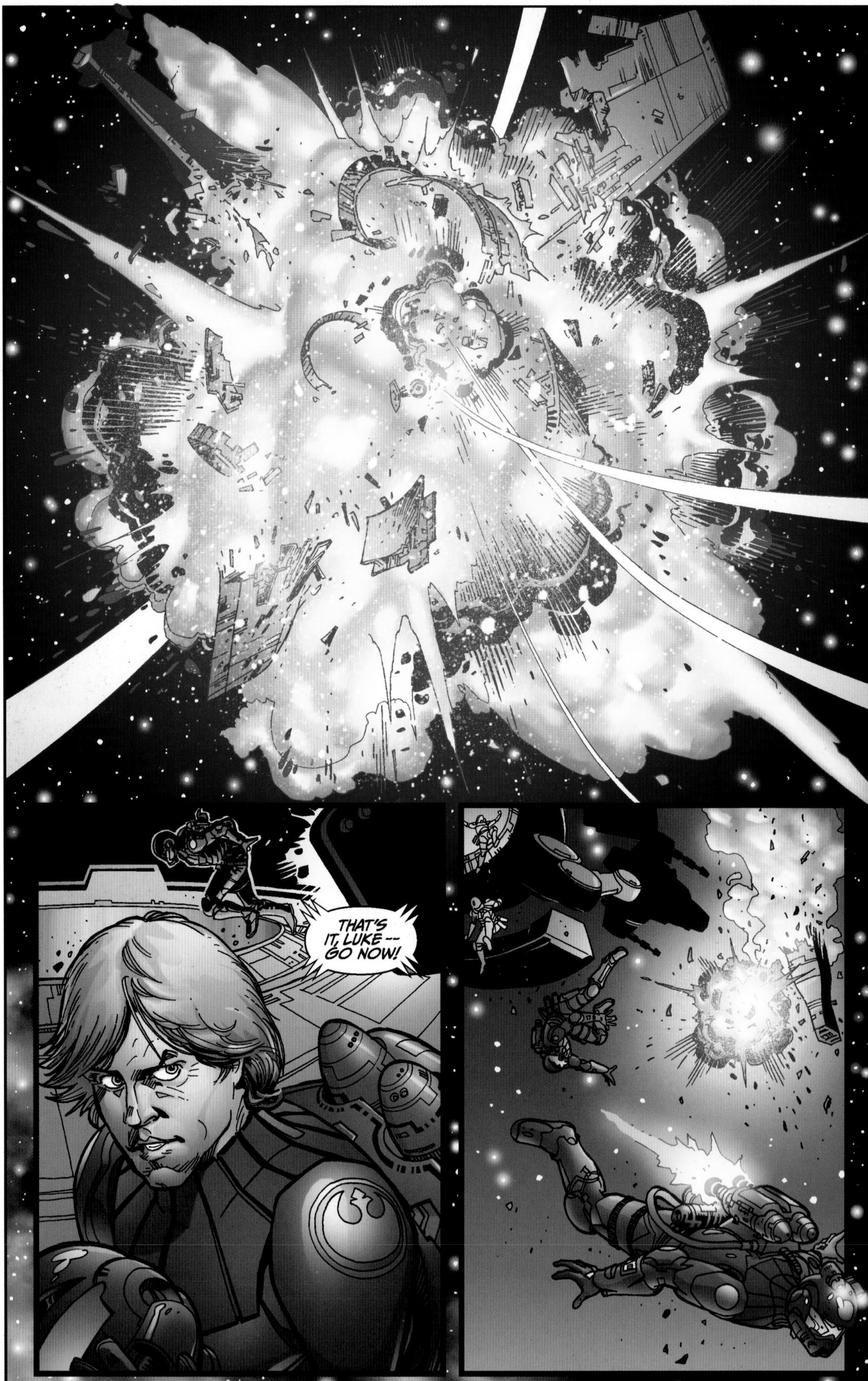
THAT'S IT, LUKE -- GO NOW!

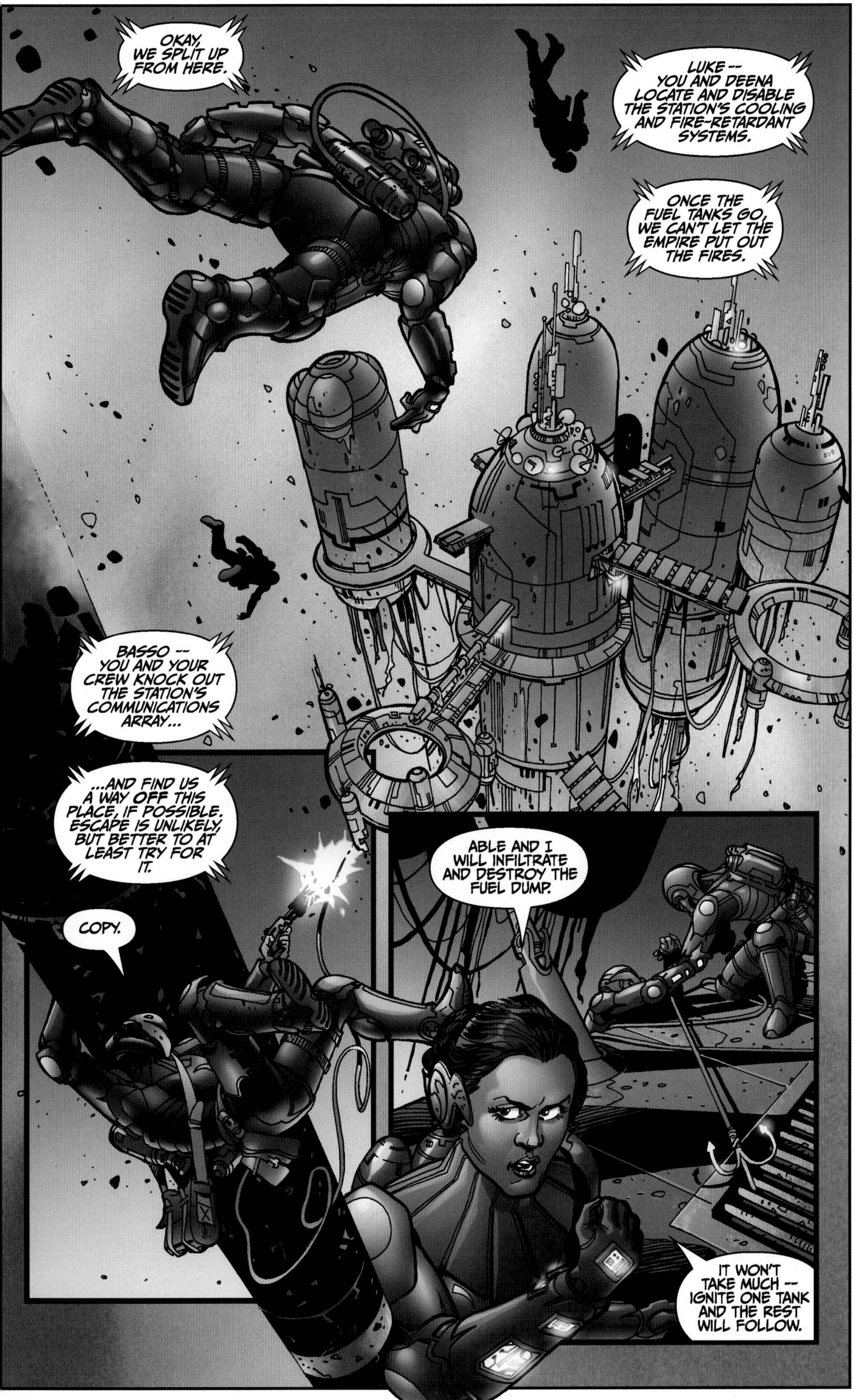
OKAY, WE SPLIT UP FROM HERE.
LUKE -- YOU AND DEENA LOCATE AND DISABLE THE STATION'S COOLING AND FIRE-RETARDANT SYSTEMS.
ONCE THE FUEL TANKS GO, WE CAN'T LET THE EMPIRE PUT OUT THE FIRES.
BASSO -- YOU AND YOUR CREW KNOCK OUT THE STATION'S COMMUNICATIONS ARRAY...
...AND FIND US A WAY OFF THIS PLACE, IF POSSIBLE. ESCAPE IS UNLIKELY, BUT BETTER TO AT LEAST TRY FOR IT.
COPY.
ABLE AND I WILL INFILTRATE AND DESTROY THE FUEL DUMP.
IT WON'T TAKE MUCH -- IGNITE ONE TANK AND THE REST WILL FOLLOW.

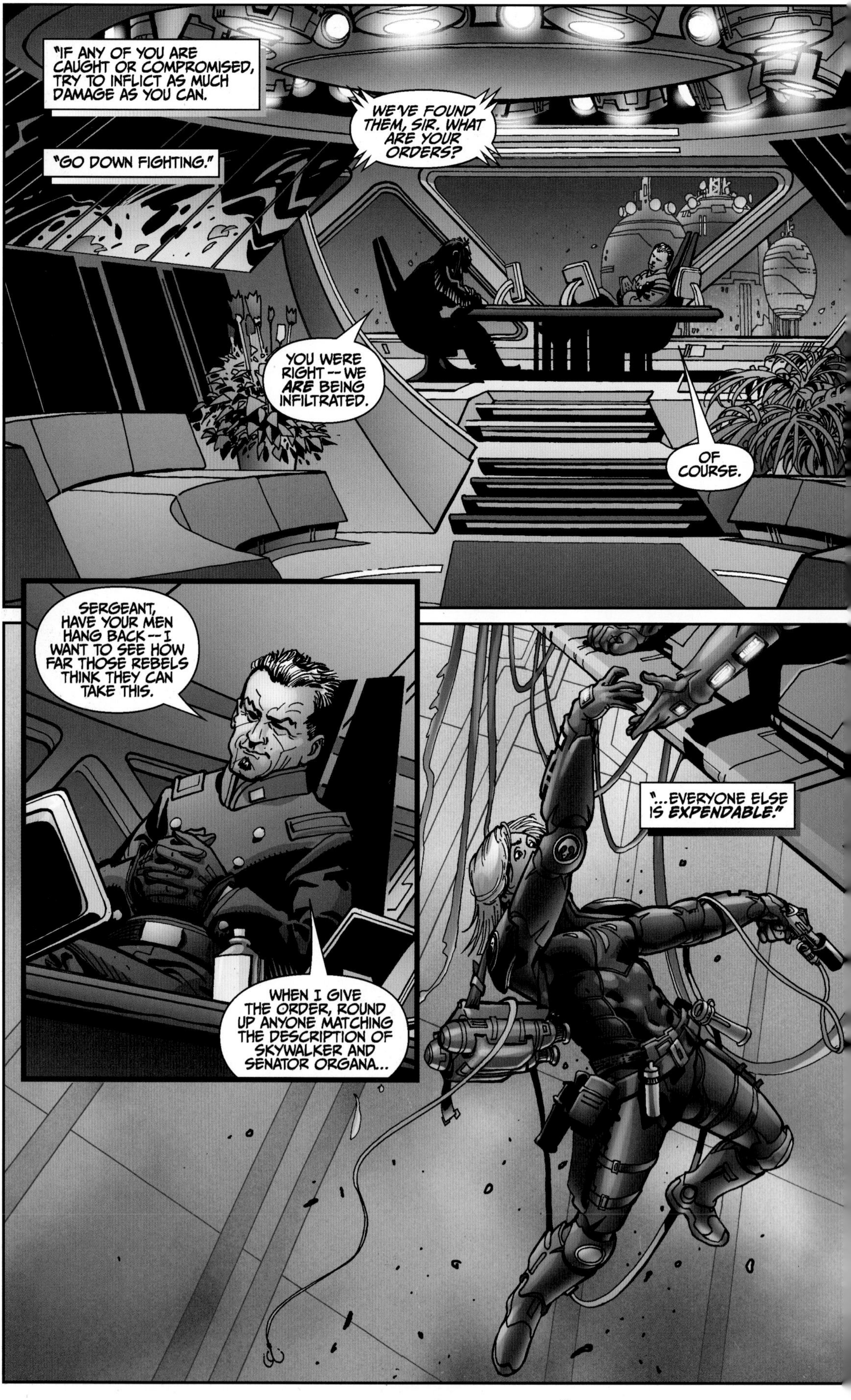
"IF ANY OF YOU ARE CAUGHT OR COMPROMISED, TRY TO INFLICT AS MUCH DAMAGE AS YOU CAN.
"GO DOWN FIGHTING."
WE'VE FOUND THEM, SIR. WHAT ARE YOUR ORDERS?
YOU WERE RIGHT -- WE ARE BEING INFILTRATED.
OF COURSE.
SERGEANT, HAVE YOUR MEN HANG BACK -- I WANT TO SEE HOW FAR THOSE REBELS THINK THEY CAN TAKE THIS.
WHEN I GIVE THE ORDER, ROUND UP ANYONE MATCHING THE DESCRIPTION OF SKYWALKER AND SENATOR ORGANA...
"...EVERYONE ELSE IS EXPENDABLE."

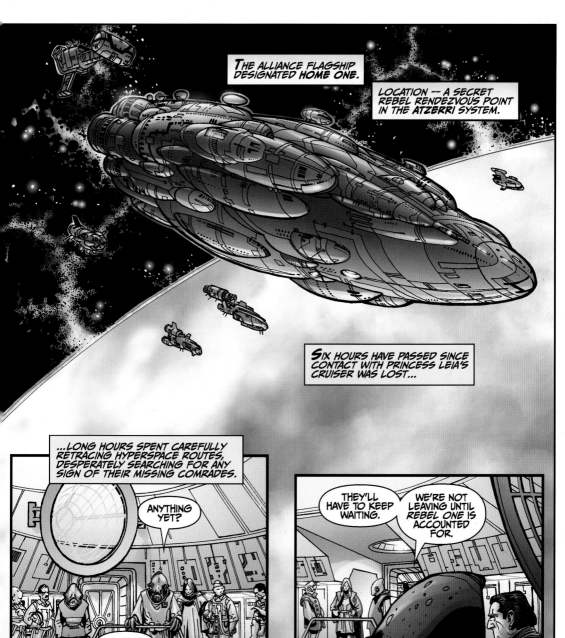

THE ALLIANCE FLAGSHIP DESIGNATED **HOME ONE.**

LOCATION -- A SECRET REBEL RENDEZVOUS POINT IN THE **ATZERRI** SYSTEM.

SIX HOURS HAVE PASSED SINCE CONTACT WITH PRINCESS LEIA'S CRUISER WAS LOST...

...LONG HOURS SPENT CAREFULLY RETRACING HYPERSPACE ROUTES, DESPERATELY SEARCHING FOR ANY SIGN OF THEIR MISSING COMRADES.

ANYTHING YET?

NOTHING, ADMIRAL.

ALL OF THE OTHER SHIPS HAVE CHECKED IN AND ARE AWAITING OUR ORDER TO JUMP.

THEY'LL HAVE TO KEEP WAITING.

WE'RE NOT LEAVING UNTIL REBEL ONE IS ACCOUNTED FOR.

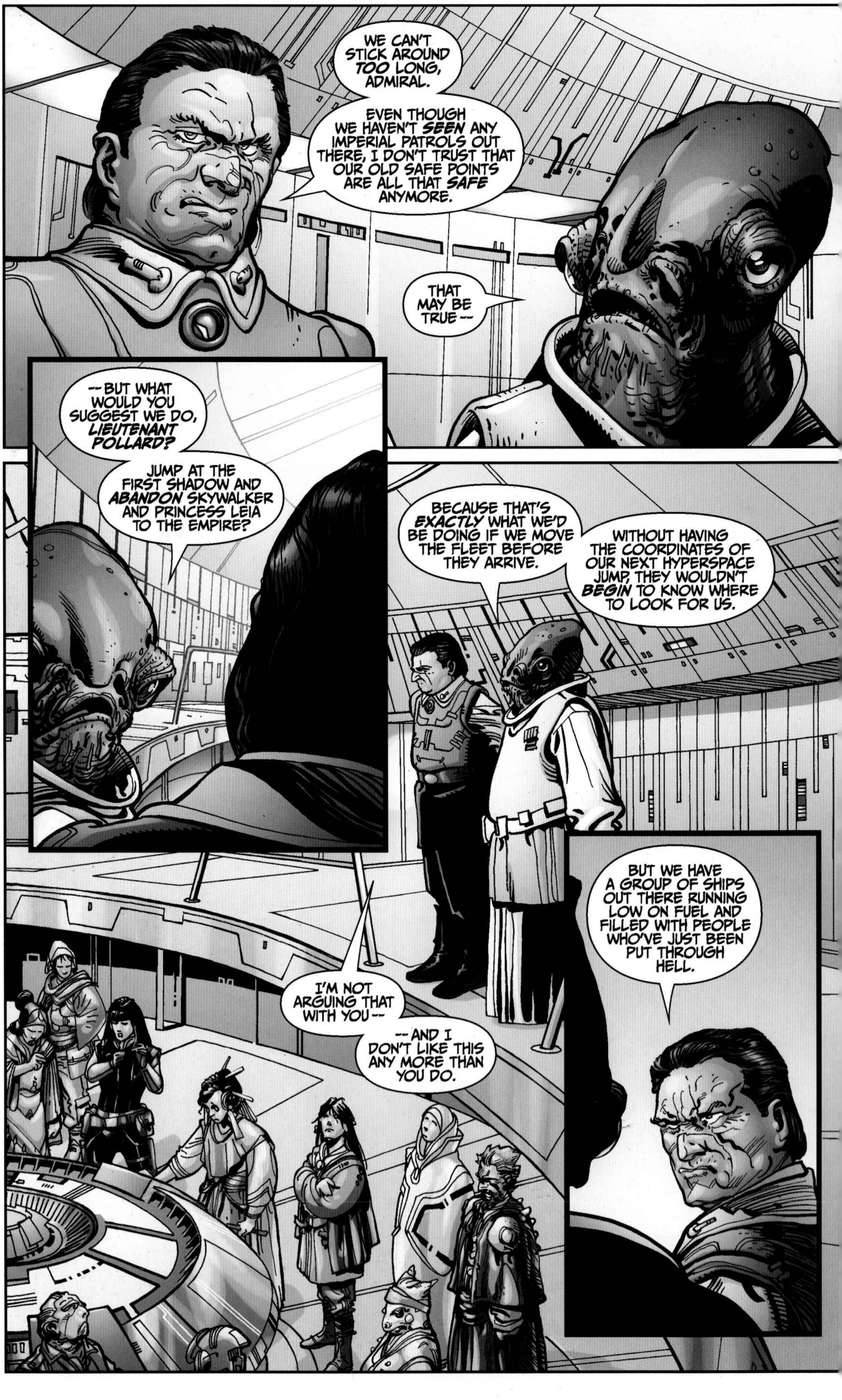

WE CAN'T STICK AROUND TOO LONG, ADMIRAL.
EVEN THOUGH WE HAVEN'T SEEN ANY IMPERIAL PATROLS OUT THERE, I DON'T TRUST THAT OUR OLD SAFE POINTS ARE ALL THAT SAFE ANYMORE.
THAT MAY BE TRUE --
-- BUT WHAT WOULD YOU SUGGEST WE DO, LIEUTENANT POLLARD?
JUMP AT THE FIRST SHADOW AND ABANDON SKYWALKER AND PRINCESS LEIA TO THE EMPIRE?
BECAUSE THAT'S EXACTLY WHAT WE'D BE DOING IF WE MOVE THE FLEET BEFORE THEY ARRIVE.
WITHOUT HAVING THE COORDINATES OF OUR NEXT HYPERSPACE JUMP, THEY WOULDN'T BEGIN TO KNOW WHERE TO LOOK FOR US.
I'M NOT ARGUING THAT WITH YOU --
-- AND I DON'T LIKE THIS ANY MORE THAN YOU DO.
BUT WE HAVE A GROUP OF SHIPS OUT THERE RUNNING LOW ON FUEL AND FILLED WITH PEOPLE WHO'VE JUST BEEN PUT THROUGH HELL.

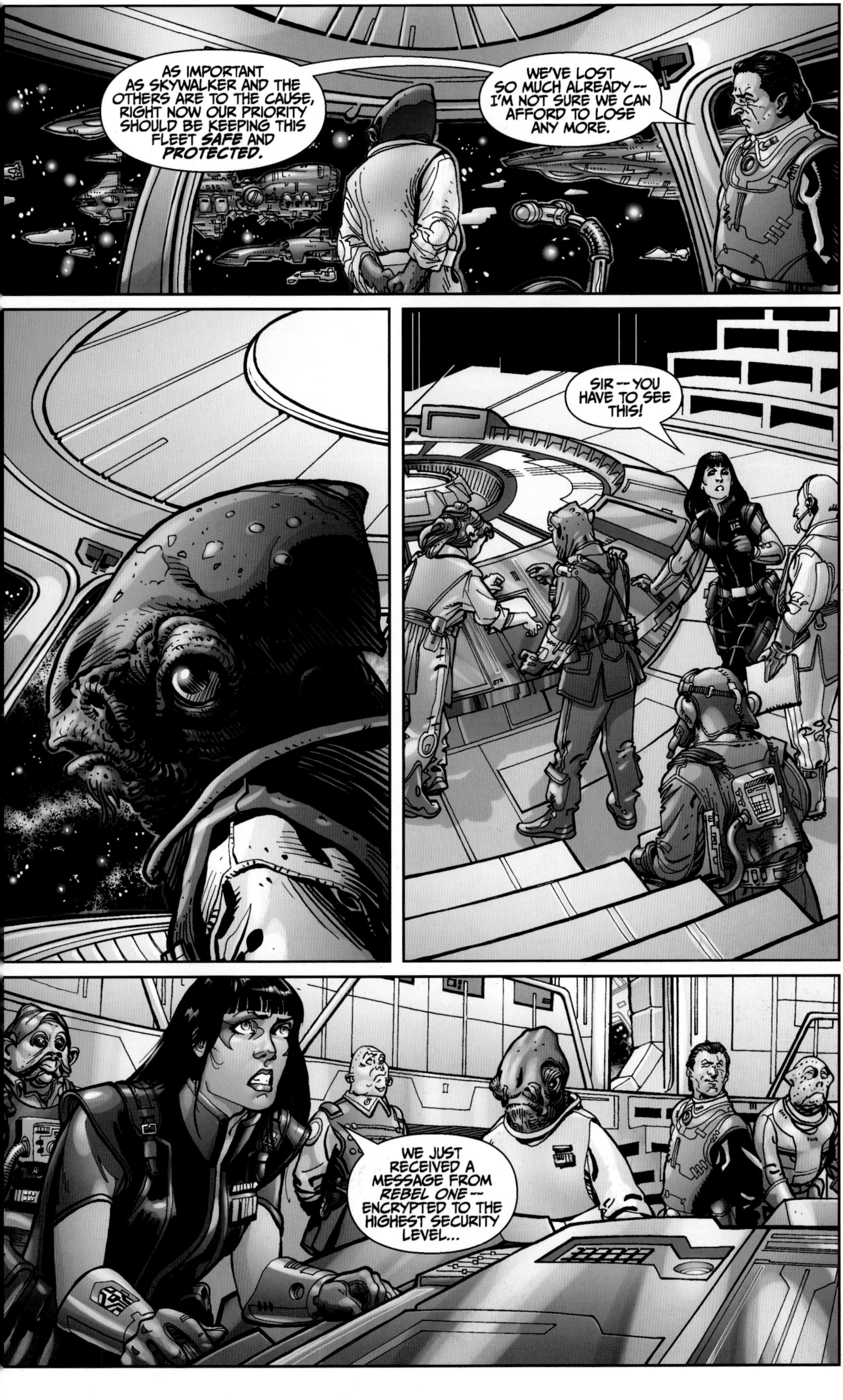
AS IMPORTANT AS SKYWALKER AND THE OTHERS ARE TO THE CAUSE, RIGHT NOW OUR PRIORITY SHOULD BE KEEPING THIS FLEET *SAFE* AND *PROTECTED.*
WE'VE LOST SO MUCH ALREADY -- I'M NOT SURE WE CAN AFFORD TO LOSE ANY MORE.
SIR -- YOU HAVE TO SEE THIS!
WE JUST RECEIVED A MESSAGE FROM *REBEL ONE* -- ENCRYPTED TO THE HIGHEST SECURITY LEVEL...

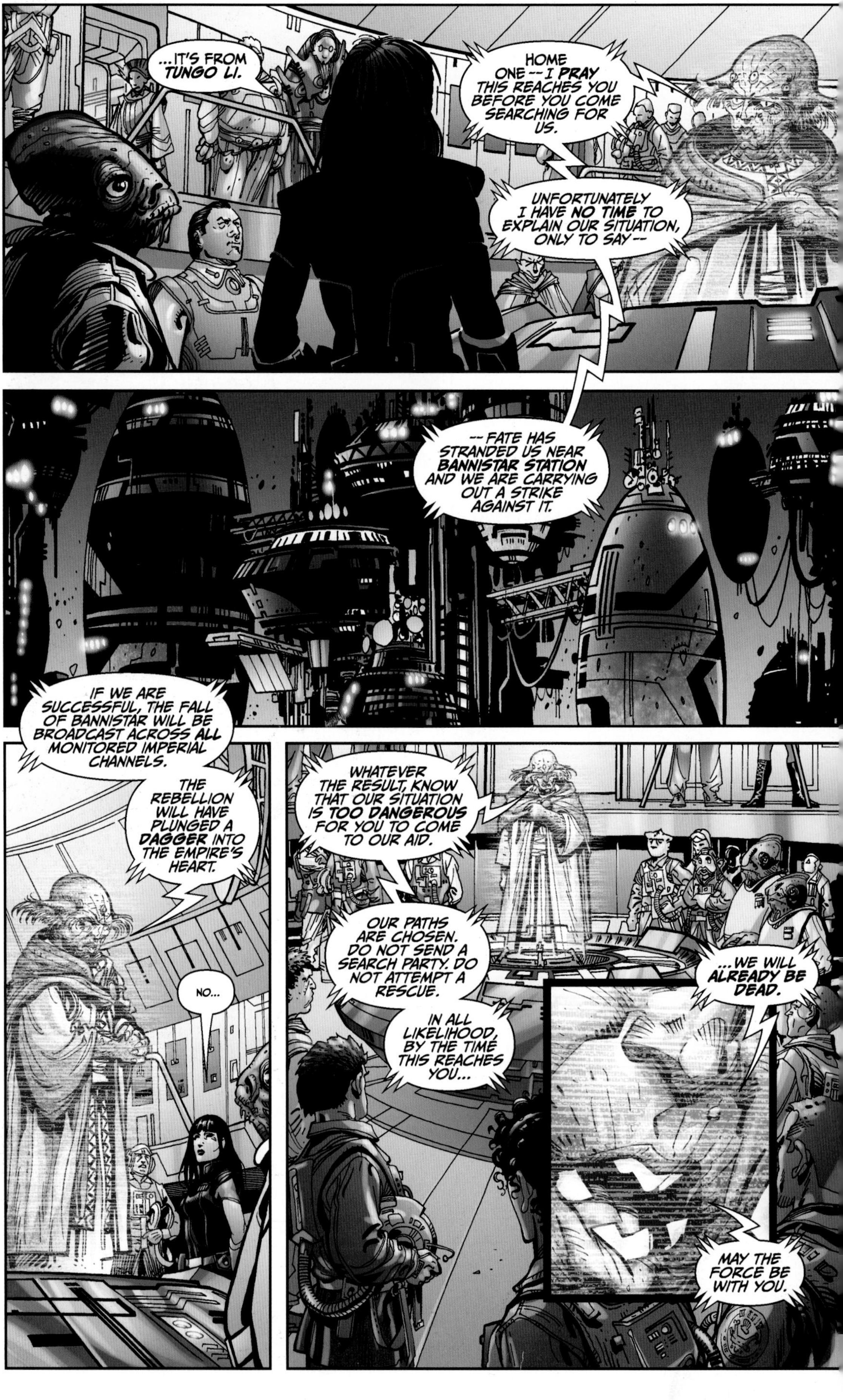

...IT'S FROM TUNGO LI.
HOME ONE -- I PRAY THIS REACHES YOU BEFORE YOU COME SEARCHING FOR US.
UNFORTUNATELY I HAVE NO TIME TO EXPLAIN OUR SITUATION, ONLY TO SAY --
-- FATE HAS STRANDED US NEAR BANNISTAR STATION AND WE ARE CARRYING OUT A STRIKE AGAINST IT.
IF WE ARE SUCCESSFUL, THE FALL OF BANNISTAR WILL BE BROADCAST ACROSS ALL MONITORED IMPERIAL CHANNELS.
THE REBELLION WILL HAVE PLUNGED A DAGGER INTO THE EMPIRE'S HEART.
NO...
WHATEVER THE RESULT, KNOW THAT OUR SITUATION IS TOO DANGEROUS FOR YOU TO COME TO OUR AID.
OUR PATHS ARE CHOSEN. DO NOT SEND A SEARCH PARTY. DO NOT ATTEMPT A RESCUE.
IN ALL LIKELIHOOD, BY THE TIME THIS REACHES YOU...
...WE WILL ALREADY BE DEAD.
MAY THE FORCE BE WITH YOU.

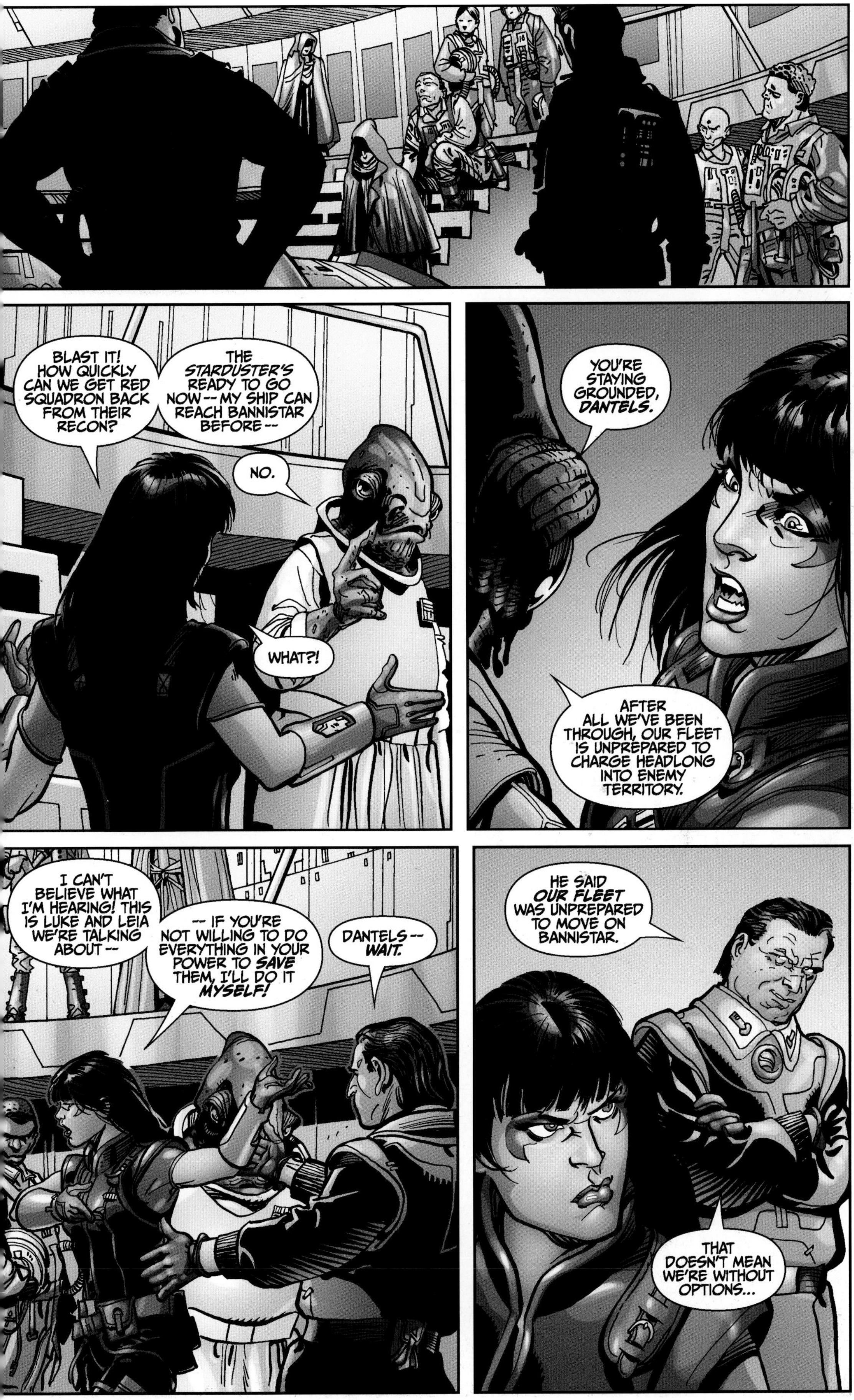
BLAST IT! HOW QUICKLY CAN WE GET RED SQUADRON BACK FROM THEIR RECON?
THE *STARDUSTER'S* READY TO GO NOW -- MY SHIP CAN REACH BANNISTAR BEFORE --
NO.
WHAT?!
YOU'RE STAYING GROUNDED, *DANTELS.*
AFTER ALL WE'VE BEEN THROUGH, OUR FLEET IS UNPREPARED TO CHARGE HEADLONG INTO ENEMY TERRITORY.
I CAN'T BELIEVE WHAT I'M HEARING! THIS IS LUKE AND LEIA WE'RE TALKING ABOUT --
-- IF YOU'RE NOT WILLING TO DO EVERYTHING IN YOUR POWER TO *SAVE* THEM, I'LL DO IT *MYSELF!*
DANTELS -- *WAIT.*
HE SAID *OUR FLEET* WAS UNPREPARED TO MOVE ON BANNISTAR.
THAT DOESN'T MEAN WE'RE WITHOUT OPTIONS...

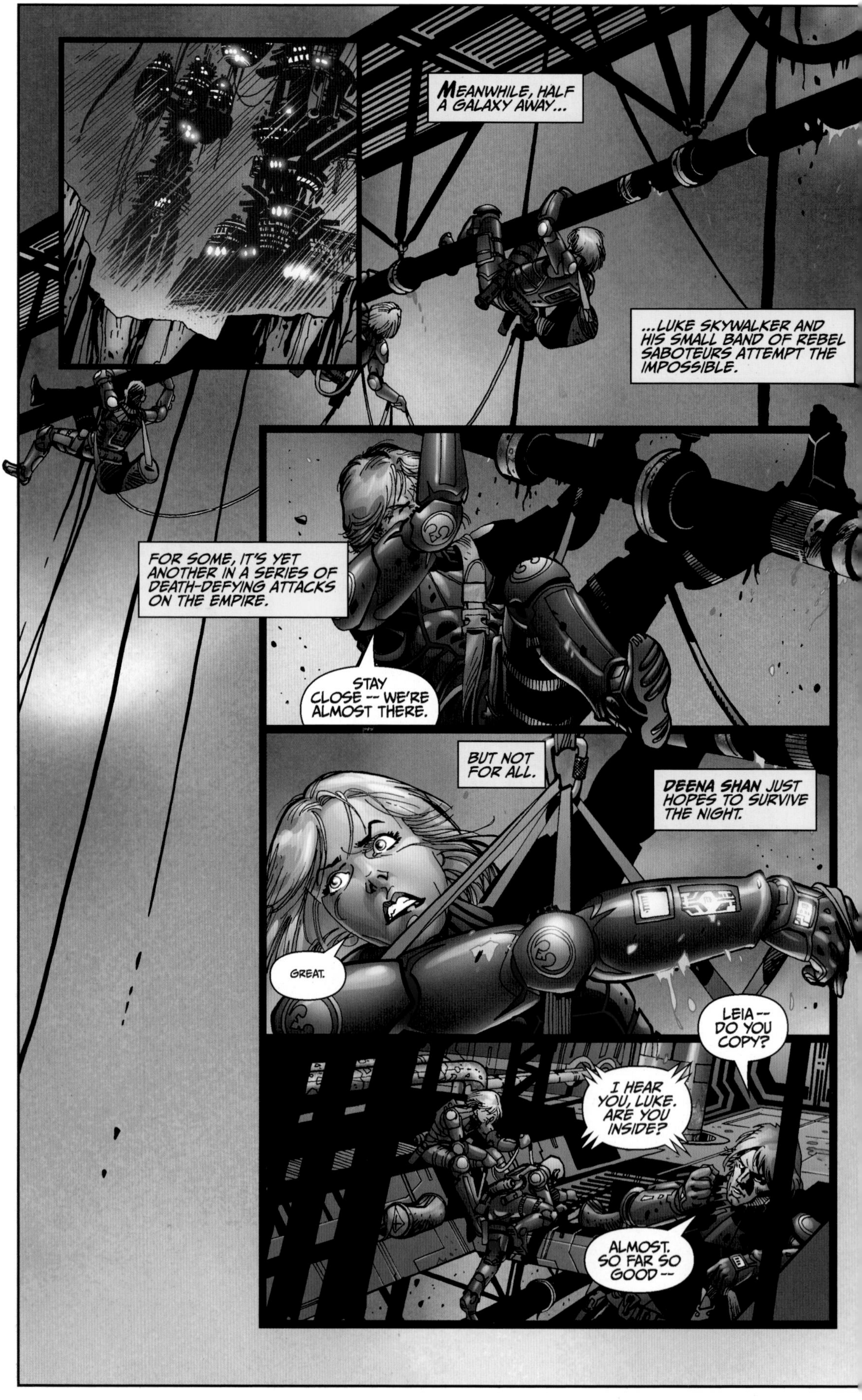
MEANWHILE, HALF A GALAXY AWAY...
...LUKE SKYWALKER AND HIS SMALL BAND OF REBEL SABOTEURS ATTEMPT THE IMPOSSIBLE.
FOR SOME, IT'S YET ANOTHER IN A SERIES OF DEATH-DEFYING ATTACKS ON THE EMPIRE.
STAY CLOSE -- WE'RE ALMOST THERE.
BUT NOT FOR ALL.
DEENA SHAN JUST HOPES TO SURVIVE THE NIGHT.
GREAT.
LEIA -- DO YOU COPY?
I HEAR YOU, LUKE. ARE YOU INSIDE?
ALMOST. SO FAR SO GOOD --

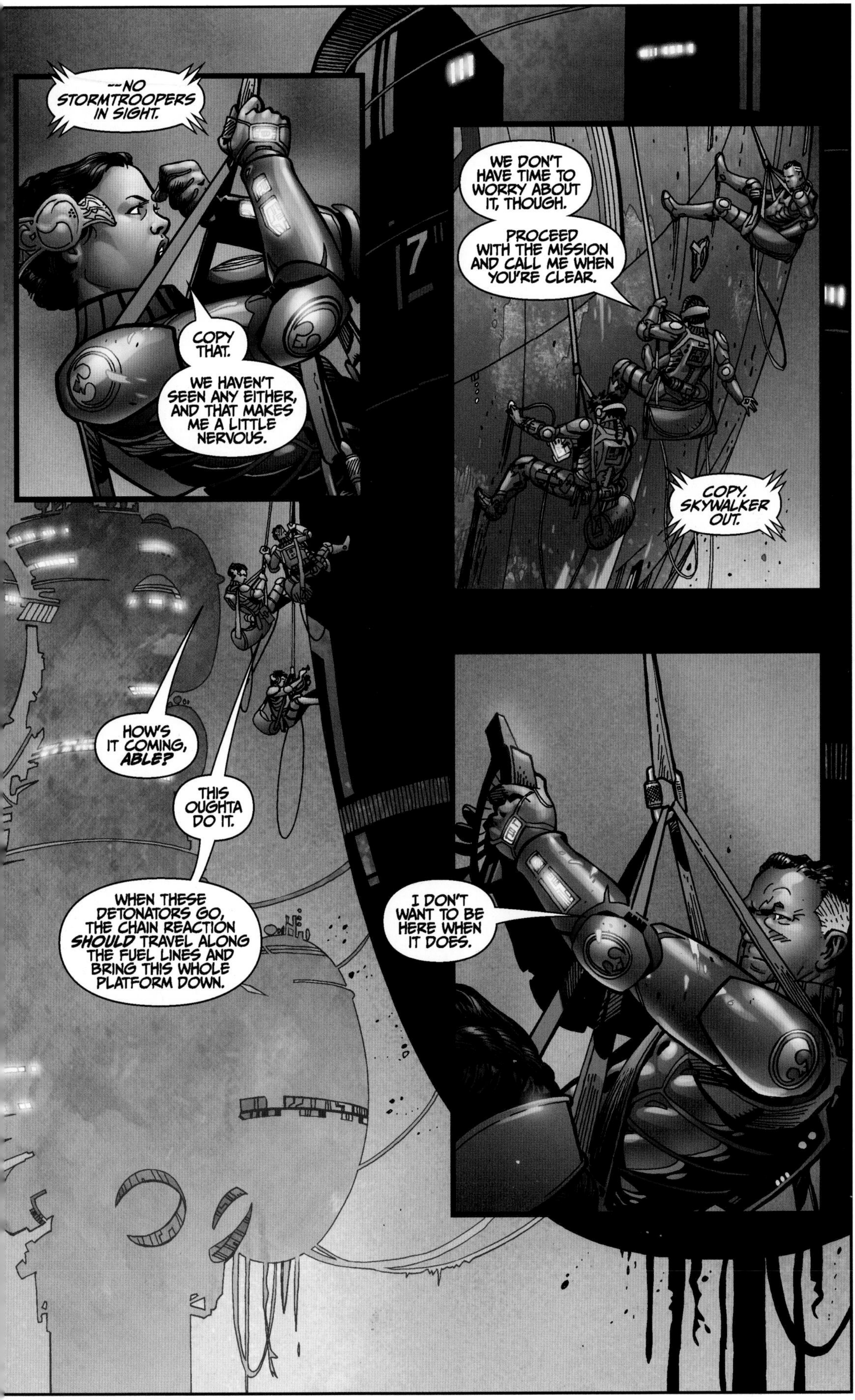
--NO STORMTROOPERS IN SIGHT.
COPY THAT.
WE HAVEN'T SEEN ANY EITHER, AND THAT MAKES ME A LITTLE NERVOUS.
WE DON'T HAVE TIME TO WORRY ABOUT IT, THOUGH.
PROCEED WITH THE MISSION AND CALL ME WHEN YOU'RE CLEAR.
COPY. SKYWALKER OUT.
HOW'S IT COMING, ABLE?
THIS OUGHTA DO IT.
WHEN THESE DETONATORS GO, THE CHAIN REACTION SHOULD TRAVEL ALONG THE FUEL LINES AND BRING THIS WHOLE PLATFORM DOWN.
I DON'T WANT TO BE HERE WHEN IT DOES.

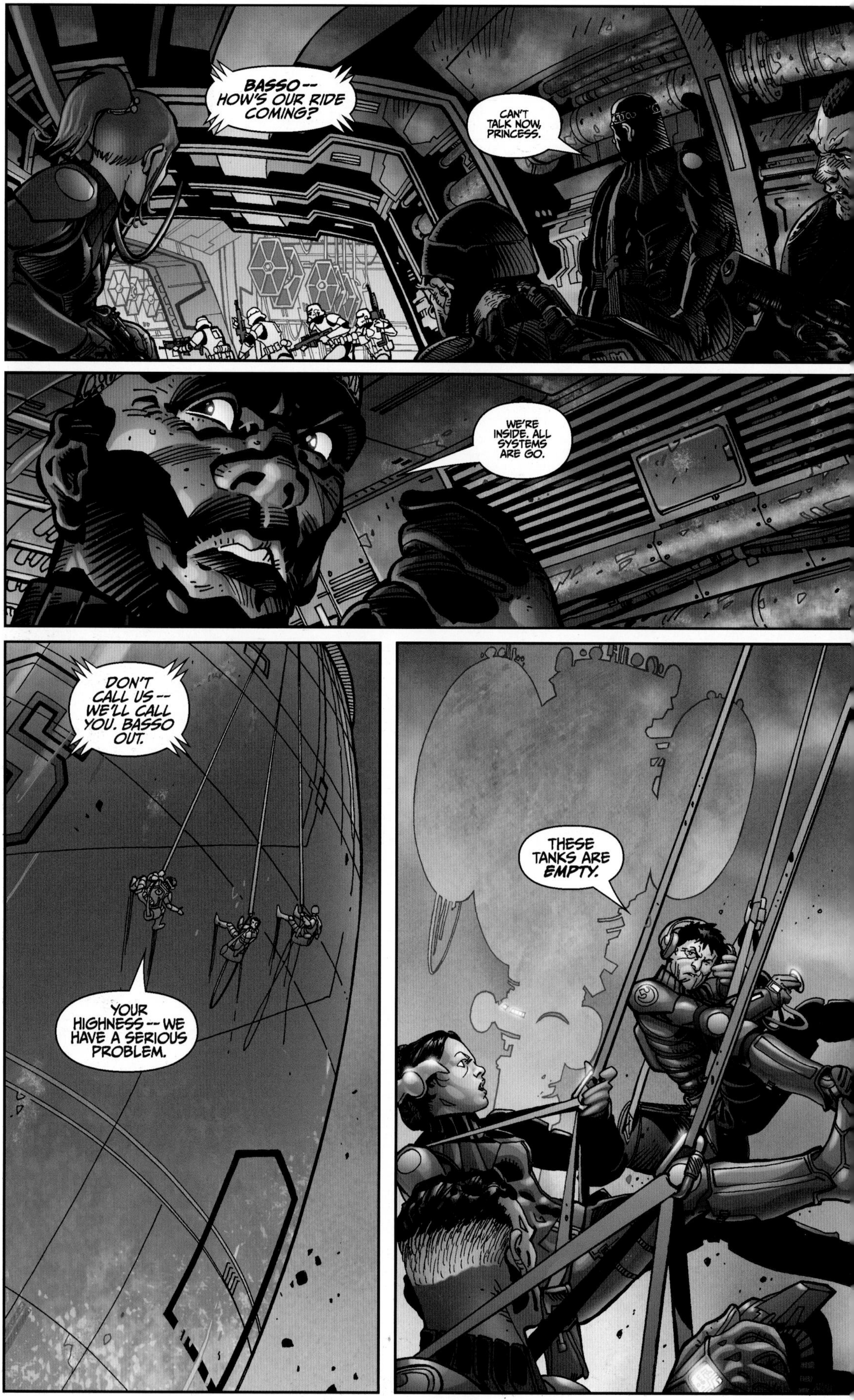
BASSO-- HOW'S OUR RIDE COMING?
CAN'T TALK NOW, PRINCESS.
WE'RE INSIDE. ALL SYSTEMS ARE GO.
DON'T CALL US-- WE'LL CALL YOU. BASSO OUT.
YOUR HIGHNESS-- WE HAVE A SERIOUS PROBLEM.
THESE TANKS ARE EMPTY.

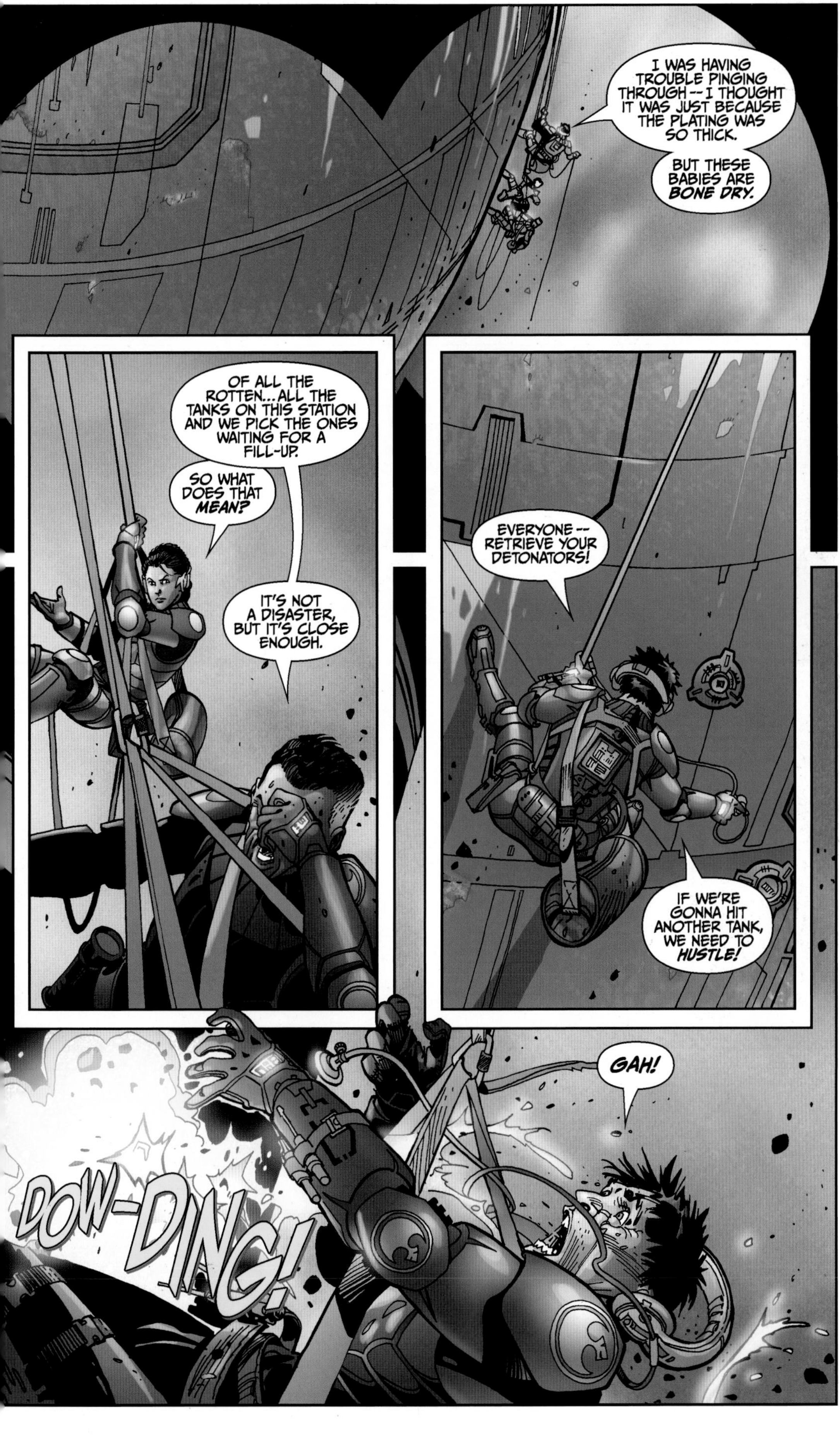
I WAS HAVING TROUBLE PINGING THROUGH -- I THOUGHT IT WAS JUST BECAUSE THE PLATING WAS SO THICK.
BUT THESE BABIES ARE *BONE DRY.*
OF ALL THE ROTTEN... ALL THE TANKS ON THIS STATION AND WE PICK THE ONES WAITING FOR A FILL-UP.
SO WHAT DOES THAT *MEAN?*
IT'S NOT A DISASTER, BUT IT'S CLOSE ENOUGH.
EVERYONE -- RETRIEVE YOUR DETONATORS!
IF WE'RE GONNA HIT ANOTHER TANK, WE NEED TO *HUSTLE!*
GAH!
DOW-DING!

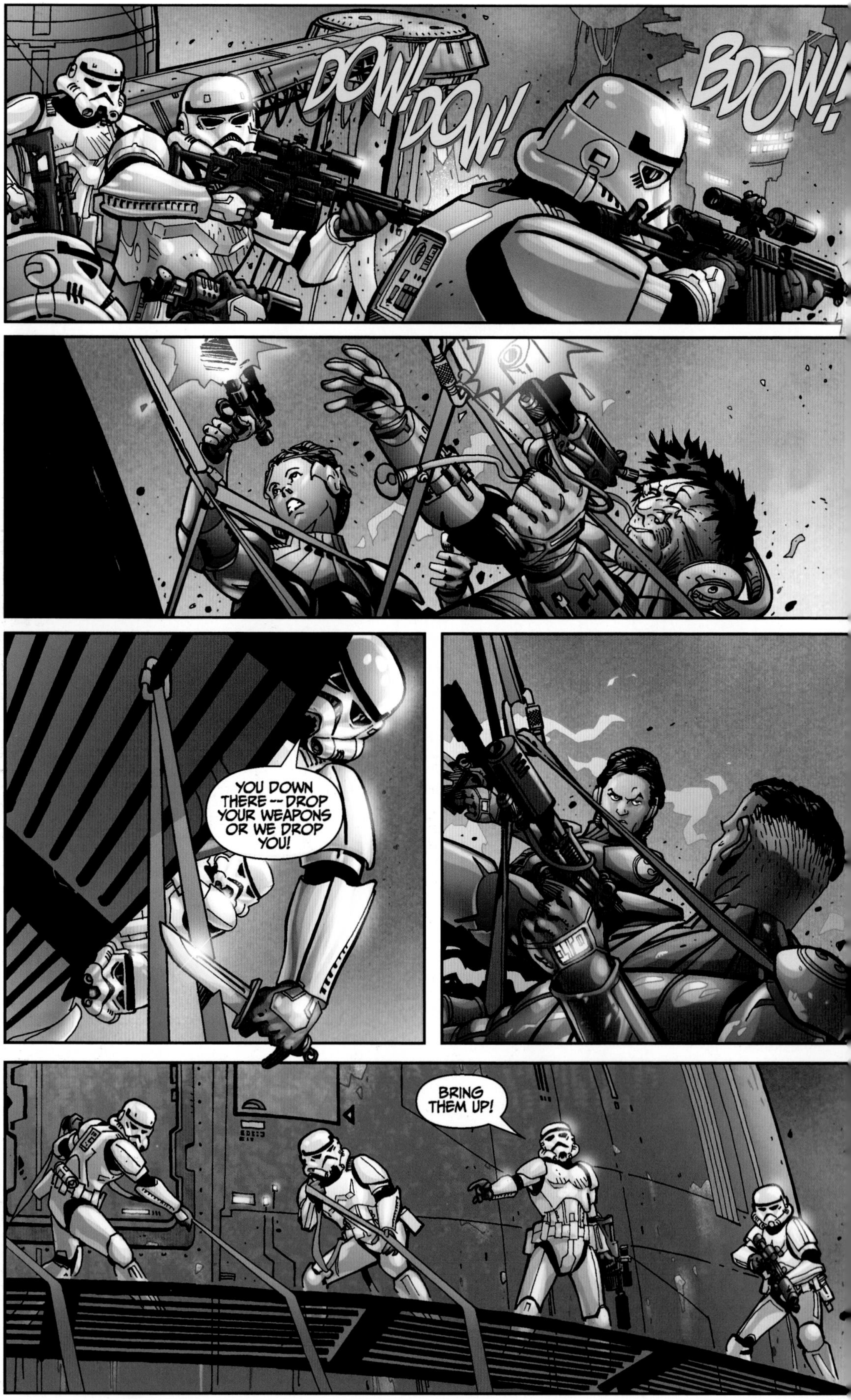
DOW! DOW!
BDOW!!
YOU DOWN THERE -- DROP YOUR WEAPONS OR WE DROP YOU!
BRING THEM UP!

AT THE SAME TIME...

WAIT -- DID YOU HEAR THAT? SOUNDED LIKE BLASTER FIRE...!

LEIA AND THE OTHERS MIGHT BE IN TROUBLE.

THEY'RE NOT THE ONLY ONES!

LOWER YOUR WEAPONS!

HANG BACK, LUKE -- LET US TAKE THIS.

BUT --

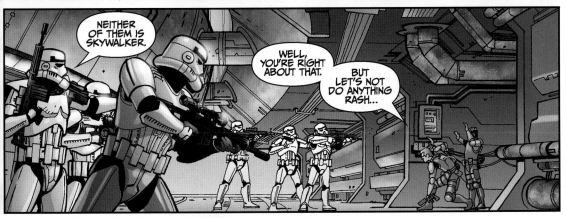

NEITHER OF THEM IS SKYWALKER.

WELL, YOU'RE RIGHT ABOUT THAT.

BUT LET'S NOT DO ANYTHING RASH...

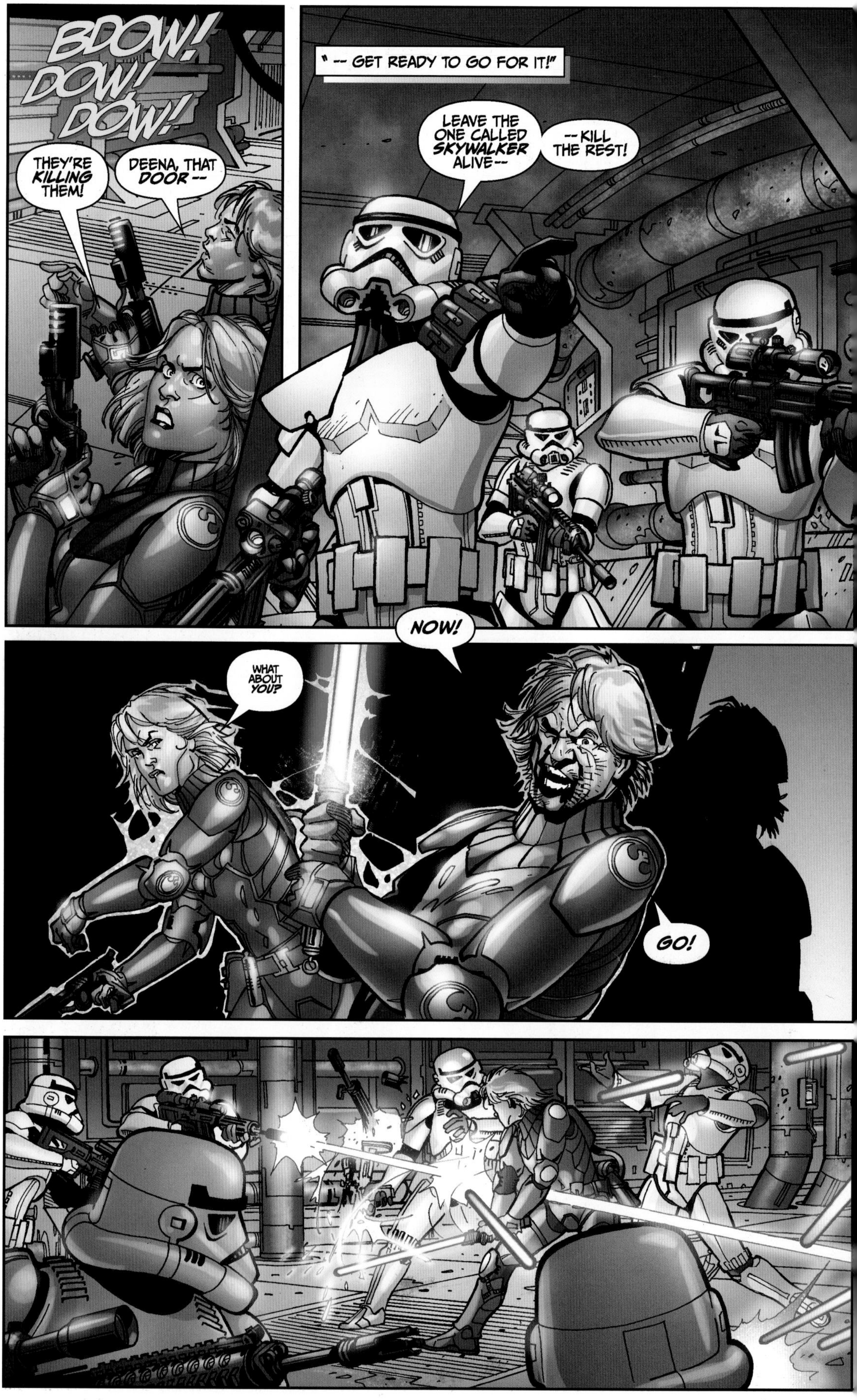
BDOW! DOW! DOW!
THEY'RE KILLING THEM!
DEENA, THAT DOOR --
" -- GET READY TO GO FOR IT!"
LEAVE THE ONE CALLED SKYWALKER ALIVE--
--KILL THE REST!
NOW!
WHAT ABOUT YOU?
GO!

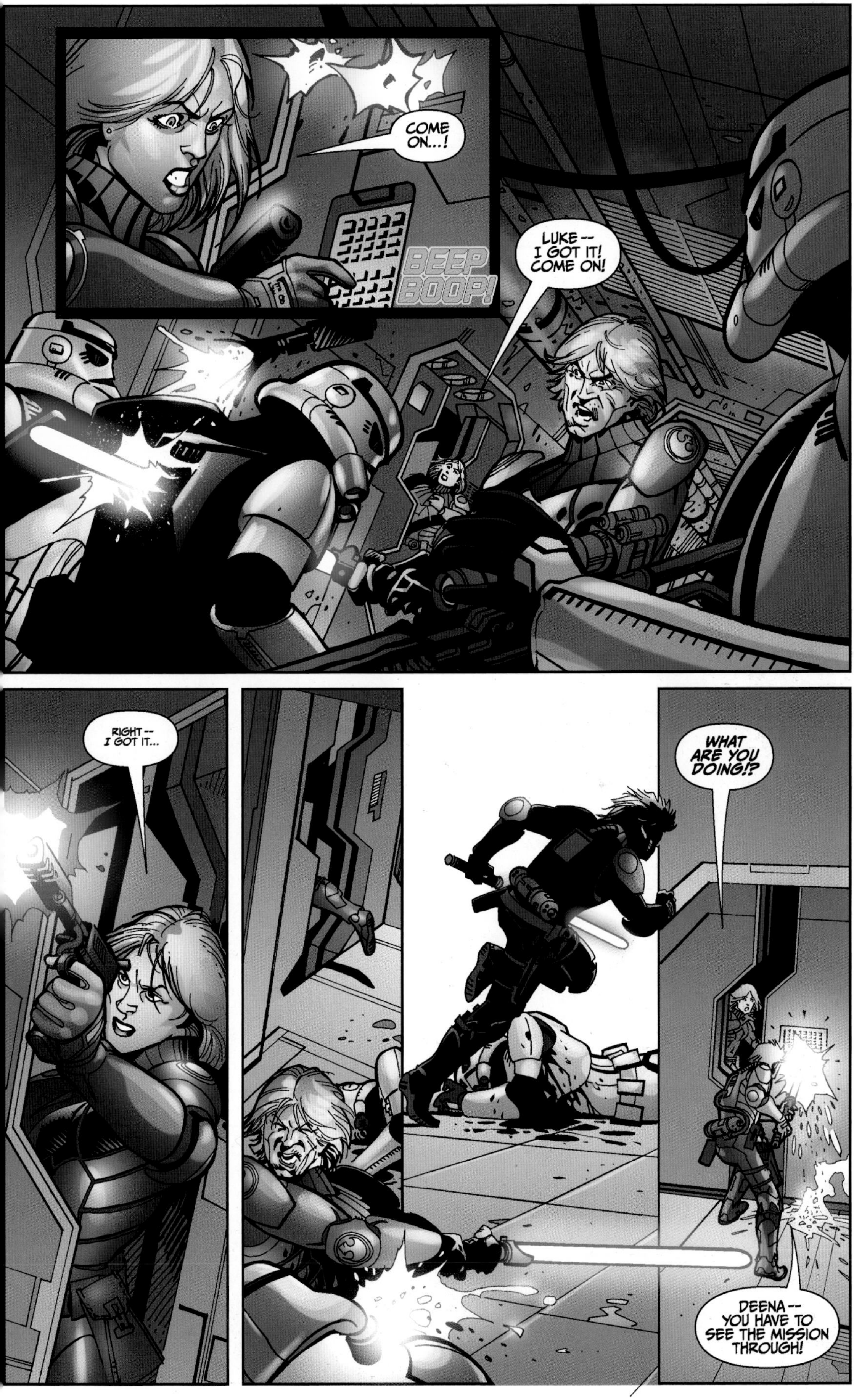
COME ON...!
BEEP BOOP!
LUKE -- I GOT IT! COME ON!
RIGHT -- I GOT IT...
WHAT ARE YOU DOING!?
DEENA -- YOU HAVE TO SEE THE MISSION THROUGH!

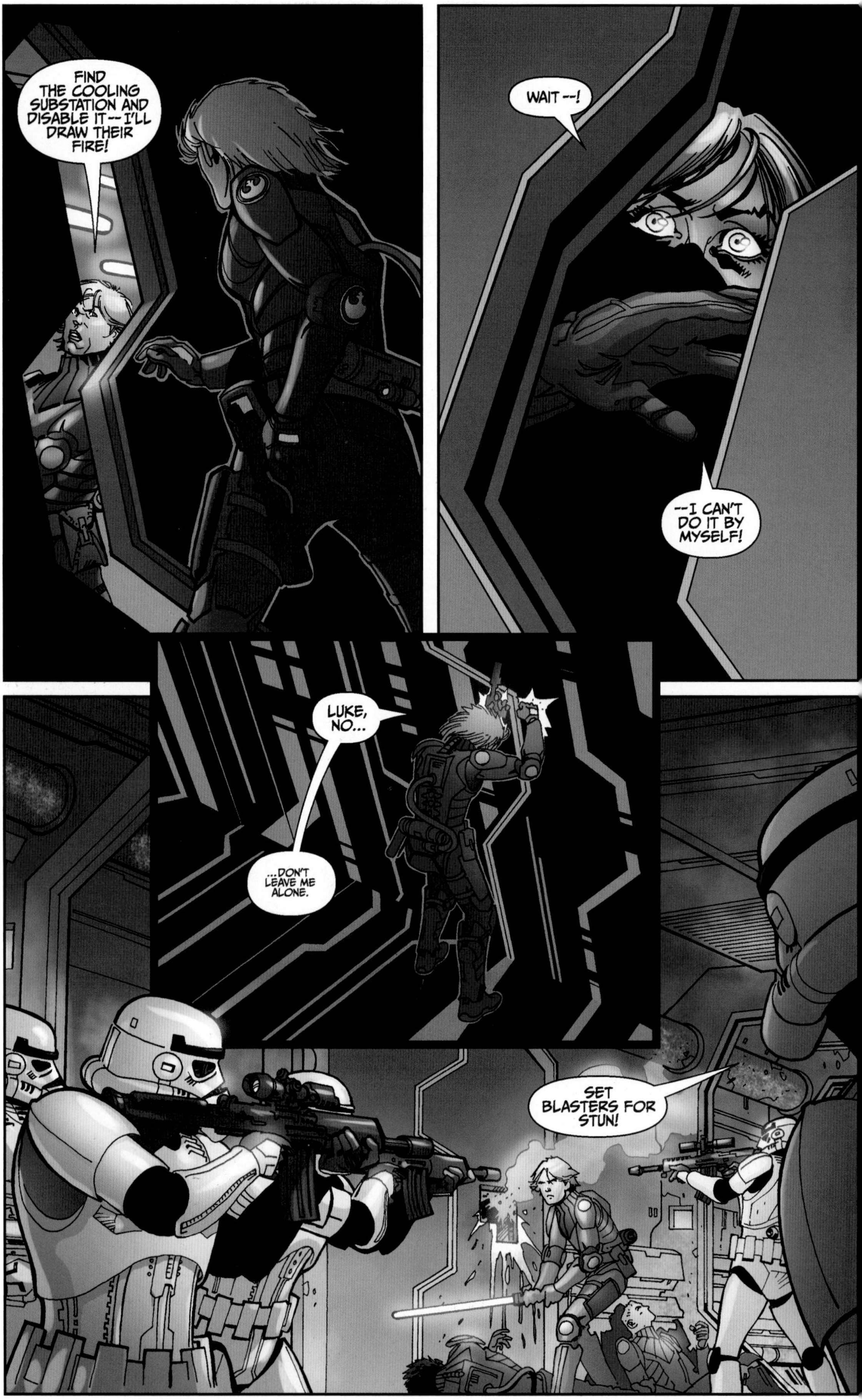
FIND THE COOLING SUBSTATION AND DISABLE IT--I'LL DRAW THEIR FIRE!
WAIT --!
--I CAN'T DO IT BY MYSELF!
LUKE, NO...
...DON'T LEAVE ME ALONE.
SET BLASTERS FOR STUN!

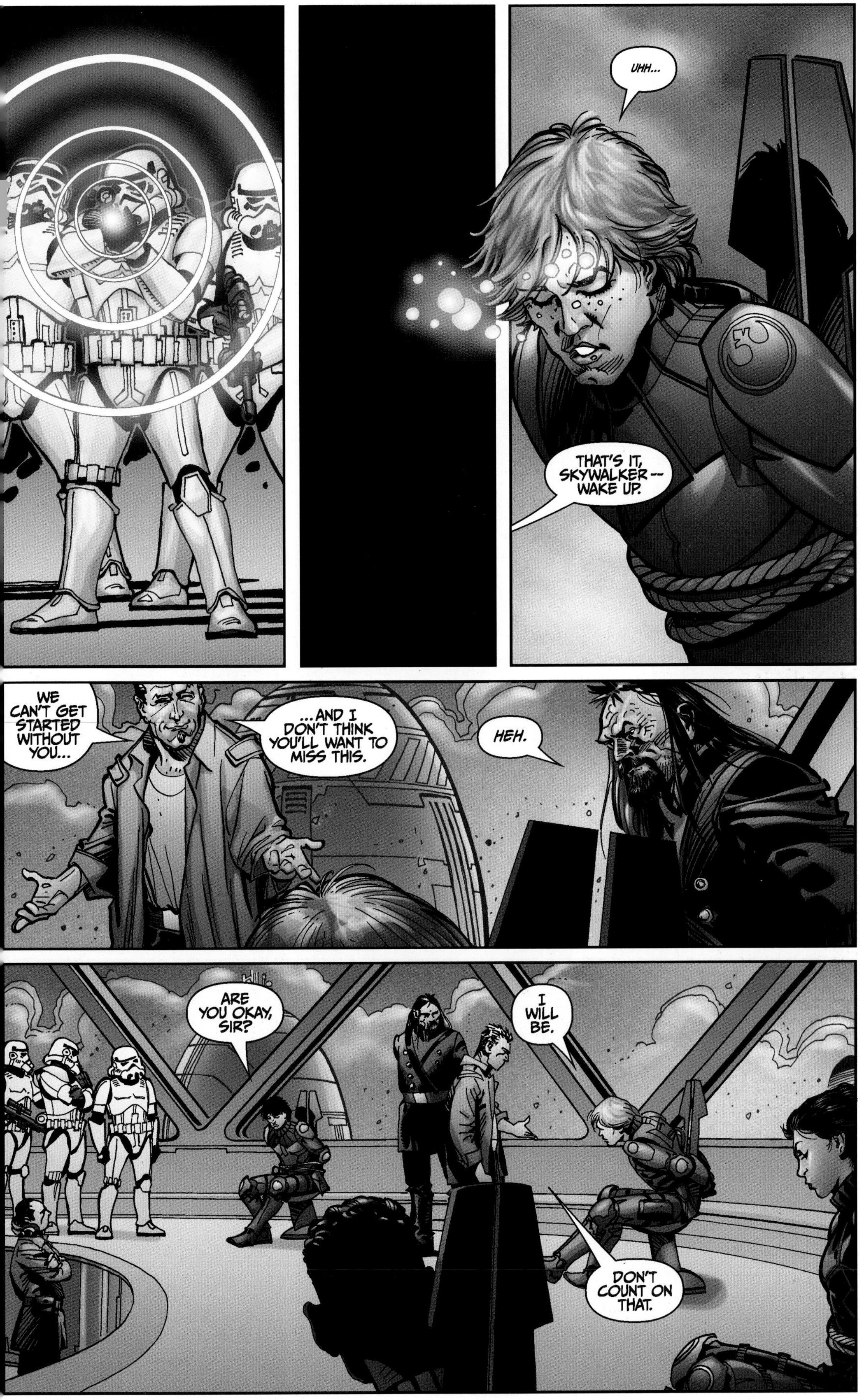
UHH...
THAT'S IT, SKYWALKER-- WAKE UP.
WE CAN'T GET STARTED WITHOUT YOU...
...AND I DON'T THINK YOU'LL WANT TO MISS THIS.
HEH.
ARE YOU OKAY, SIR?
I WILL BE.
DON'T COUNT ON THAT.

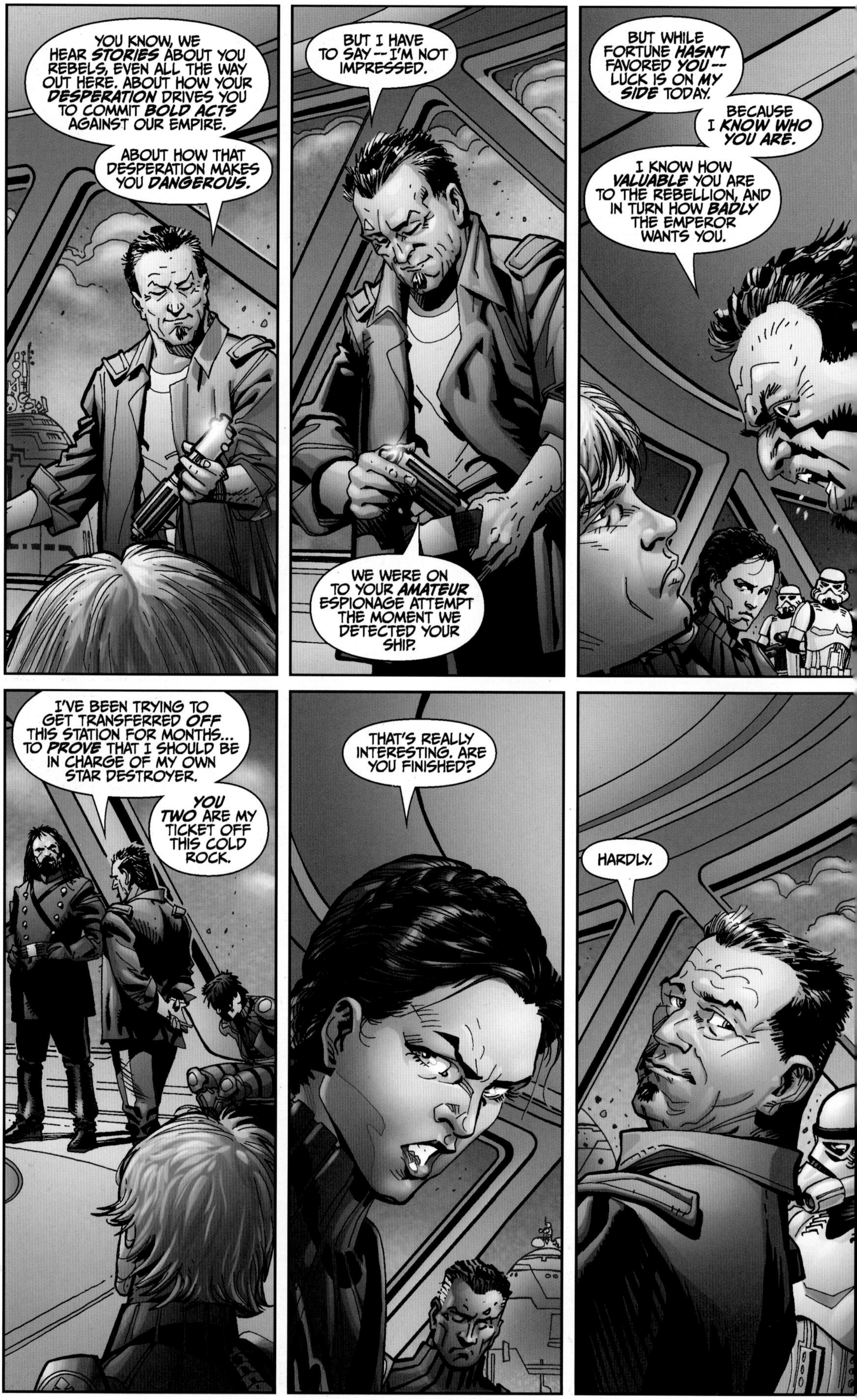
YOU KNOW, WE HEAR STORIES ABOUT YOU REBELS, EVEN ALL THE WAY OUT HERE. ABOUT HOW YOUR DESPERATION DRIVES YOU TO COMMIT BOLD ACTS AGAINST OUR EMPIRE.
ABOUT HOW THAT DESPERATION MAKES YOU DANGEROUS.
BUT I HAVE TO SAY -- I'M NOT IMPRESSED.
WE WERE ON TO YOUR AMATEUR ESPIONAGE ATTEMPT THE MOMENT WE DETECTED YOUR SHIP.
BUT WHILE FORTUNE HASN'T FAVORED YOU -- LUCK IS ON MY SIDE TODAY.
BECAUSE I KNOW WHO YOU ARE.
I KNOW HOW VALUABLE YOU ARE TO THE REBELLION, AND IN TURN HOW BADLY THE EMPEROR WANTS YOU.
I'VE BEEN TRYING TO GET TRANSFERRED OFF THIS STATION FOR MONTHS... TO PROVE THAT I SHOULD BE IN CHARGE OF MY OWN STAR DESTROYER.
YOU TWO ARE MY TICKET OFF THIS COLD ROCK.
THAT'S REALLY INTERESTING. ARE YOU FINISHED?
HARDLY.

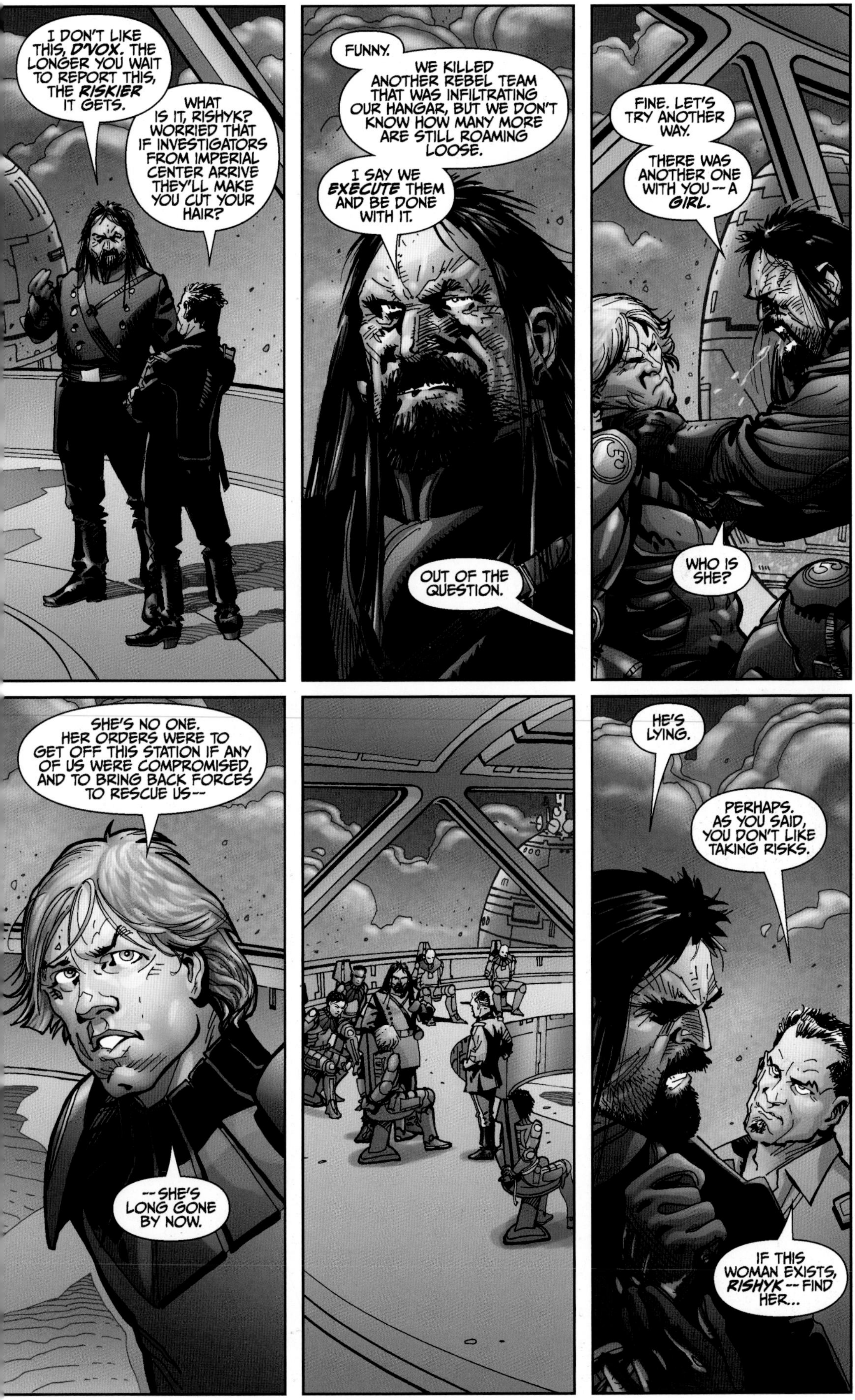
I DON'T LIKE THIS, D'VOX. THE LONGER YOU WAIT TO REPORT THIS, THE RISKIER IT GETS.
WHAT IS IT, RISHYK? WORRIED THAT IF INVESTIGATORS FROM IMPERIAL CENTER ARRIVE THEY'LL MAKE YOU CUT YOUR HAIR?
FUNNY.
WE KILLED ANOTHER REBEL TEAM THAT WAS INFILTRATING OUR HANGAR, BUT WE DON'T KNOW HOW MANY MORE ARE STILL ROAMING LOOSE.
I SAY WE EXECUTE THEM AND BE DONE WITH IT.
OUT OF THE QUESTION.
FINE. LET'S TRY ANOTHER WAY.
THERE WAS ANOTHER ONE WITH YOU -- A GIRL.
WHO IS SHE?
SHE'S NO ONE. HER ORDERS WERE TO GET OFF THIS STATION IF ANY OF US WERE COMPROMISED, AND TO BRING BACK FORCES TO RESCUE US--
--SHE'S LONG GONE BY NOW.
HE'S LYING.
PERHAPS. AS YOU SAID, YOU DON'T LIKE TAKING RISKS.
IF THIS WOMAN EXISTS, RISHYK -- FIND HER...

"...OR THAT 'HAIRCUT' WILL START AT YOUR NECK."

≠SOB≠

IN TRAINING, YOU'RE TAUGHT TO HOPE FOR THE BEST BUT PLAN FOR THE WORST.

"HOPE." IT'S A FUNNY THING. A REAL CRACK-UP.

JUST A FEW SHORT HOURS AGO, DEENA'S HOPE WAS THAT BY JOINING LUKE SKYWALKER ON THIS MISSION, SHE'D REDISCOVER HER OWN INNER COURAGE.

BRAVERY BY OSMOSIS.

JUST STICK CLOSE TO THE FARMBOY AND EVERYTHING WOULD BE FINE.

THIS IS ALL HIS FAULT ANYWAY. IF HE'D HAVE LET HER LEAVE LIKE SHE WANTED TO...

NO. NO -- SHE GOT HERSELF INTO THIS.

ANGER IS A STEP UP FROM DESPAIR, BUT GETTING MAD AT LUKE WON'T HELP ANYONE.

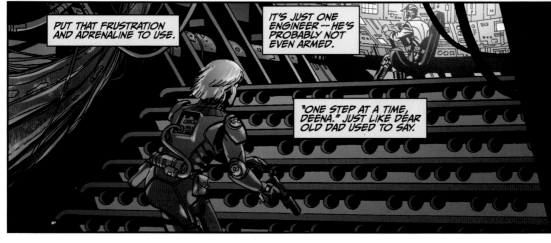

PUT THAT FRUSTRATION AND ADRENALINE TO USE.

IT'S JUST ONE ENGINEER -- HE'S PROBABLY NOT EVEN ARMED.

"ONE STEP AT A TIME, DEENA." JUST LIKE DEAR OLD DAD USED TO SAY.

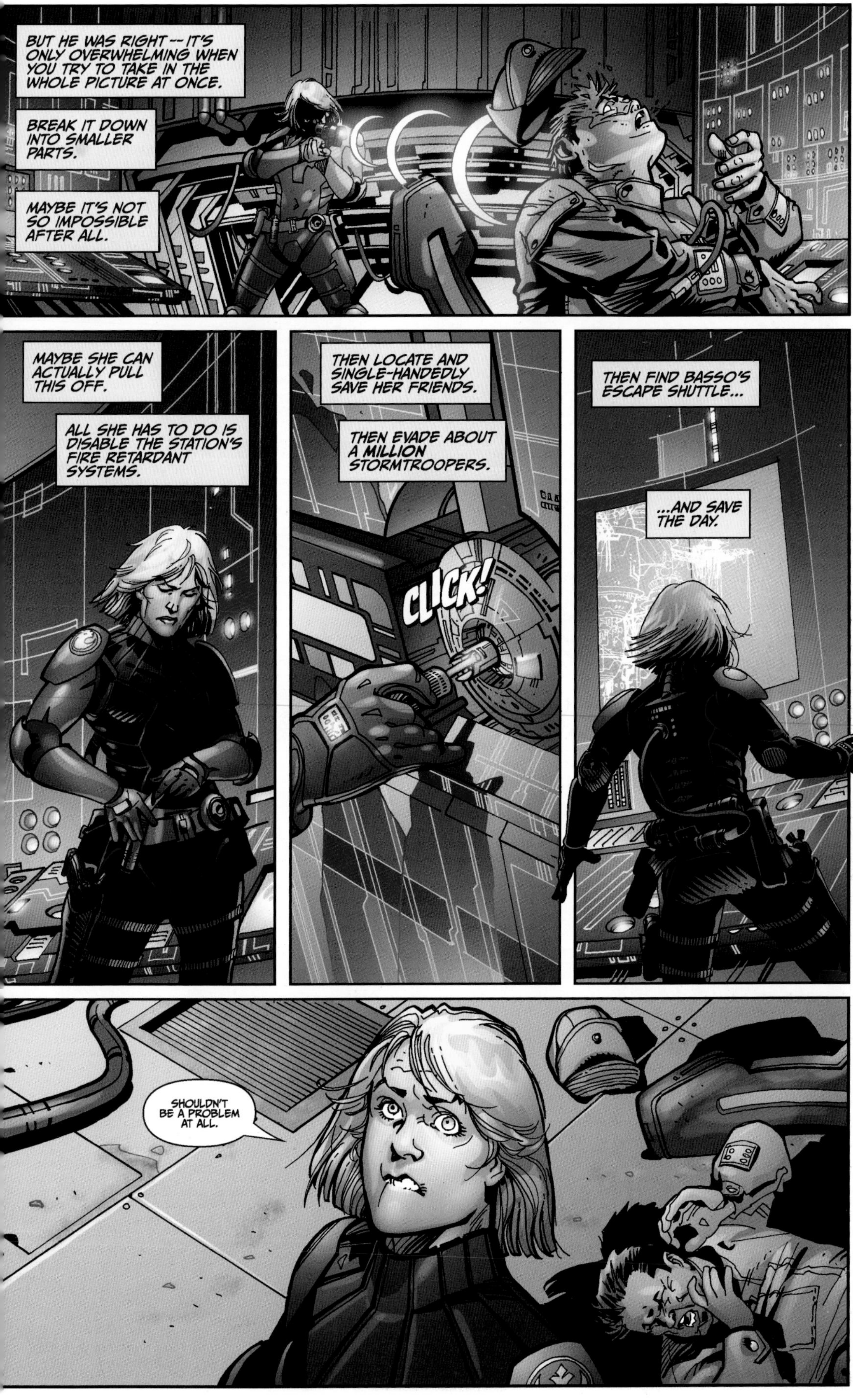
BUT HE WAS RIGHT -- IT'S ONLY OVERWHELMING WHEN YOU TRY TO TAKE IN THE WHOLE PICTURE AT ONCE.
BREAK IT DOWN INTO SMALLER PARTS.
MAYBE IT'S NOT SO IMPOSSIBLE AFTER ALL.
MAYBE SHE CAN ACTUALLY PULL THIS OFF.
ALL SHE HAS TO DO IS DISABLE THE STATION'S FIRE RETARDANT SYSTEMS.
THEN LOCATE AND SINGLE-HANDEDLY SAVE HER FRIENDS.
THEN EVADE ABOUT A MILLION STORMTROOPERS.
CLICK!
THEN FIND BASSO'S ESCAPE SHUTTLE...
...AND SAVE THE DAY.
SHOULDN'T BE A PROBLEM AT ALL.

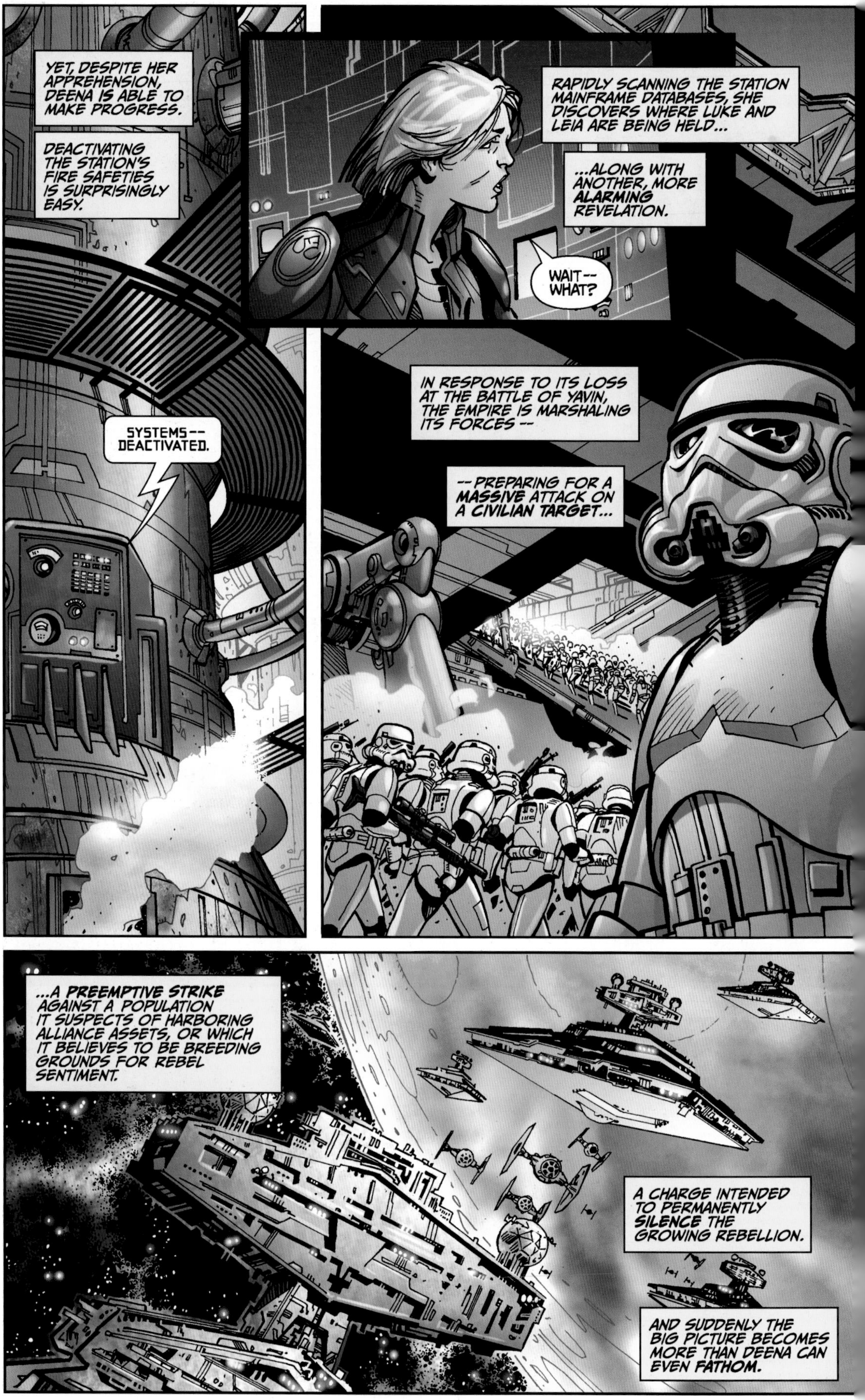
YET, DESPITE HER APPREHENSION, DEENA IS ABLE TO MAKE PROGRESS.
DEACTIVATING THE STATION'S FIRE SAFETIES IS SURPRISINGLY EASY.
RAPIDLY SCANNING THE STATION MAINFRAME DATABASES, SHE DISCOVERS WHERE LUKE AND LEIA ARE BEING HELD...
...ALONG WITH ANOTHER, MORE ALARMING REVELATION.
WAIT-- WHAT?
SYSTEMS-- DEACTIVATED.
IN RESPONSE TO ITS LOSS AT THE BATTLE OF YAVIN, THE EMPIRE IS MARSHALING ITS FORCES --
-- PREPARING FOR A MASSIVE ATTACK ON A CIVILIAN TARGET...
...A PREEMPTIVE STRIKE AGAINST A POPULATION IT SUSPECTS OF HARBORING ALLIANCE ASSETS, OR WHICH IT BELIEVES TO BE BREEDING GROUNDS FOR REBEL SENTIMENT.
A CHARGE INTENDED TO PERMANENTLY SILENCE THE GROWING REBELLION.
AND SUDDENLY THE BIG PICTURE BECOMES MORE THAN DEENA CAN EVEN FATHOM.

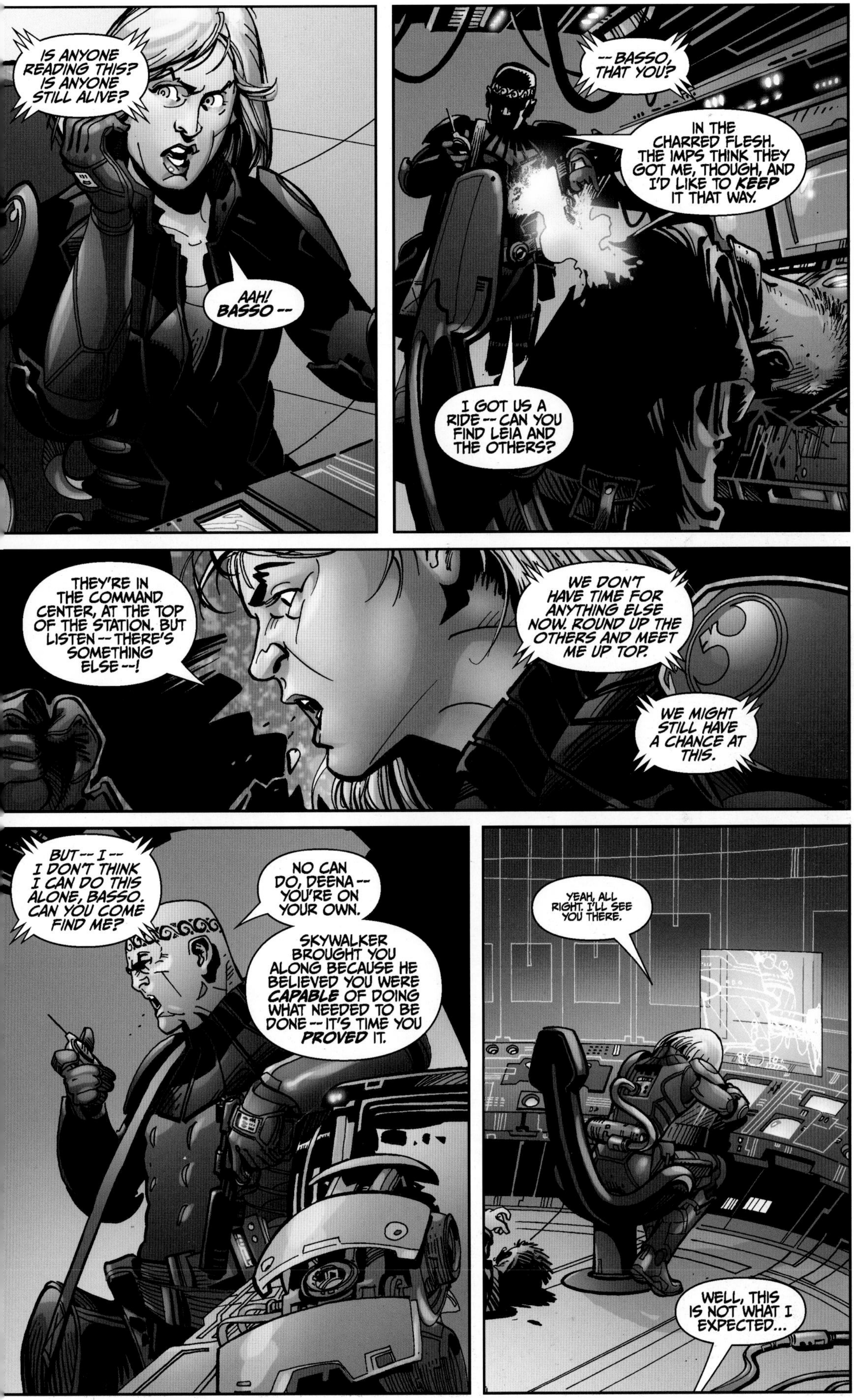
IS ANYONE READING THIS? IS ANYONE STILL ALIVE?
AAH! BASSO --
-- BASSO, THAT YOU?
IN THE CHARRED FLESH. THE IMPS THINK THEY GOT ME, THOUGH, AND I'D LIKE TO KEEP IT THAT WAY.
I GOT US A RIDE -- CAN YOU FIND LEIA AND THE OTHERS?
THEY'RE IN THE COMMAND CENTER, AT THE TOP OF THE STATION. BUT LISTEN -- THERE'S SOMETHING ELSE --!
WE DON'T HAVE TIME FOR ANYTHING ELSE NOW. ROUND UP THE OTHERS AND MEET ME UP TOP.
WE MIGHT STILL HAVE A CHANCE AT THIS.
BUT -- I -- I DON'T THINK I CAN DO THIS ALONE, BASSO. CAN YOU COME FIND ME?
NO CAN DO, DEENA -- YOU'RE ON YOUR OWN.
SKYWALKER BROUGHT YOU ALONG BECAUSE HE BELIEVED YOU WERE CAPABLE OF DOING WHAT NEEDED TO BE DONE -- IT'S TIME YOU PROVED IT.
YEAH, ALL RIGHT. I'LL SEE YOU THERE.
WELL, THIS IS NOT WHAT I EXPECTED...

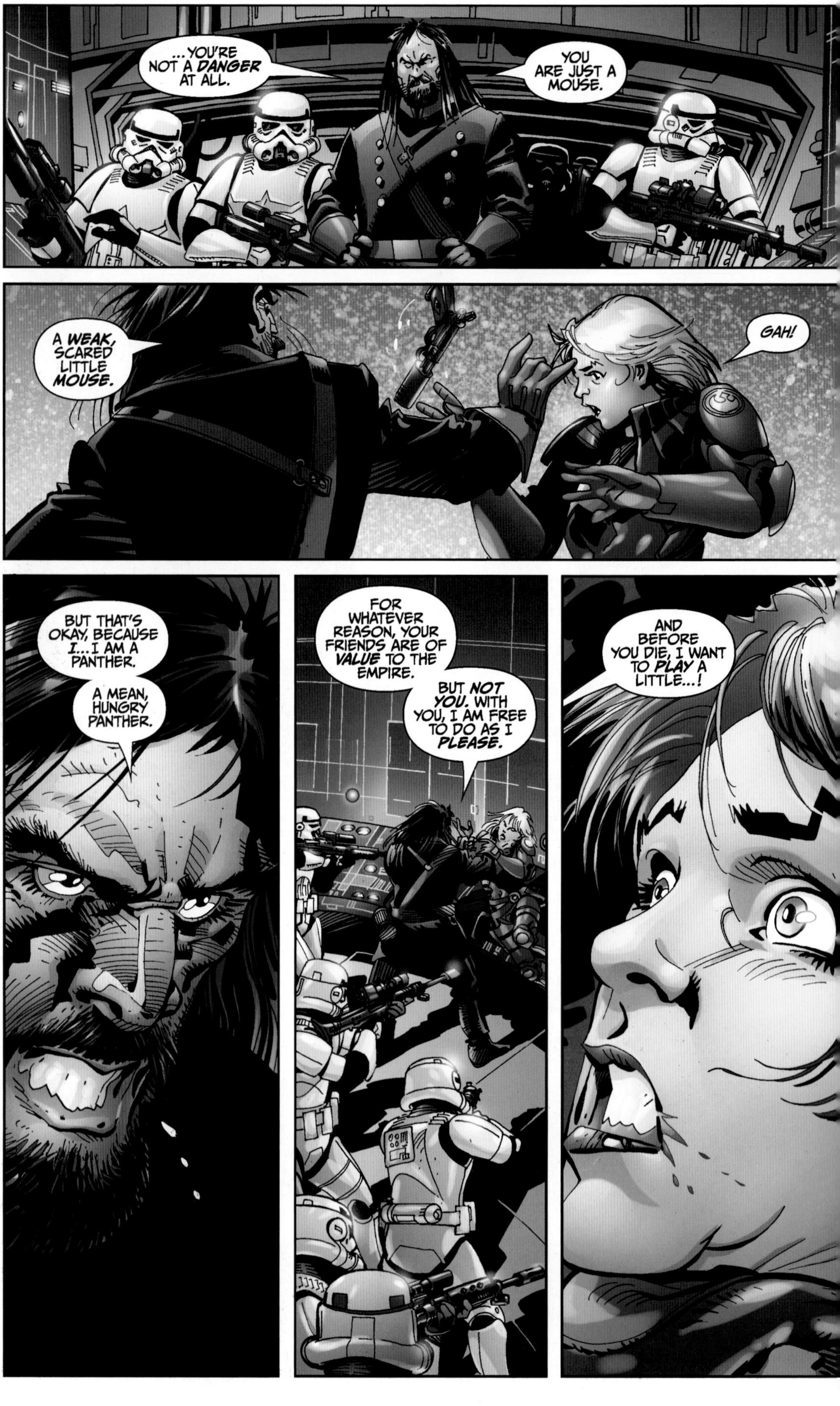
...YOU'RE NOT A DANGER AT ALL.
YOU ARE JUST A MOUSE.
A WEAK, SCARED LITTLE MOUSE.
GAH!
BUT THAT'S OKAY, BECAUSE I...I AM A PANTHER.
A MEAN, HUNGRY PANTHER.
FOR WHATEVER REASON, YOUR FRIENDS ARE OF VALUE TO THE EMPIRE.
BUT NOT YOU. WITH YOU, I AM FREE TO DO AS I PLEASE.
AND BEFORE YOU DIE, I WANT TO PLAY A LITTLE...!

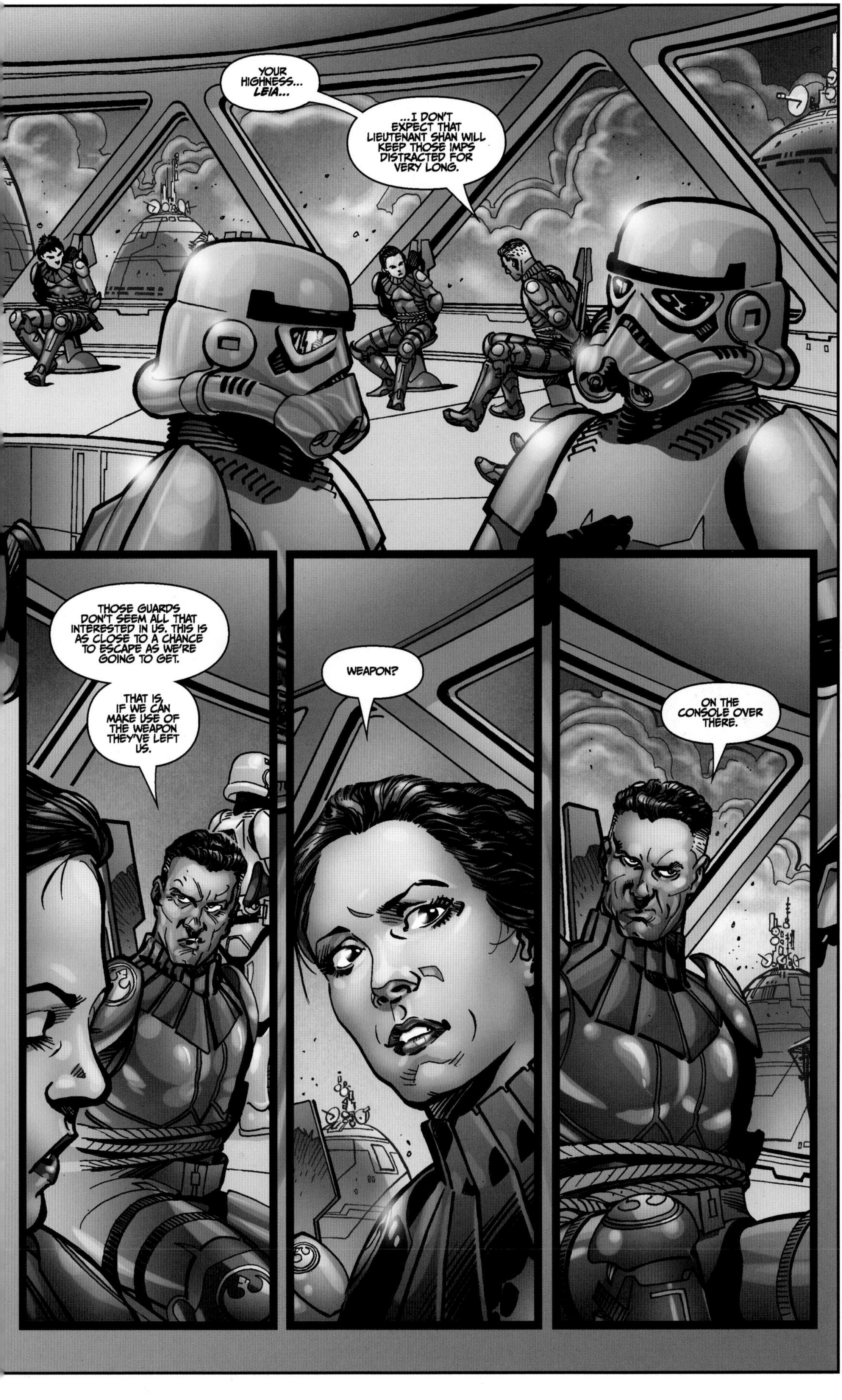
YOUR HIGHNESS... *LEIA*...
...I DON'T EXPECT THAT LIEUTENANT SHAN WILL KEEP THOSE IMPS DISTRACTED FOR VERY LONG.
THOSE GUARDS DON'T SEEM ALL THAT INTERESTED IN US. THIS IS AS CLOSE TO A CHANCE TO ESCAPE AS WE'RE GOING TO GET.
THAT IS, IF WE CAN MAKE USE OF THE WEAPON THEY'VE LEFT US.
WEAPON?
ON THE CONSOLE OVER THERE.

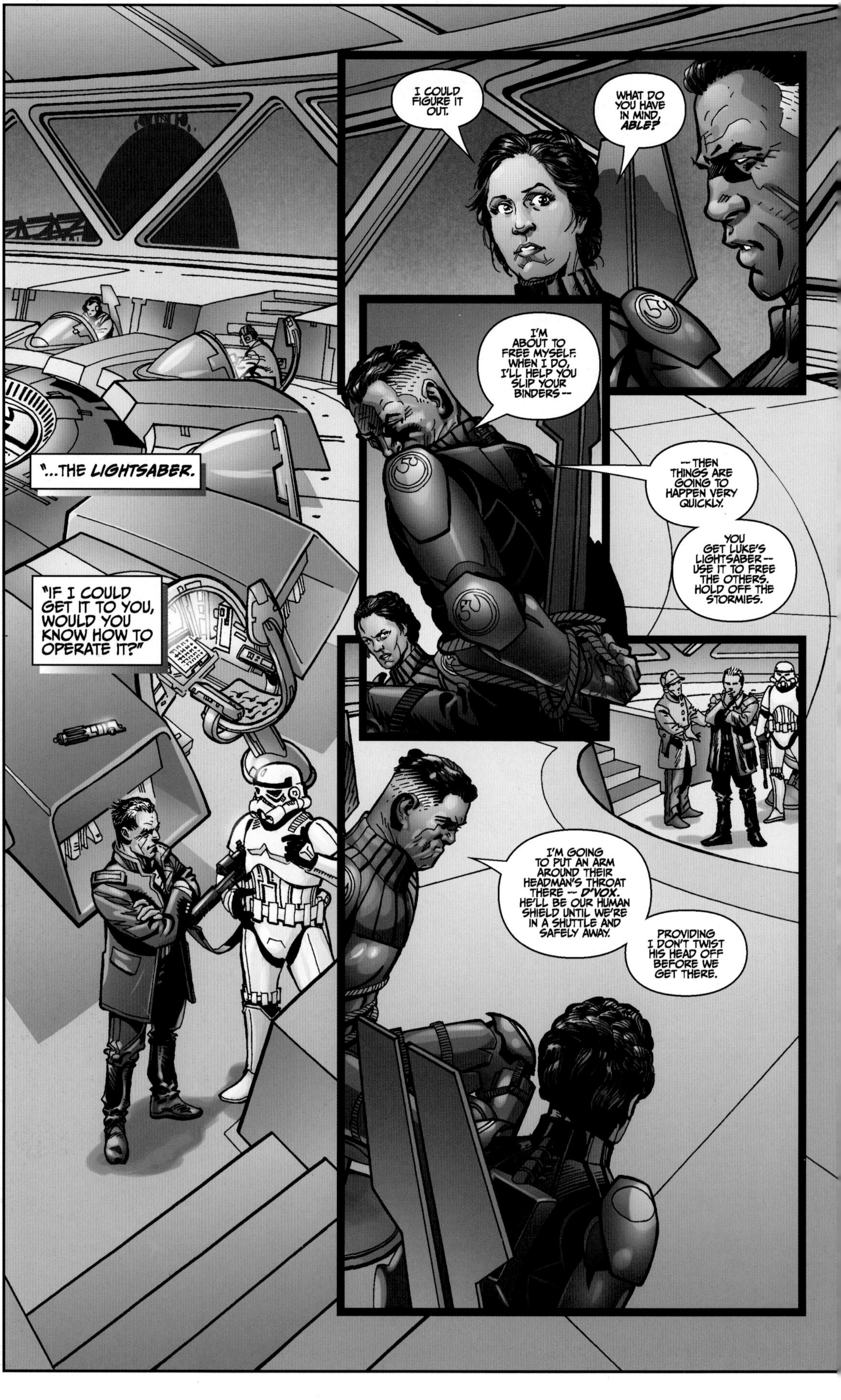
"...THE LIGHTSABER.
"IF I COULD GET IT TO YOU, WOULD YOU KNOW HOW TO OPERATE IT?"
I COULD FIGURE IT OUT.
WHAT DO YOU HAVE IN MIND, ABLE?
I'M ABOUT TO FREE MYSELF. WHEN I DO, I'LL HELP YOU SLIP YOUR BINDERS --
-- THEN THINGS ARE GOING TO HAPPEN VERY QUICKLY.
YOU GET LUKE'S LIGHTSABER -- USE IT TO FREE THE OTHERS. HOLD OFF THE STORMIES.
I'M GOING TO PUT AN ARM AROUND THEIR HEADMAN'S THROAT THERE -- D'VOX. HE'LL BE OUR HUMAN SHIELD UNTIL WE'RE IN A SHUTTLE AND SAFELY AWAY.
PROVIDING I DON'T TWIST HIS HEAD OFF BEFORE WE GET THERE.

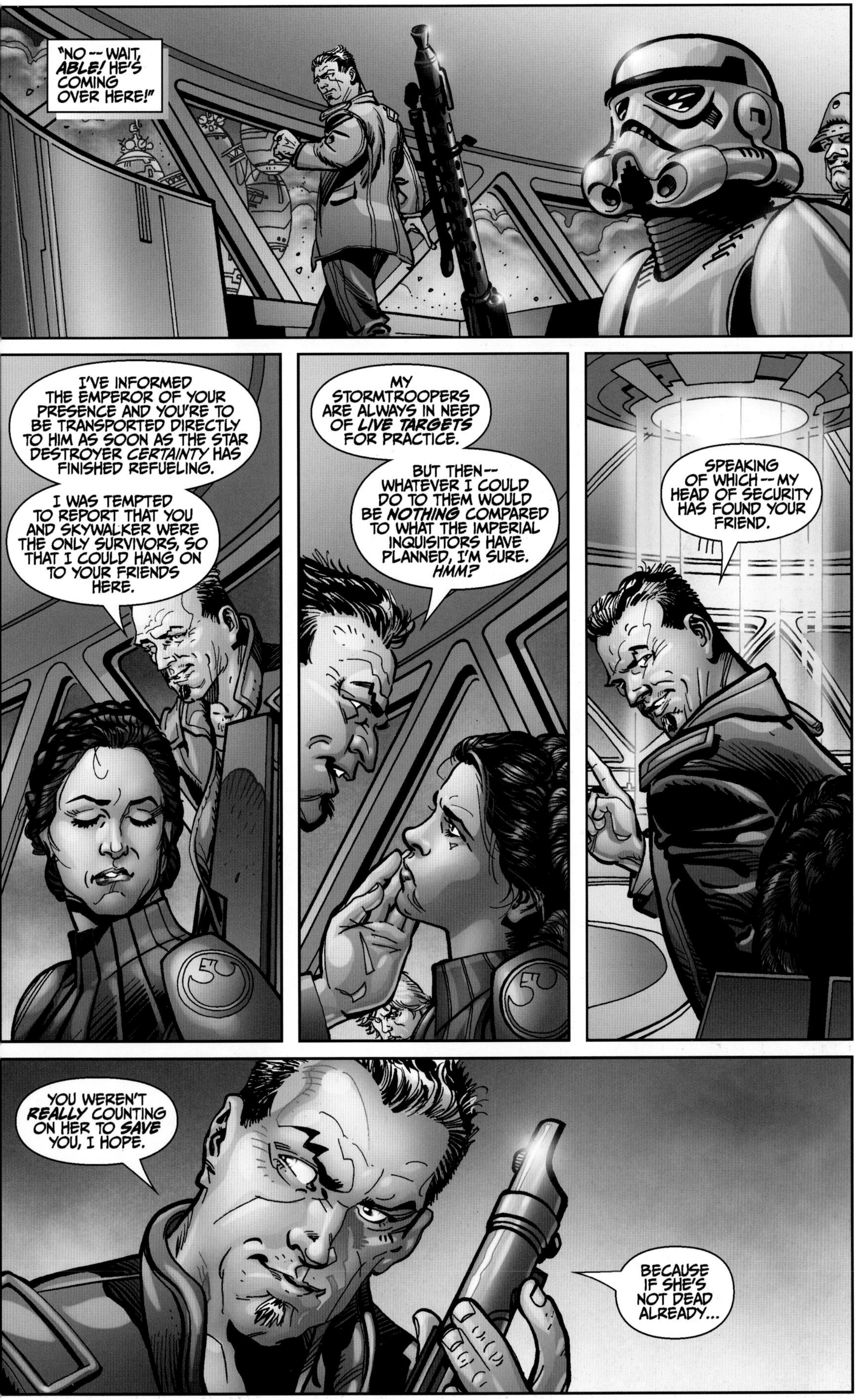
"NO -- WAIT, ABLE! HE'S COMING OVER HERE!"
I'VE INFORMED THE EMPEROR OF YOUR PRESENCE AND YOU'RE TO BE TRANSPORTED DIRECTLY TO HIM AS SOON AS THE STAR DESTROYER CERTAINTY HAS FINISHED REFUELING.
I WAS TEMPTED TO REPORT THAT YOU AND SKYWALKER WERE THE ONLY SURVIVORS, SO THAT I COULD HANG ON TO YOUR FRIENDS HERE.
MY STORMTROOPERS ARE ALWAYS IN NEED OF LIVE TARGETS FOR PRACTICE.
BUT THEN-- WHATEVER I COULD DO TO THEM WOULD BE NOTHING COMPARED TO WHAT THE IMPERIAL INQUISITORS HAVE PLANNED, I'M SURE. HMM?
SPEAKING OF WHICH -- MY HEAD OF SECURITY HAS FOUND YOUR FRIEND.
YOU WEREN'T REALLY COUNTING ON HER TO SAVE YOU, I HOPE.
BECAUSE IF SHE'S NOT DEAD ALREADY...

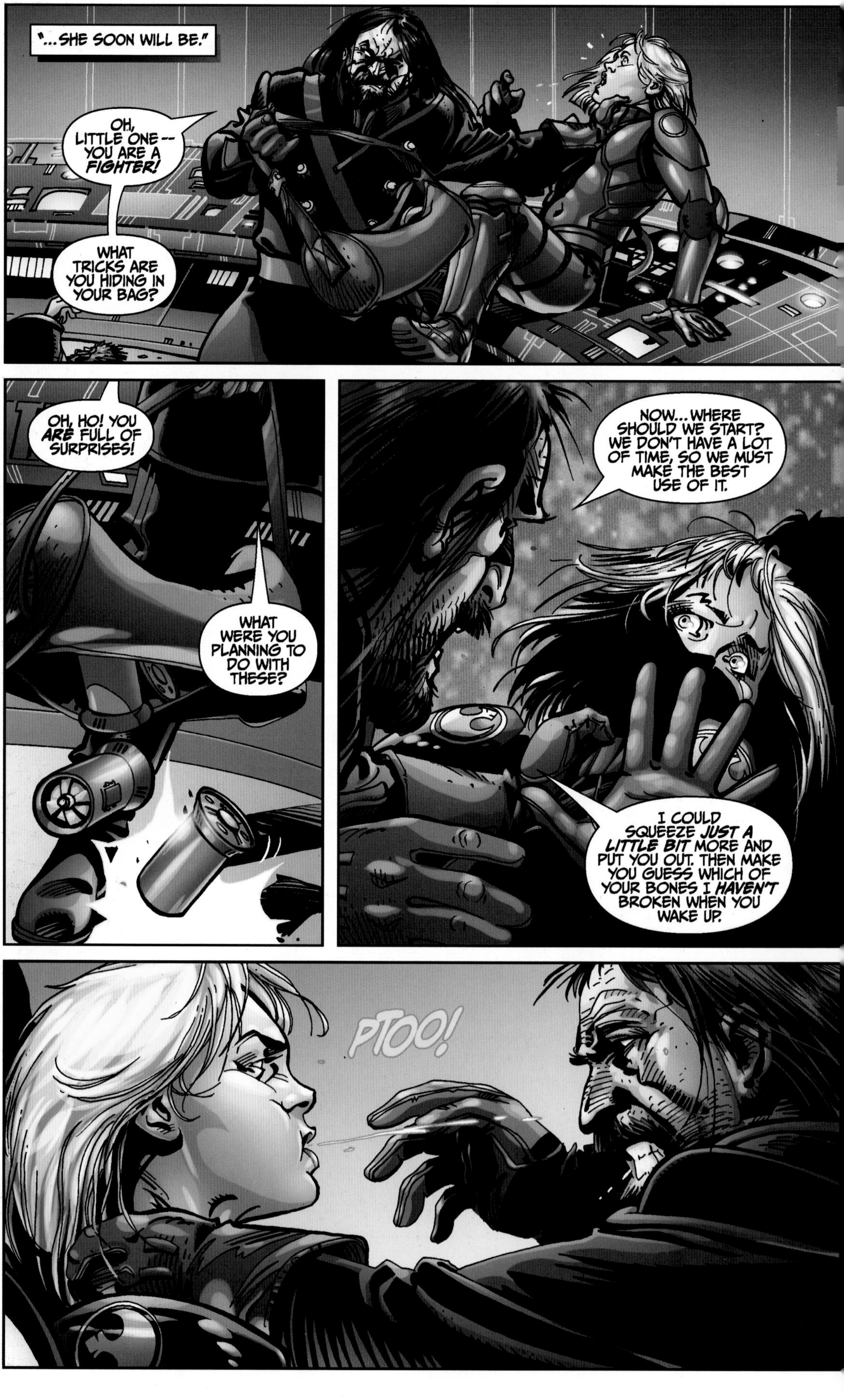
"...SHE SOON WILL BE."
OH, LITTLE ONE -- YOU ARE A FIGHTER!
WHAT TRICKS ARE YOU HIDING IN YOUR BAG?
OH, HO! YOU ARE FULL OF SURPRISES!
WHAT WERE YOU PLANNING TO DO WITH THESE?
NOW... WHERE SHOULD WE START? WE DON'T HAVE A LOT OF TIME, SO WE MUST MAKE THE BEST USE OF IT.
I COULD SQUEEZE JUST A LITTLE BIT MORE AND PUT YOU OUT. THEN MAKE YOU GUESS WHICH OF YOUR BONES I HAVEN'T BROKEN WHEN YOU WAKE UP.
PTOO!

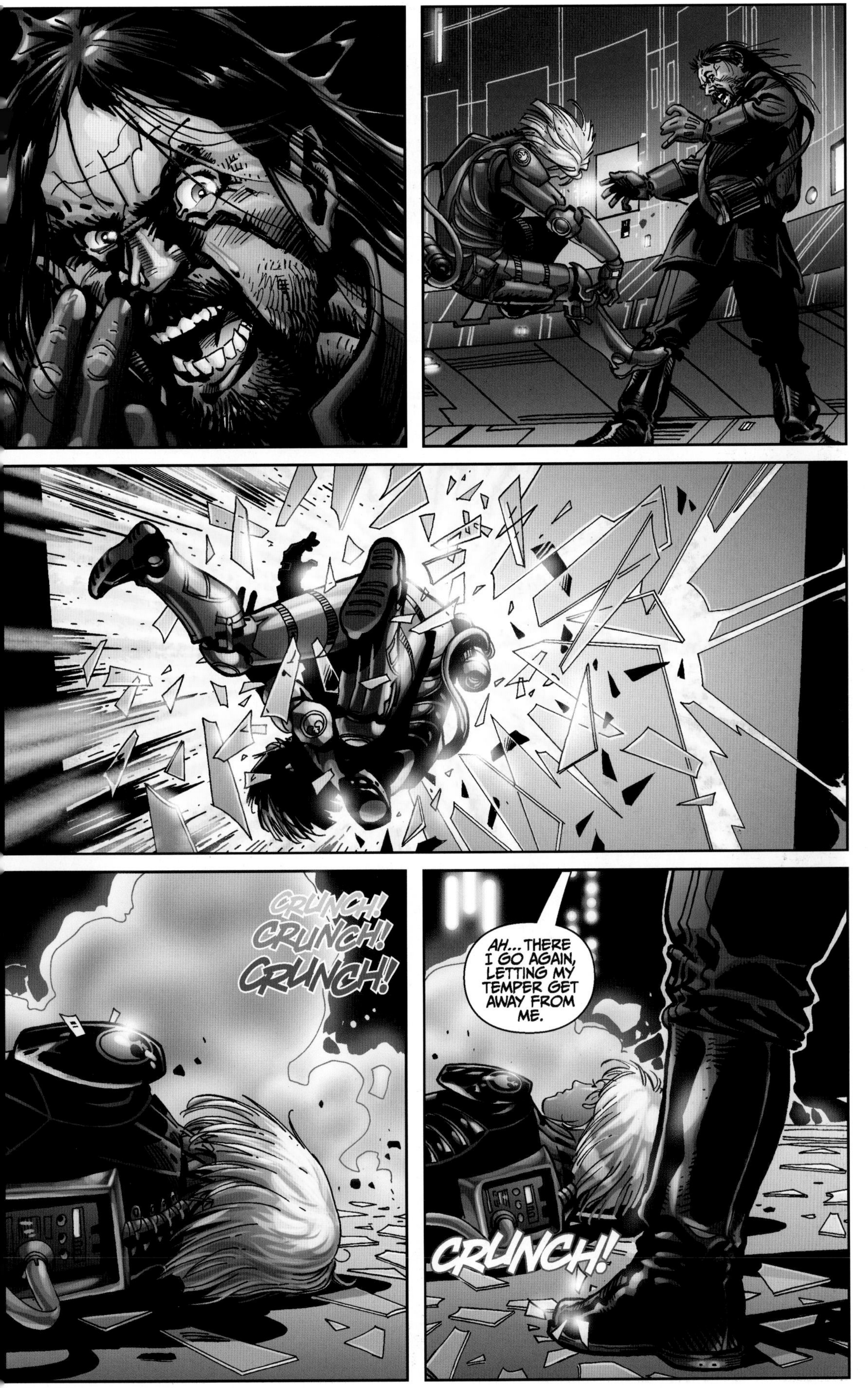
CRUNCH!
CRUNCH!
CRUNCH!
AH... THERE I GO AGAIN, LETTING MY TEMPER GET AWAY FROM ME.
CRUNCH!

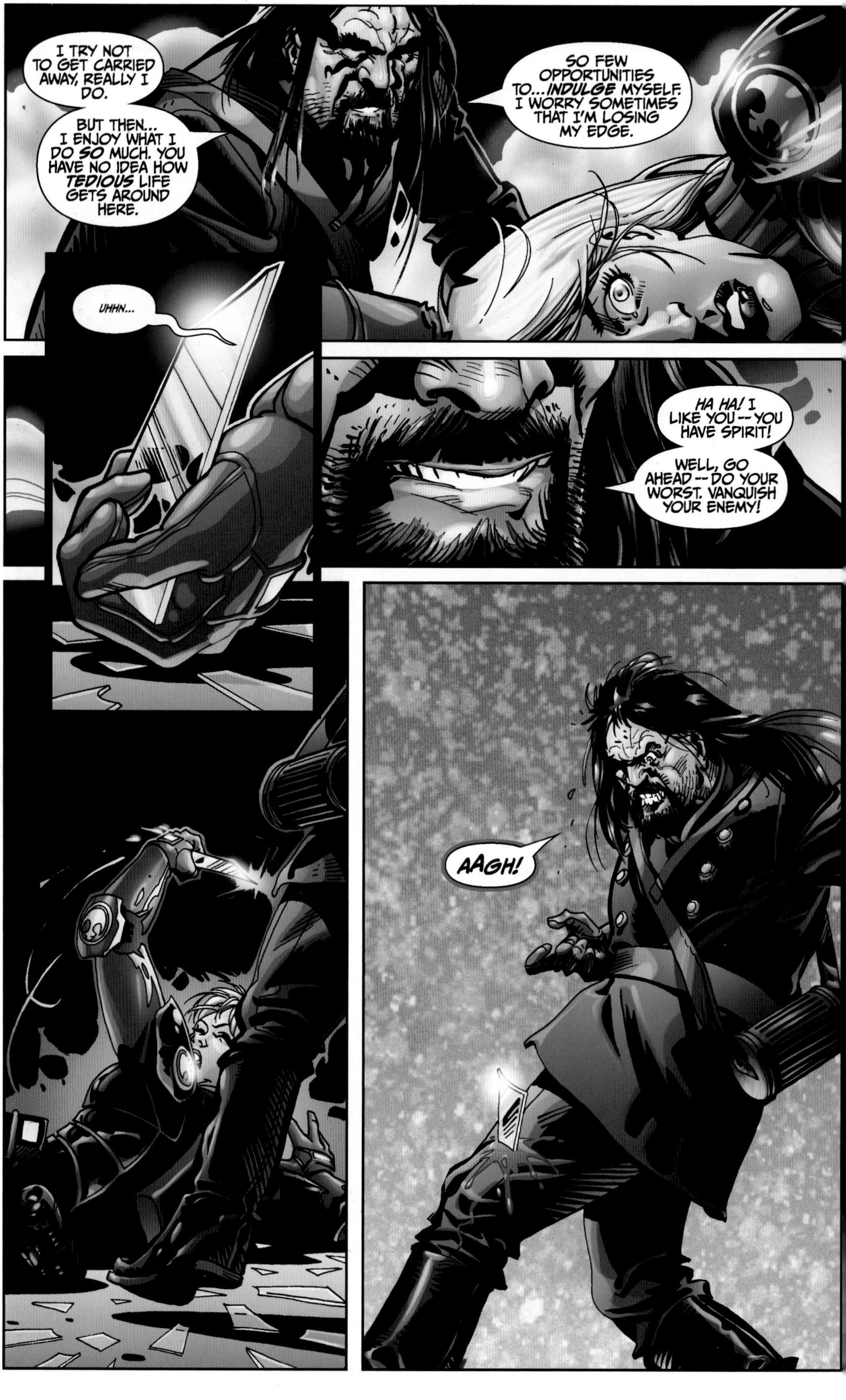
I TRY NOT TO GET CARRIED AWAY, REALLY I DO.
BUT THEN... I ENJOY WHAT I DO SO MUCH. YOU HAVE NO IDEA HOW TEDIOUS LIFE GETS AROUND HERE.
SO FEW OPPORTUNITIES TO...INDULGE MYSELF. I WORRY SOMETIMES THAT I'M LOSING MY EDGE.
UHHN...
HA HA! I LIKE YOU -- YOU HAVE SPIRIT!
WELL, GO AHEAD -- DO YOUR WORST. VANQUISH YOUR ENEMY!
AAGH!

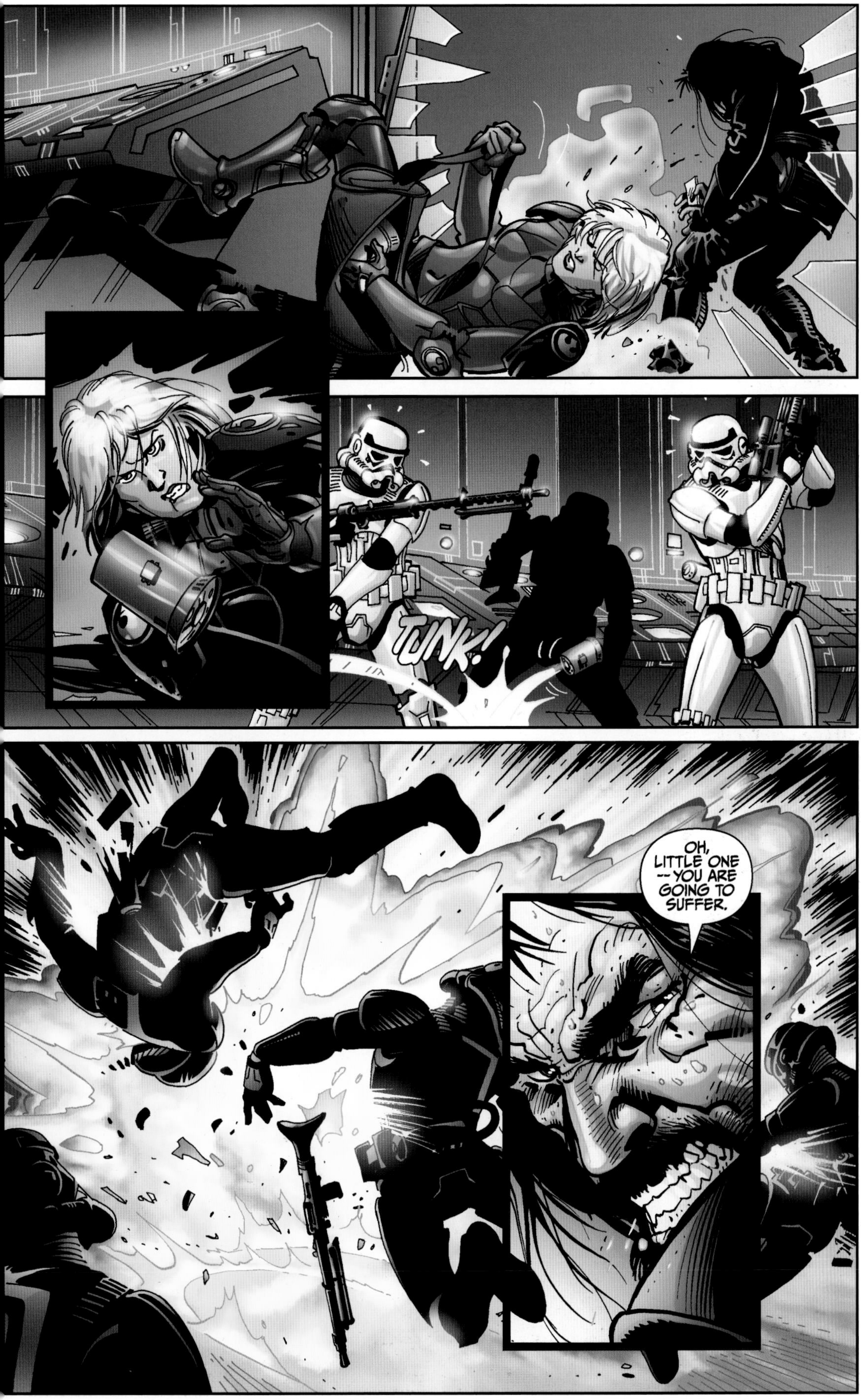
TUNK!
OH, LITTLE ONE --YOU ARE GOING TO SUFFER.

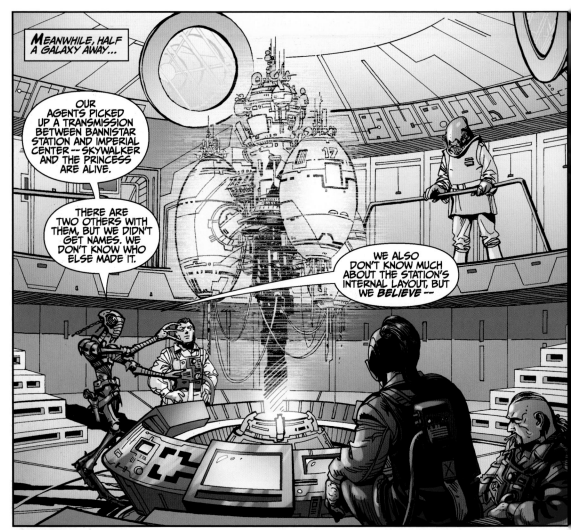

MEANWHILE, HALF A GALAXY AWAY...
OUR AGENTS PICKED UP A TRANSMISSION BETWEEN BANNISTAR STATION AND IMPERIAL CENTER -- SKYWALKER AND THE PRINCESS ARE ALIVE.
THERE ARE TWO OTHERS WITH THEM, BUT WE DIDN'T GET NAMES. WE DON'T KNOW WHO ELSE MADE IT.
WE ALSO DON'T KNOW MUCH ABOUT THE STATION'S INTERNAL LAYOUT, BUT WE BELIEVE --
-- THAT OUR FRIENDS ARE BEING HELD IN THE COMMAND CENTER -- HERE.
THEY'RE SCHEDULED TO BE TRANSPORTED AWAY FROM THE STATION WITHIN ONE STANDARD DAY, WHICH IS JUST ABOUT AS MUCH TIME AS IT WOULD TAKE FOR US TO GET THERE.
SO IF WE'RE GOING TO DO THIS --
IT HAS TO BE A SIMPLE SMASH AND GRAB.
WE GET IN, WE GET OUR FRIENDS, WE GET OUT BEFORE THEY KNOW WHAT HIT THEM.
I'M NOT SURE ABOUT THIS...

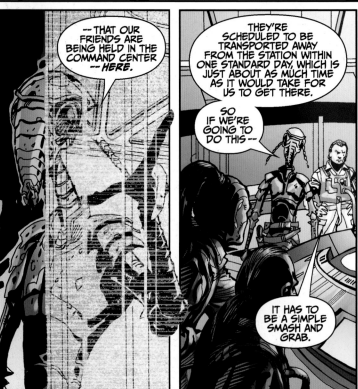

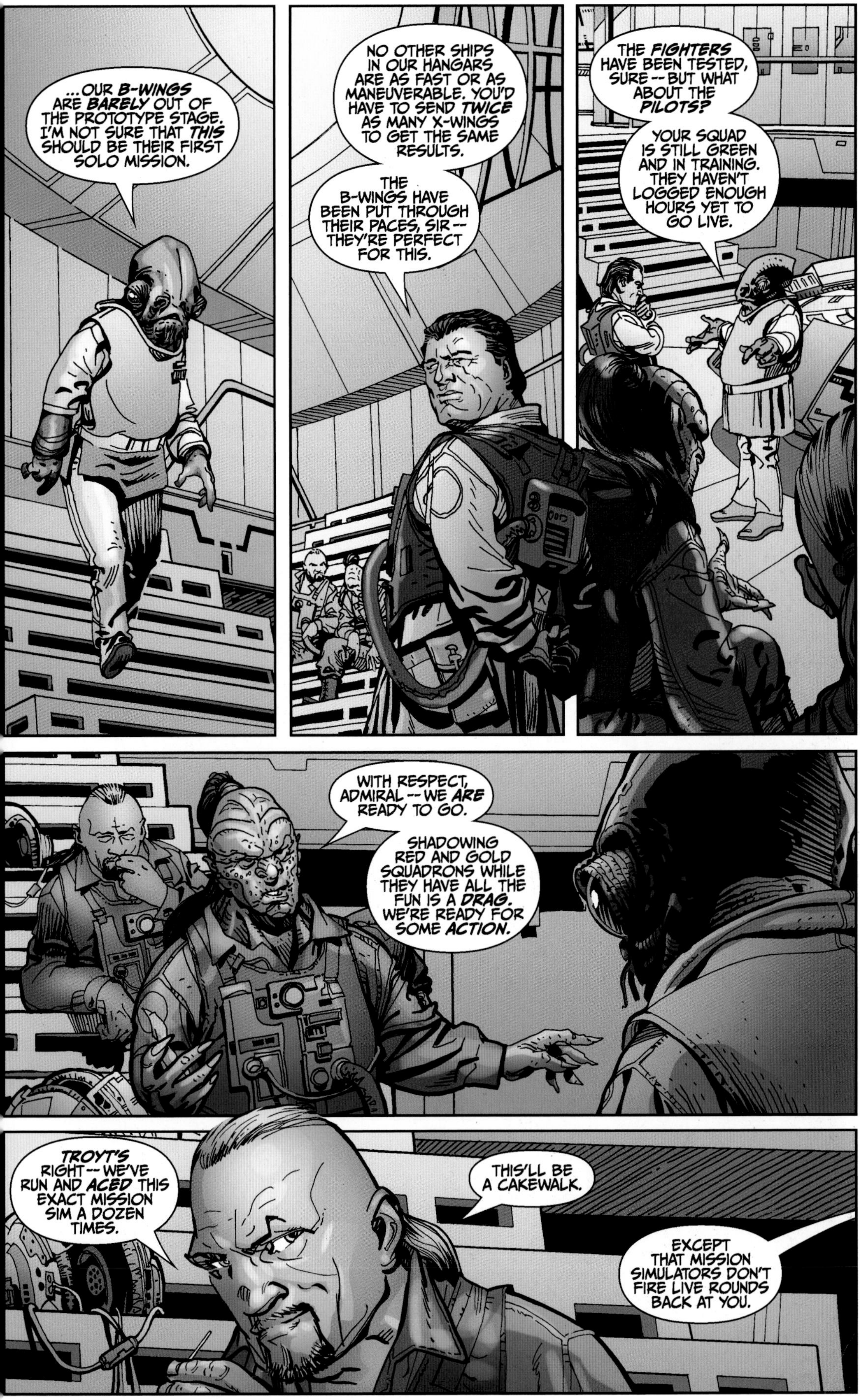
...OUR B-WINGS ARE BARELY OUT OF THE PROTOTYPE STAGE. I'M NOT SURE THAT THIS SHOULD BE THEIR FIRST SOLO MISSION.
NO OTHER SHIPS IN OUR HANGARS ARE AS FAST OR AS MANEUVERABLE. YOU'D HAVE TO SEND TWICE AS MANY X-WINGS TO GET THE SAME RESULTS.
THE B-WINGS HAVE BEEN PUT THROUGH THEIR PACES, SIR -- THEY'RE PERFECT FOR THIS.
THE FIGHTERS HAVE BEEN TESTED, SURE -- BUT WHAT ABOUT THE PILOTS?
YOUR SQUAD IS STILL GREEN AND IN TRAINING. THEY HAVEN'T LOGGED ENOUGH HOURS YET TO GO LIVE.
WITH RESPECT, ADMIRAL -- WE ARE READY TO GO.
SHADOWING RED AND GOLD SQUADRONS WHILE THEY HAVE ALL THE FUN IS A DRAG. WE'RE READY FOR SOME ACTION.
TROYT'S RIGHT -- WE'VE RUN AND ACED THIS EXACT MISSION SIM A DOZEN TIMES.
THIS'LL BE A CAKEWALK.
EXCEPT THAT MISSION SIMULATORS DON'T FIRE LIVE ROUNDS BACK AT YOU.

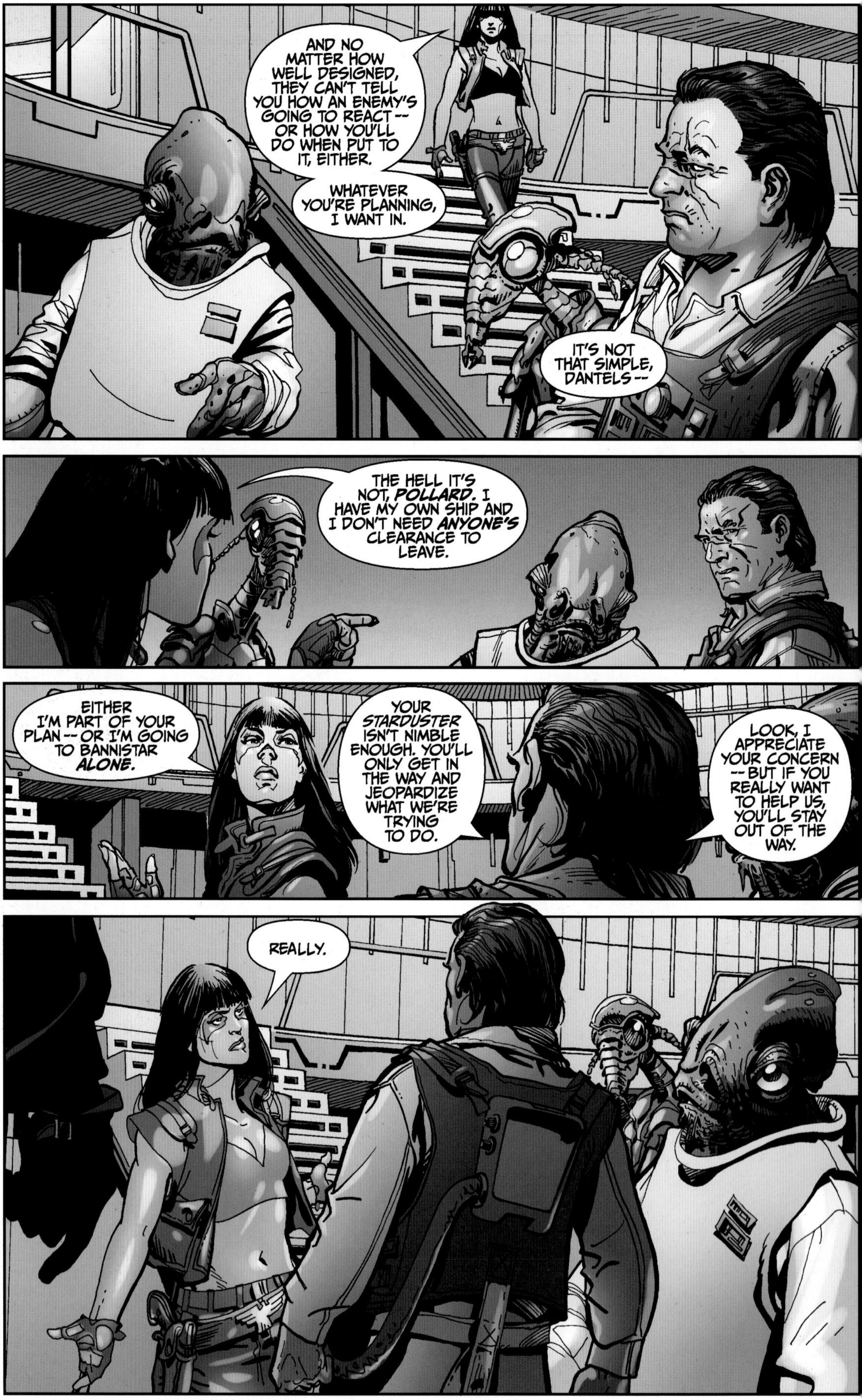
AND NO MATTER HOW WELL DESIGNED, THEY CAN'T TELL YOU HOW AN ENEMY'S GOING TO REACT -- OR HOW YOU'LL DO WHEN PUT TO IT, EITHER.
WHATEVER YOU'RE PLANNING, I WANT IN.
IT'S NOT THAT SIMPLE, DANTELS --
THE HELL IT'S NOT, POLLARD. I HAVE MY OWN SHIP AND I DON'T NEED ANYONE'S CLEARANCE TO LEAVE.
EITHER I'M PART OF YOUR PLAN -- OR I'M GOING TO BANNISTAR ALONE.
YOUR STARDUSTER ISN'T NIMBLE ENOUGH. YOU'LL ONLY GET IN THE WAY AND JEOPARDIZE WHAT WE'RE TRYING TO DO.
LOOK, I APPRECIATE YOUR CONCERN -- BUT IF YOU REALLY WANT TO HELP US, YOU'LL STAY OUT OF THE WAY.
REALLY.

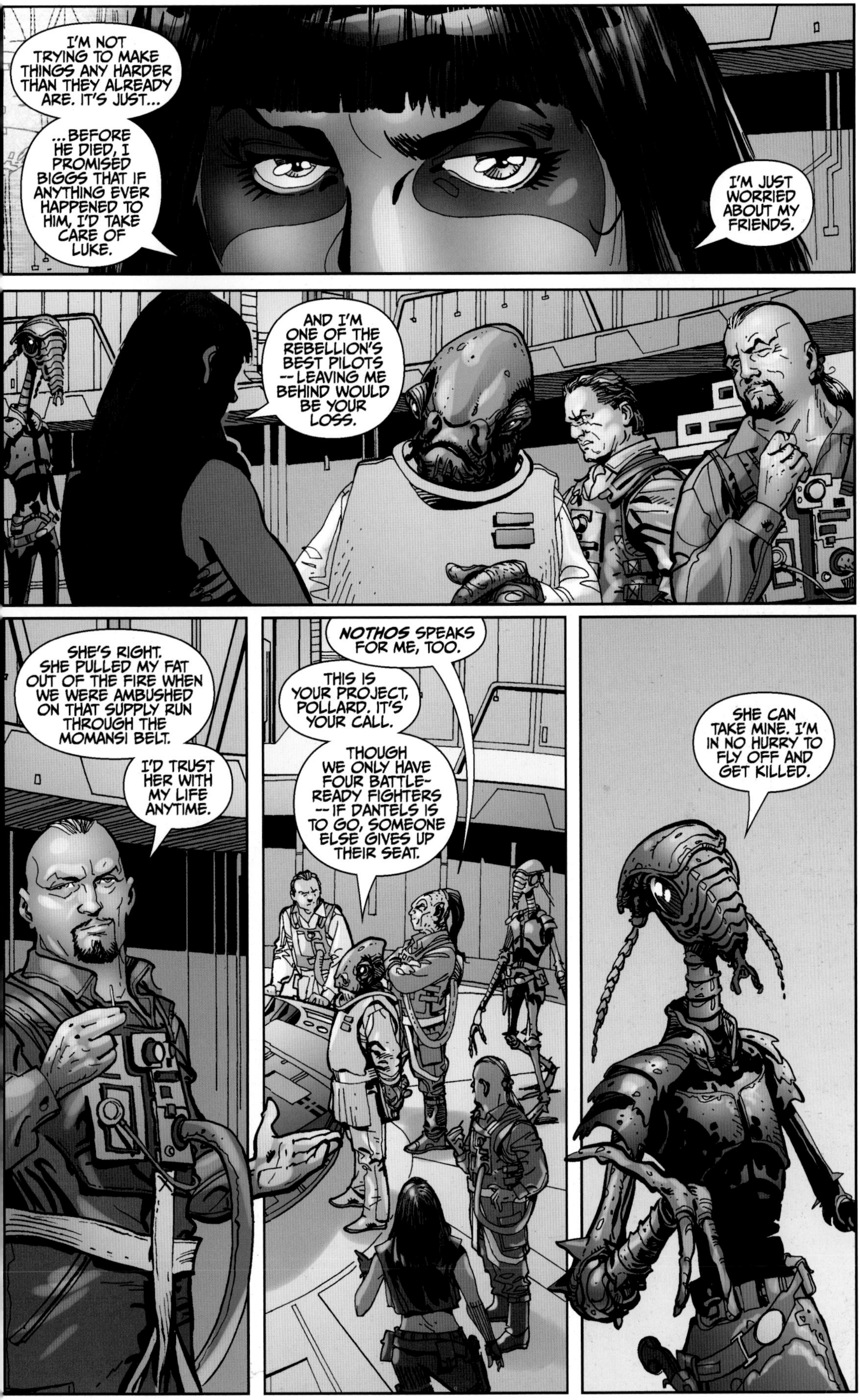
I'M NOT TRYING TO MAKE THINGS ANY HARDER THAN THEY ALREADY ARE. IT'S JUST...
...BEFORE HE DIED, I PROMISED BIGGS THAT IF ANYTHING EVER HAPPENED TO HIM, I'D TAKE CARE OF LUKE.
I'M JUST WORRIED ABOUT MY FRIENDS.
AND I'M ONE OF THE REBELLION'S BEST PILOTS --LEAVING ME BEHIND WOULD BE YOUR LOSS.
SHE'S RIGHT. SHE PULLED MY FAT OUT OF THE FIRE WHEN WE WERE AMBUSHED ON THAT SUPPLY RUN THROUGH THE MOMANSI BELT.
I'D TRUST HER WITH MY LIFE ANYTIME.
NOTHOS SPEAKS FOR ME, TOO.
THIS IS YOUR PROJECT, POLLARD. IT'S YOUR CALL.
THOUGH WE ONLY HAVE FOUR BATTLE-READY FIGHTERS --IF DANTELS IS TO GO, SOMEONE ELSE GIVES UP THEIR SEAT.
SHE CAN TAKE MINE. I'M IN NO HURRY TO FLY OFF AND GET KILLED.

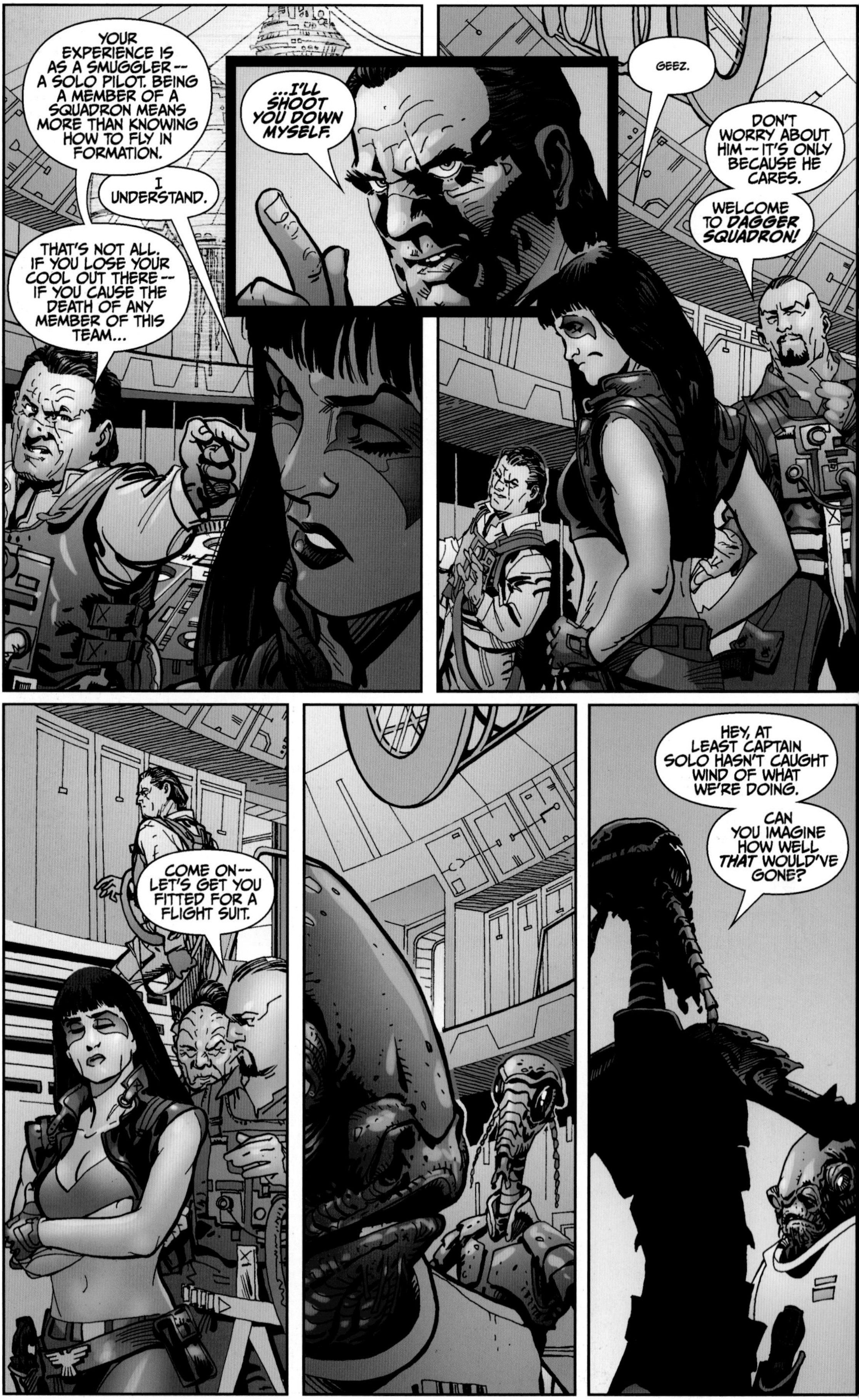
YOUR EXPERIENCE IS AS A SMUGGLER-- A SOLO PILOT. BEING A MEMBER OF A SQUADRON MEANS MORE THAN KNOWING HOW TO FLY IN FORMATION.
I UNDERSTAND.
THAT'S NOT ALL. IF YOU LOSE YOUR COOL OUT THERE-- IF YOU CAUSE THE DEATH OF ANY MEMBER OF THIS TEAM...
...I'LL SHOOT YOU DOWN MYSELF.
GEEZ.
DON'T WORRY ABOUT HIM--IT'S ONLY BECAUSE HE CARES.
WELCOME TO DAGGER SQUADRON!
COME ON-- LET'S GET YOU FITTED FOR A FLIGHT SUIT.
HEY, AT LEAST CAPTAIN SOLO HASN'T CAUGHT WIND OF WHAT WE'RE DOING.
CAN YOU IMAGINE HOW WELL THAT WOULD'VE GONE?

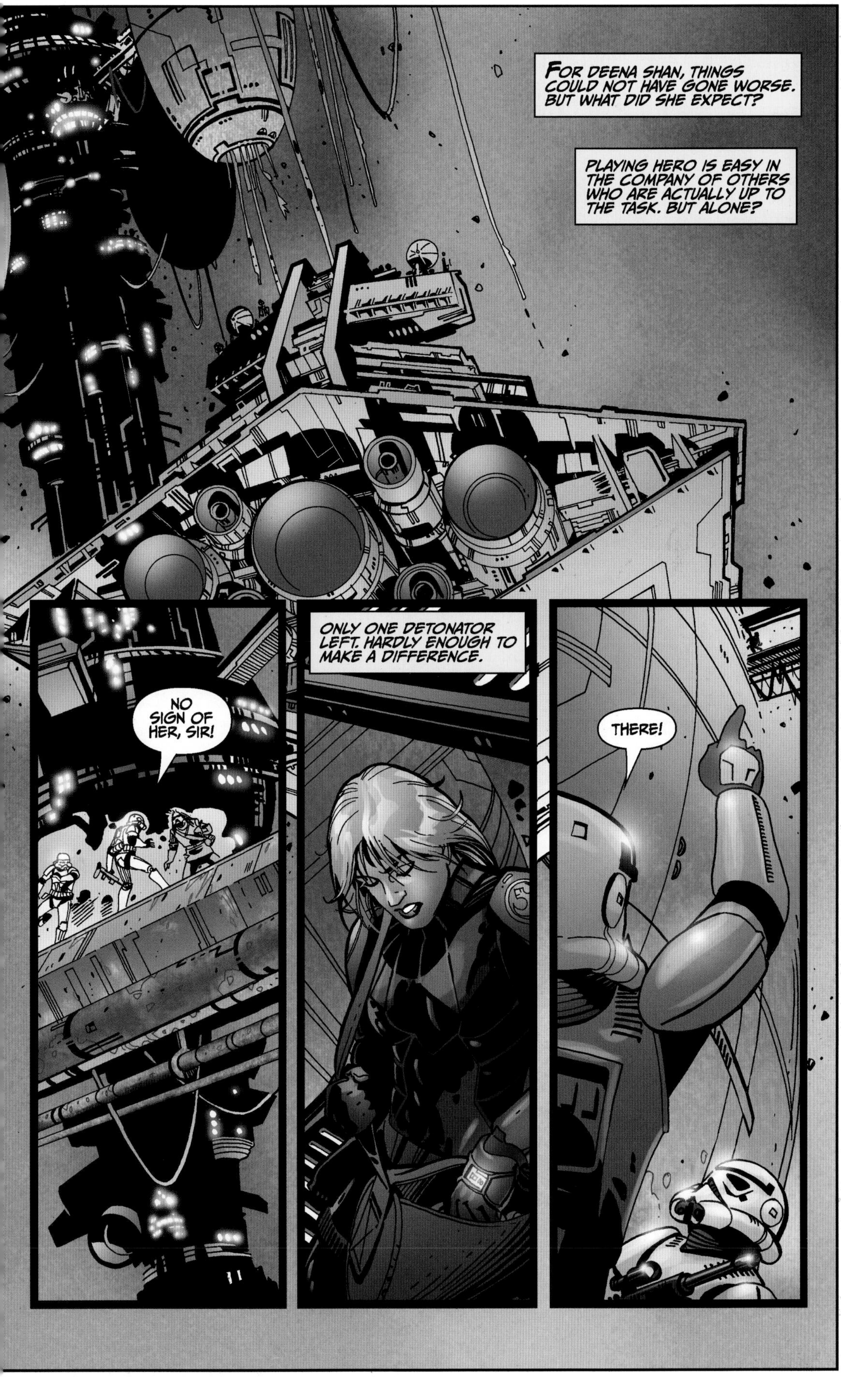
FOR DEENA SHAN, THINGS COULD NOT HAVE GONE WORSE. BUT WHAT DID SHE EXPECT?
PLAYING HERO IS EASY IN THE COMPANY OF OTHERS WHO ARE ACTUALLY UP TO THE TASK. BUT ALONE?
NO SIGN OF HER, SIR!
ONLY ONE DETONATOR LEFT. HARDLY ENOUGH TO MAKE A DIFFERENCE.
THERE!

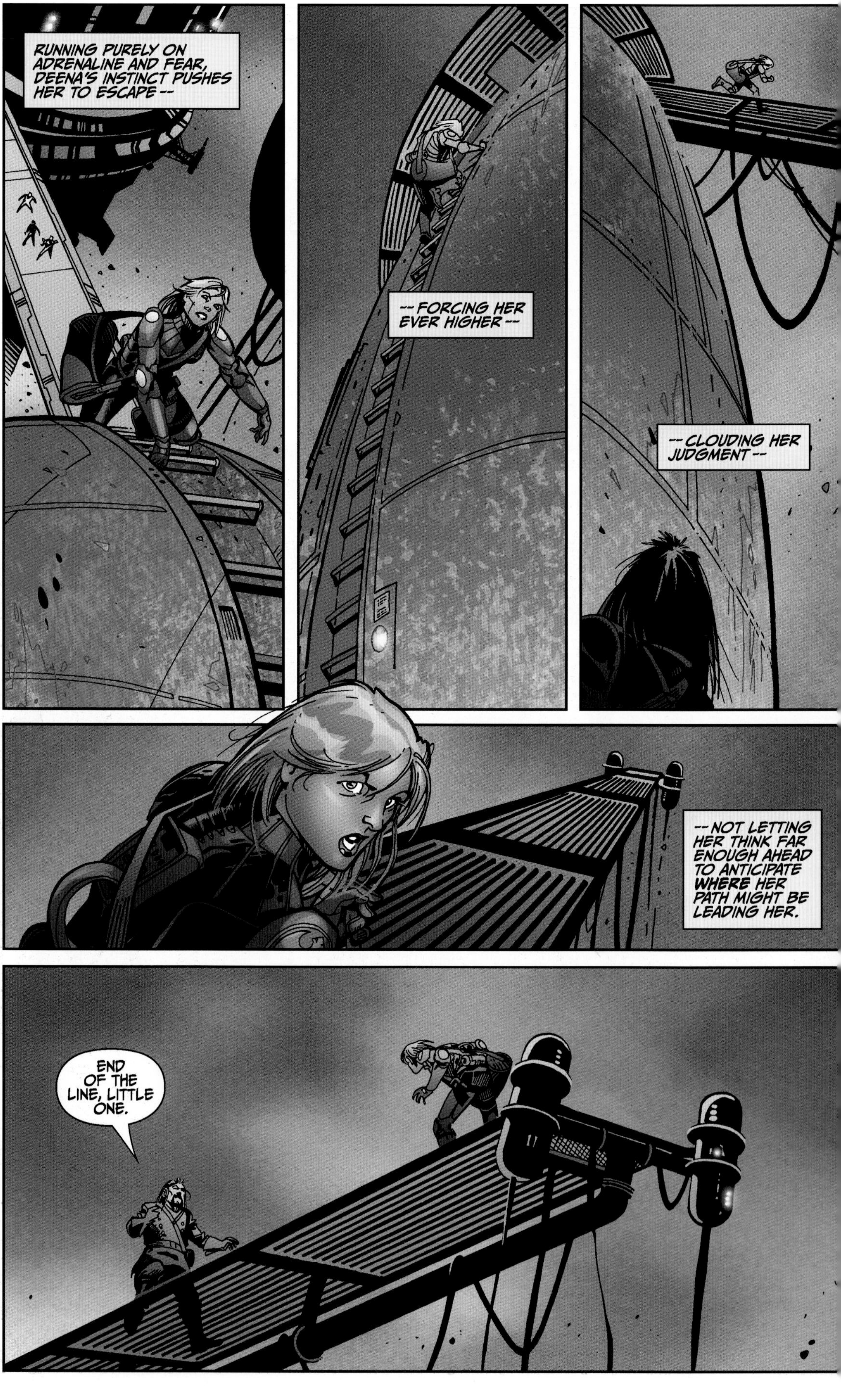
RUNNING PURELY ON ADRENALINE AND FEAR, DEENA'S INSTINCT PUSHES HER TO ESCAPE --
-- FORCING HER EVER HIGHER --
-- CLOUDING HER JUDGMENT --
-- NOT LETTING HER THINK FAR ENOUGH AHEAD TO ANTICIPATE WHERE HER PATH MIGHT BE LEADING HER.
END OF THE LINE, LITTLE ONE.

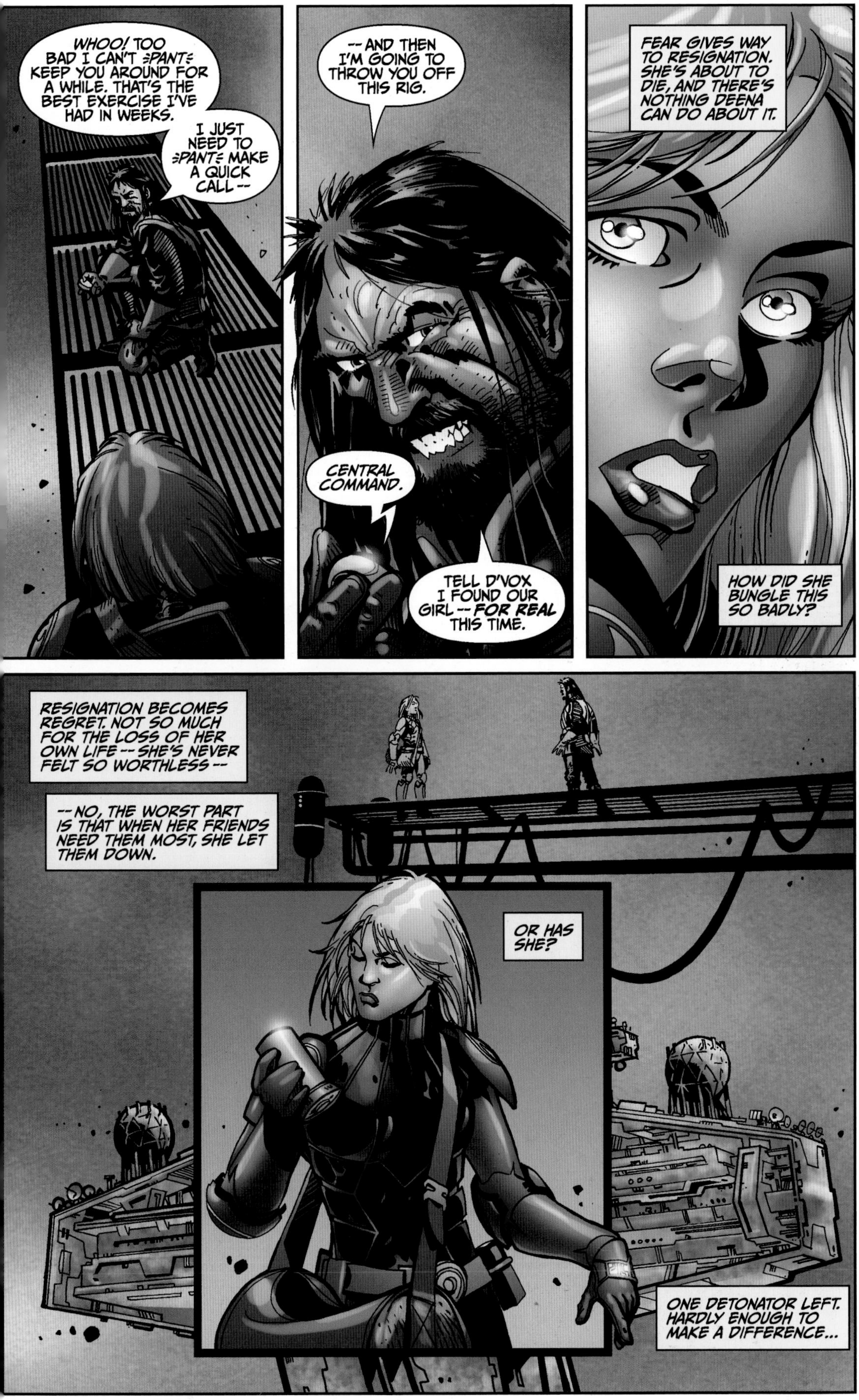

WHOO! TOO BAD I CAN'T =PANT= KEEP YOU AROUND FOR A WHILE. THAT'S THE BEST EXERCISE I'VE HAD IN WEEKS.
I JUST NEED TO =PANT= MAKE A QUICK CALL --
-- AND THEN I'M GOING TO THROW YOU OFF THIS RIG.
CENTRAL COMMAND.
TELL D'VOX I FOUND OUR GIRL -- FOR REAL THIS TIME.
FEAR GIVES WAY TO RESIGNATION. SHE'S ABOUT TO DIE, AND THERE'S NOTHING DEENA CAN DO ABOUT IT.
HOW DID SHE BUNGLE THIS SO BADLY?
RESIGNATION BECOMES REGRET. NOT SO MUCH FOR THE LOSS OF HER OWN LIFE -- SHE'S NEVER FELT SO WORTHLESS --
-- NO, THE WORST PART IS THAT WHEN HER FRIENDS NEED THEM MOST, SHE LET THEM DOWN.
OR HAS SHE?
ONE DETONATOR LEFT. HARDLY ENOUGH TO MAKE A DIFFERENCE...

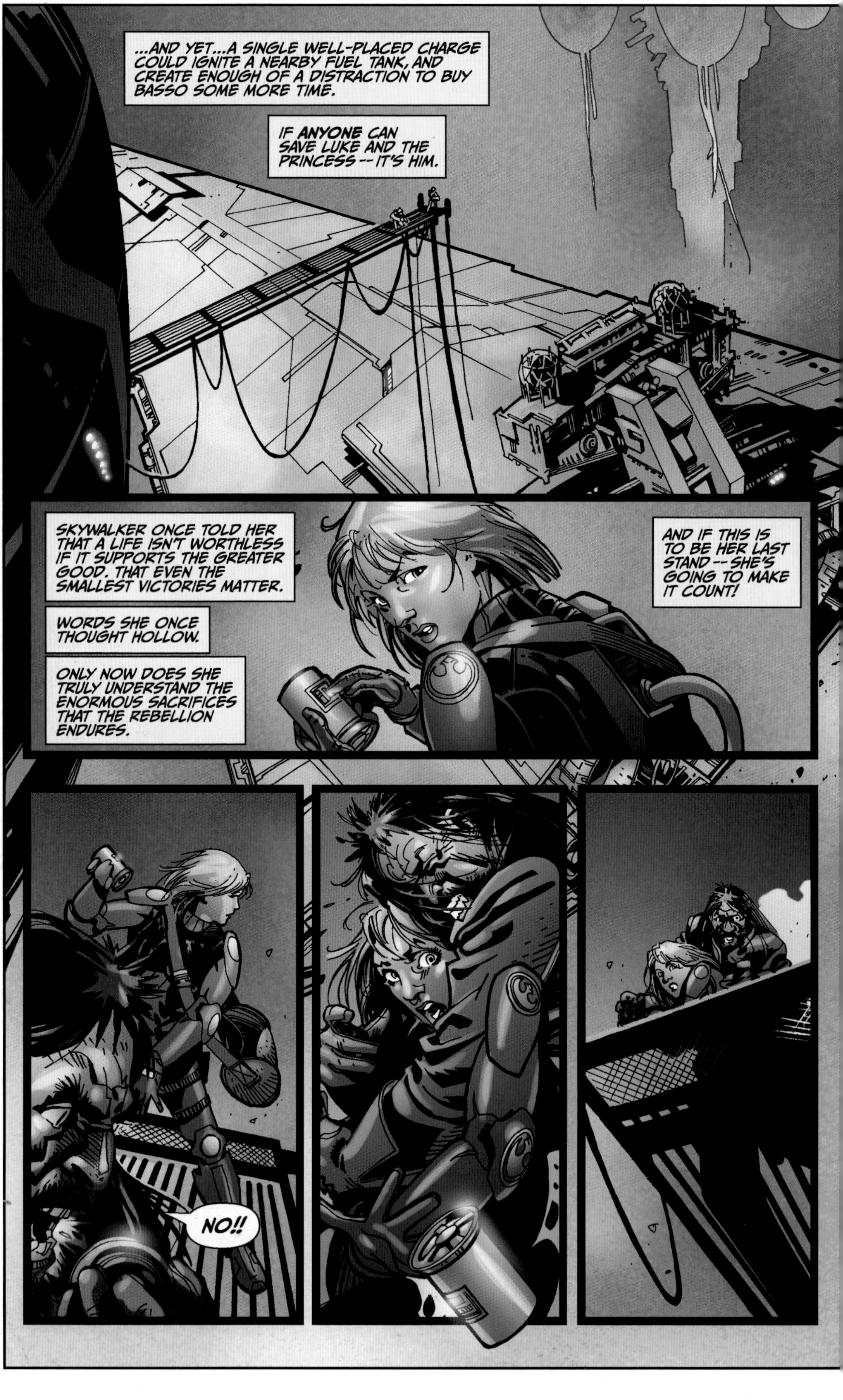
...AND YET...A SINGLE WELL-PLACED CHARGE COULD IGNITE A NEARBY FUEL TANK, AND CREATE ENOUGH OF A DISTRACTION TO BUY BASSO SOME MORE TIME.
IF ANYONE CAN SAVE LUKE AND THE PRINCESS--IT'S HIM.
SKYWALKER ONCE TOLD HER THAT A LIFE ISN'T WORTHLESS IF IT SUPPORTS THE GREATER GOOD. THAT EVEN THE SMALLEST VICTORIES MATTER.
WORDS SHE ONCE THOUGHT HOLLOW.
ONLY NOW DOES SHE TRULY UNDERSTAND THE ENORMOUS SACRIFICES THAT THE REBELLION ENDURES.
AND IF THIS IS TO BE HER LAST STAND--SHE'S GOING TO MAKE IT COUNT!
NO!!

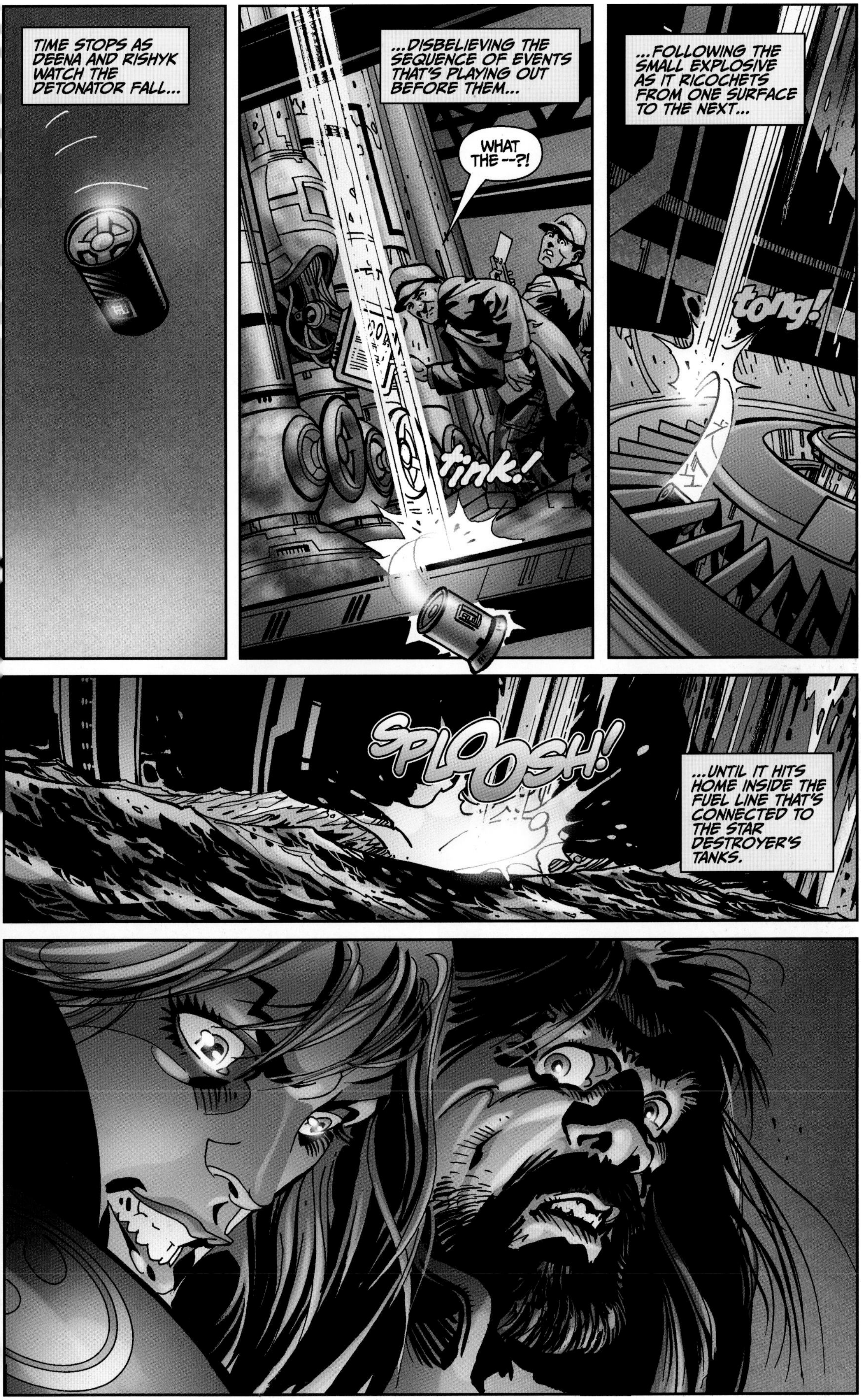
TIME STOPS AS DEENA AND RISHYK WATCH THE DETONATOR FALL...
...DISBELIEVING THE SEQUENCE OF EVENTS THAT'S PLAYING OUT BEFORE THEM...
WHAT THE --?!
tink!
...FOLLOWING THE SMALL EXPLOSIVE AS IT RICOCHETS FROM ONE SURFACE TO THE NEXT...
tong!
SPLOOOSH!
...UNTIL IT HITS HOME INSIDE THE FUEL LINE THAT'S CONNECTED TO THE STAR DESTROYER'S TANKS.

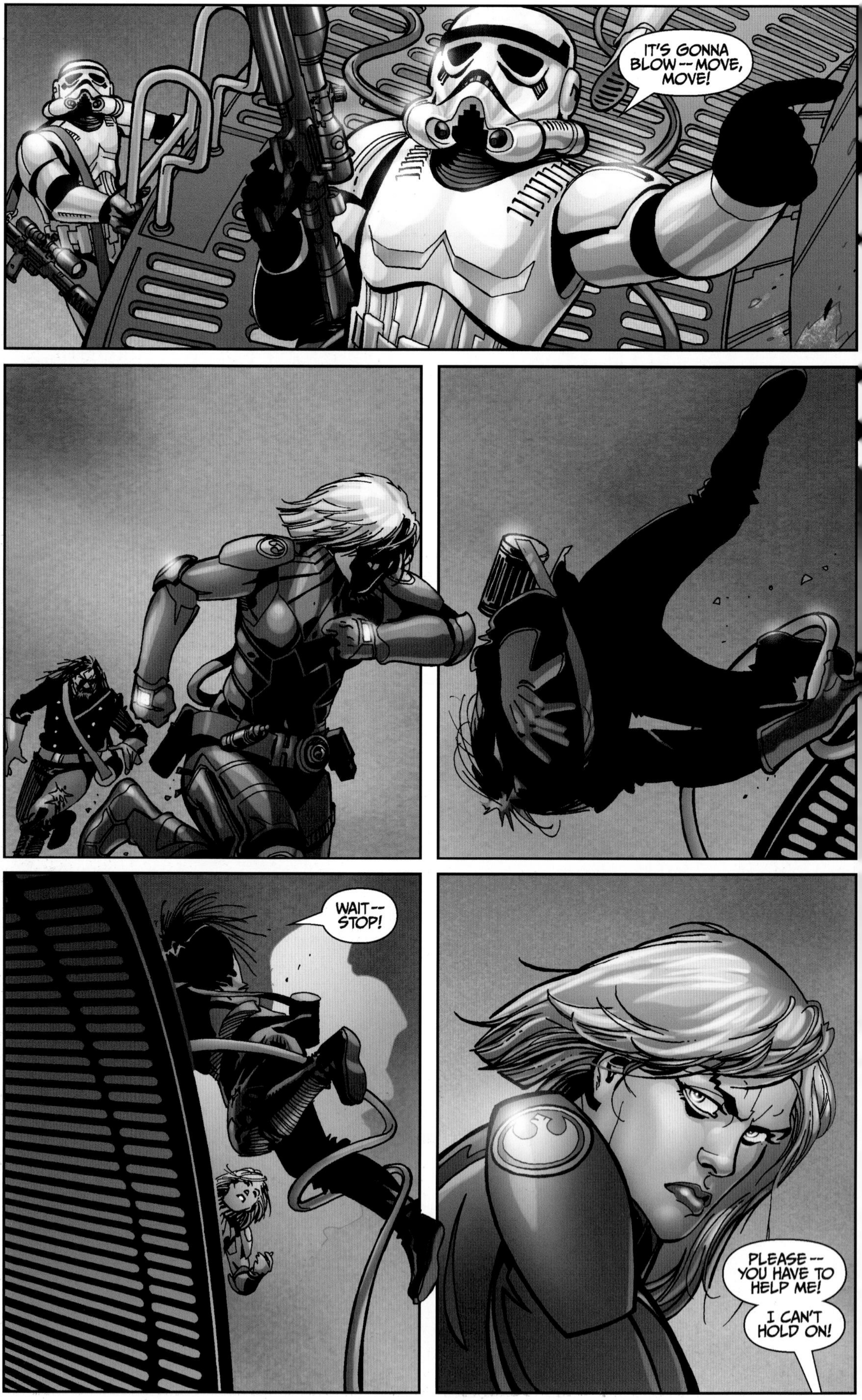
IT'S GONNA BLOW--MOVE, MOVE!
WAIT--STOP!
PLEASE--YOU HAVE TO HELP ME!
I CAN'T HOLD ON!

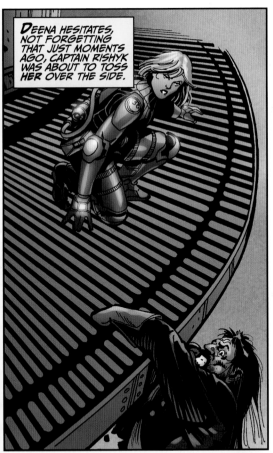

DEENA HESITATES, NOT FORGETTING THAT JUST MOMENTS AGO, CAPTAIN RISHYK WAS ABOUT TO TOSS HER OVER THE SIDE.

BUT SHE ALSO CAN'T CHANGE WHO SHE IS.

TAKE MY HAND -- HURRY!

I'M NOT GOING TO DIE HERE, WOMAN -- YOU ARE!

CHAK!

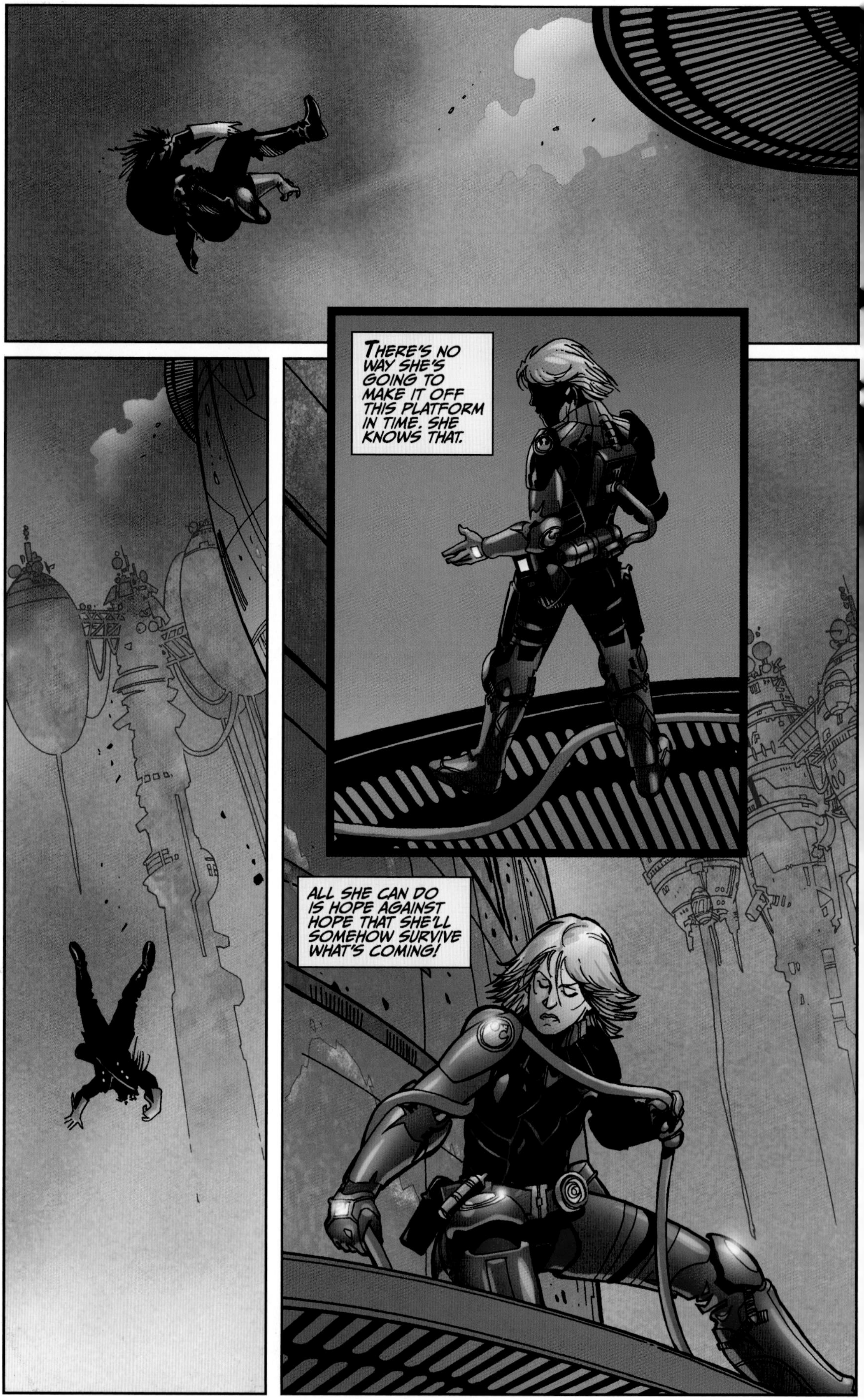
THERE'S NO WAY SHE'S GOING TO MAKE IT OFF THIS PLATFORM IN TIME. SHE KNOWS THAT.
ALL SHE CAN DO IS HOPE AGAINST HOPE THAT SHE'LL SOMEHOW SURVIVE WHAT'S COMING!

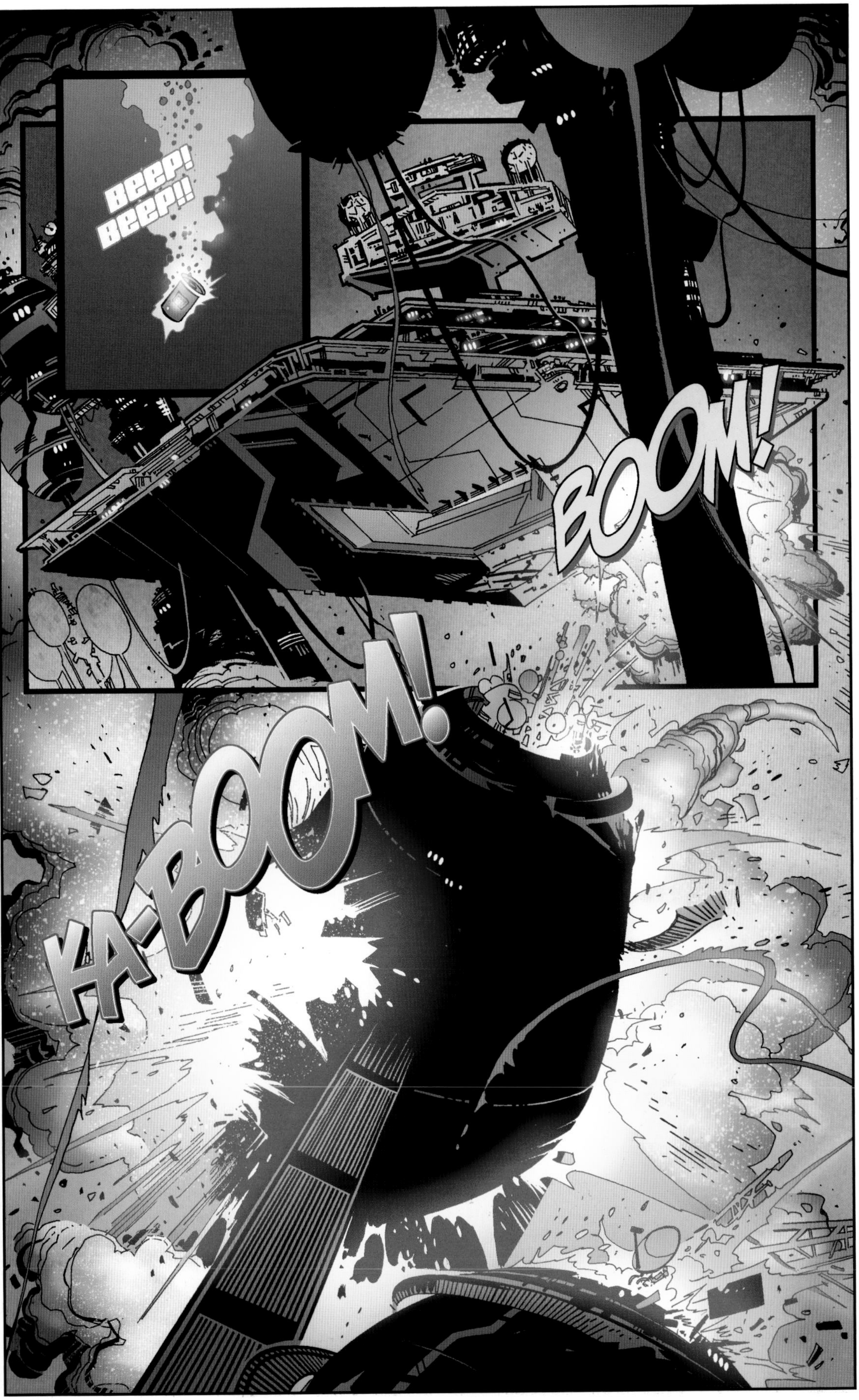

BEEP!
BEEP!!
BOOM!
KA-BOOM!

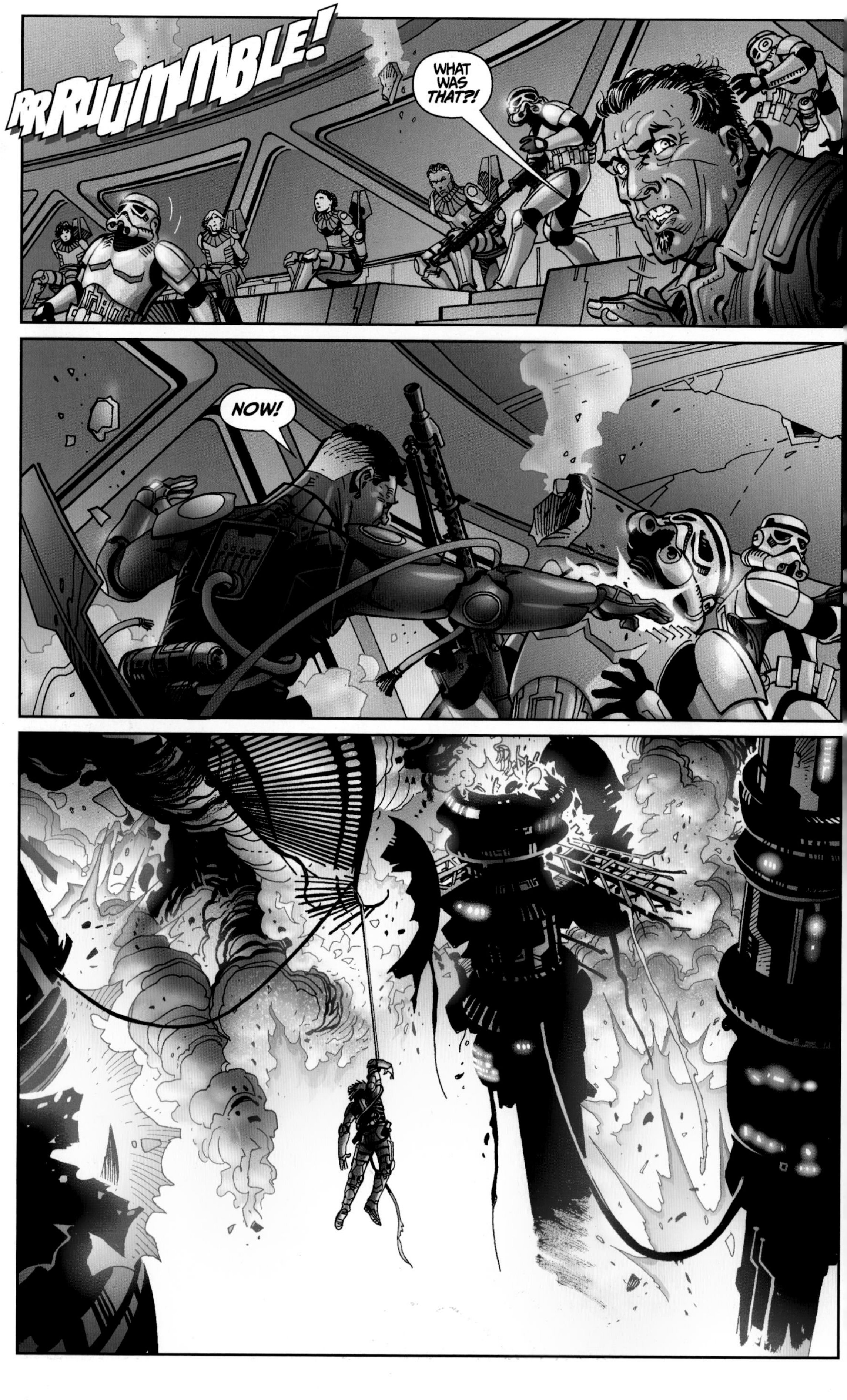
RRRUUUMMBLE!
WHAT WAS THAT?!
NOW!

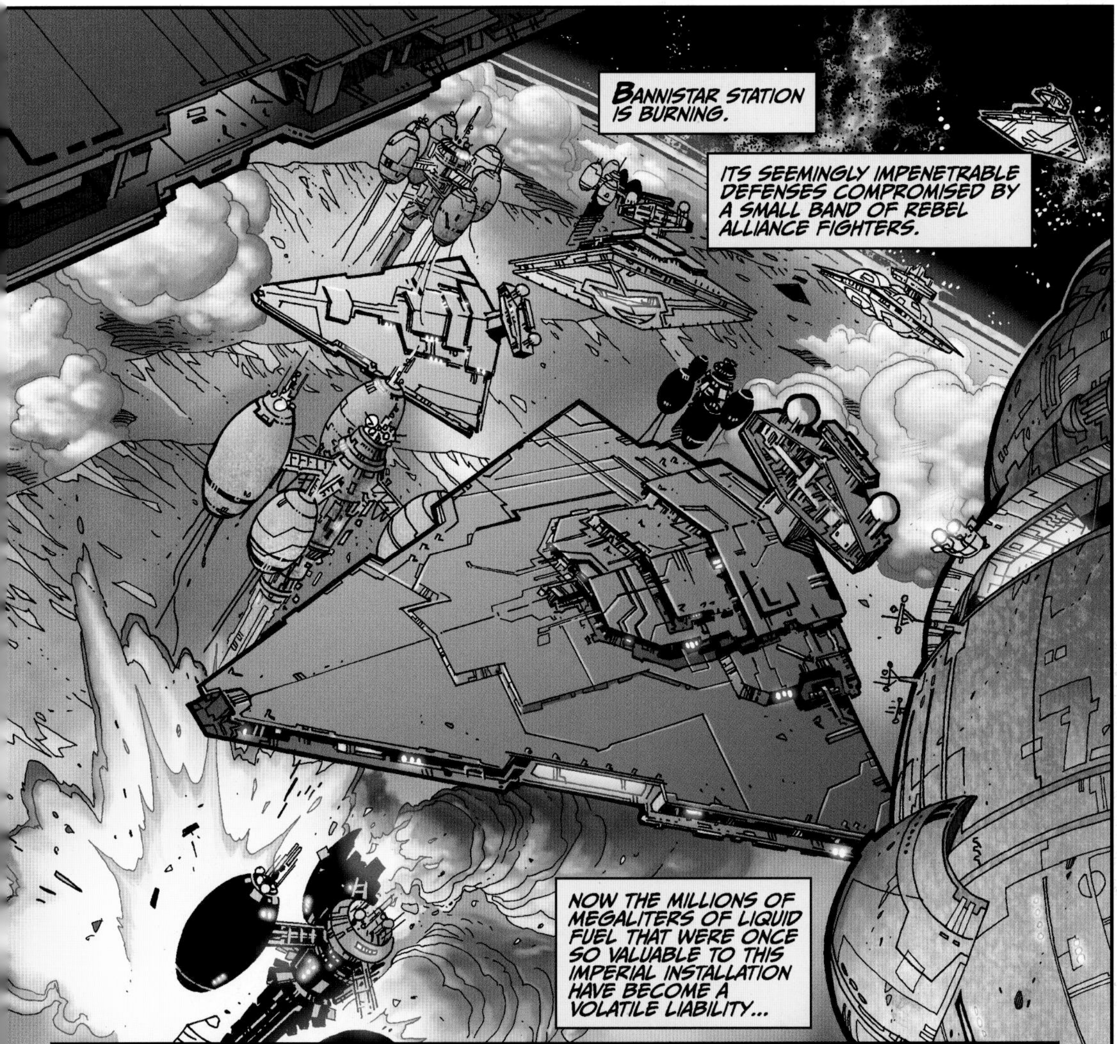
BANNISTAR STATION IS BURNING.
ITS SEEMINGLY IMPENETRABLE DEFENSES COMPROMISED BY A SMALL BAND OF REBEL ALLIANCE FIGHTERS.
NOW THE MILLIONS OF MEGALITERS OF LIQUID FUEL THAT WERE ONCE SO VALUABLE TO THIS IMPERIAL INSTALLATION HAVE BECOME A VOLATILE LIABILITY...
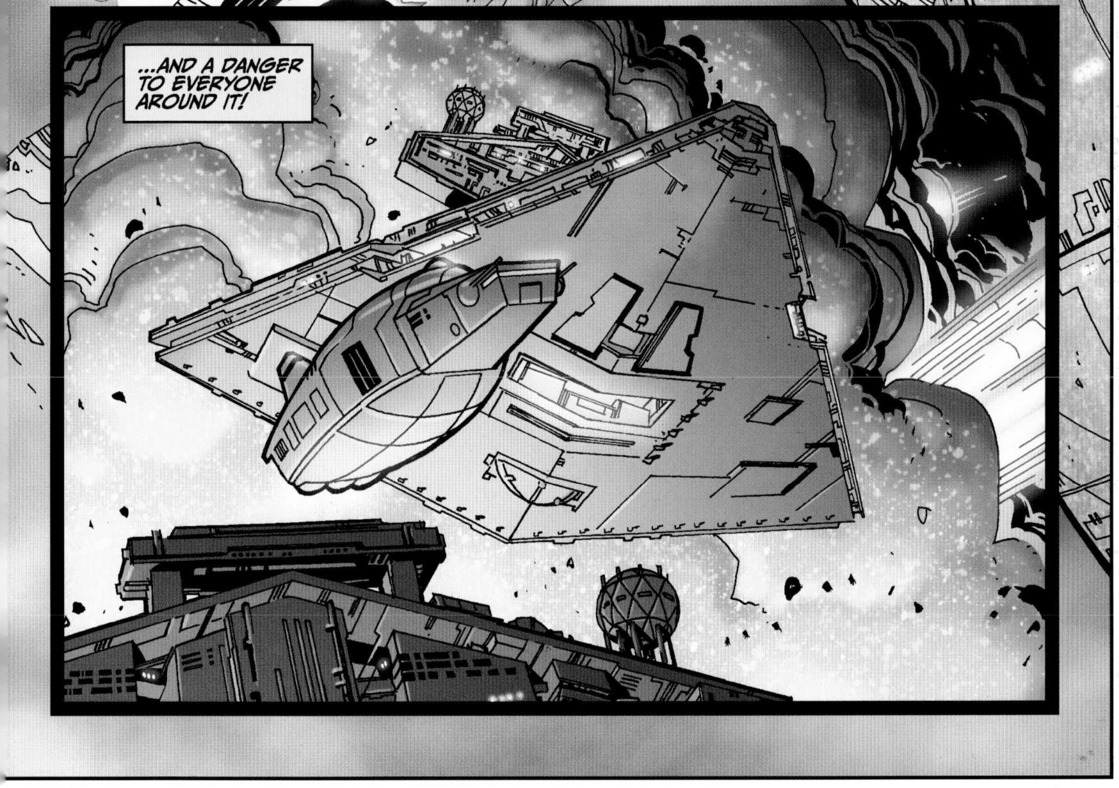
...AND A DANGER TO EVERYONE AROUND IT!

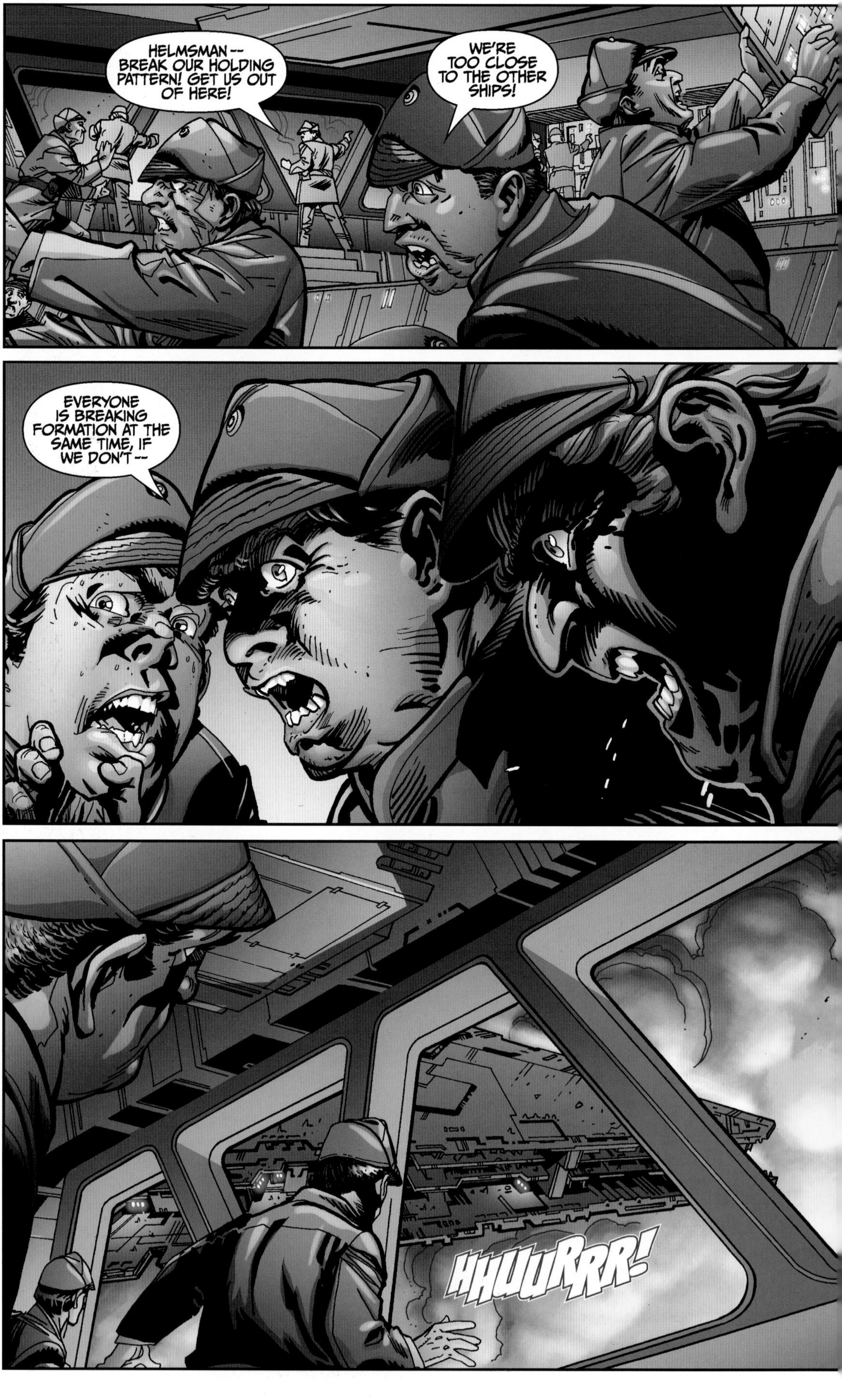
HELMSMAN -- BREAK OUR HOLDING PATTERN! GET US OUT OF HERE!
WE'RE TOO CLOSE TO THE OTHER SHIPS!
EVERYONE IS BREAKING FORMATION AT THE SAME TIME, IF WE DON'T --
HHUURRR!

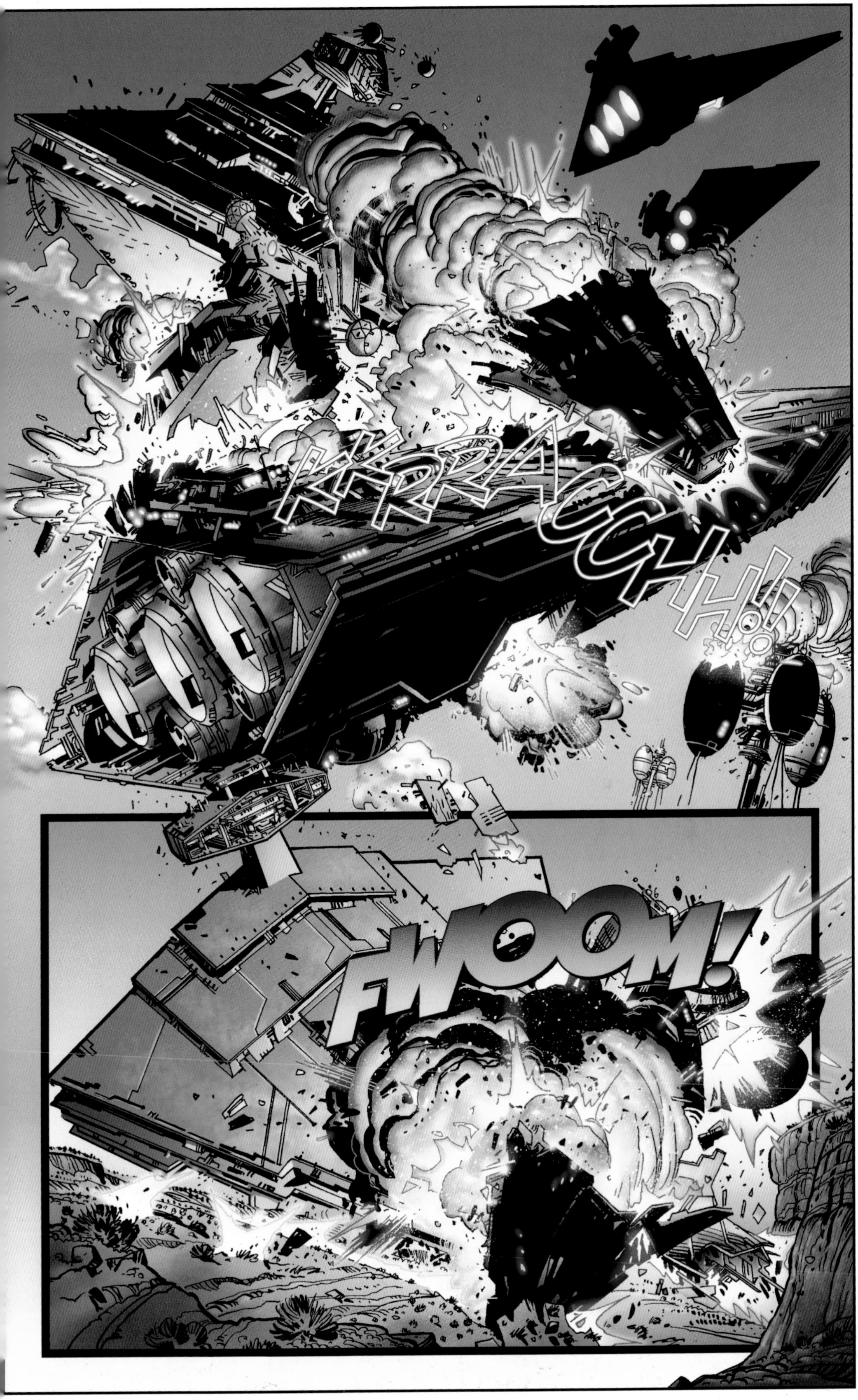

K'KRRACCH!!
FWOOM!

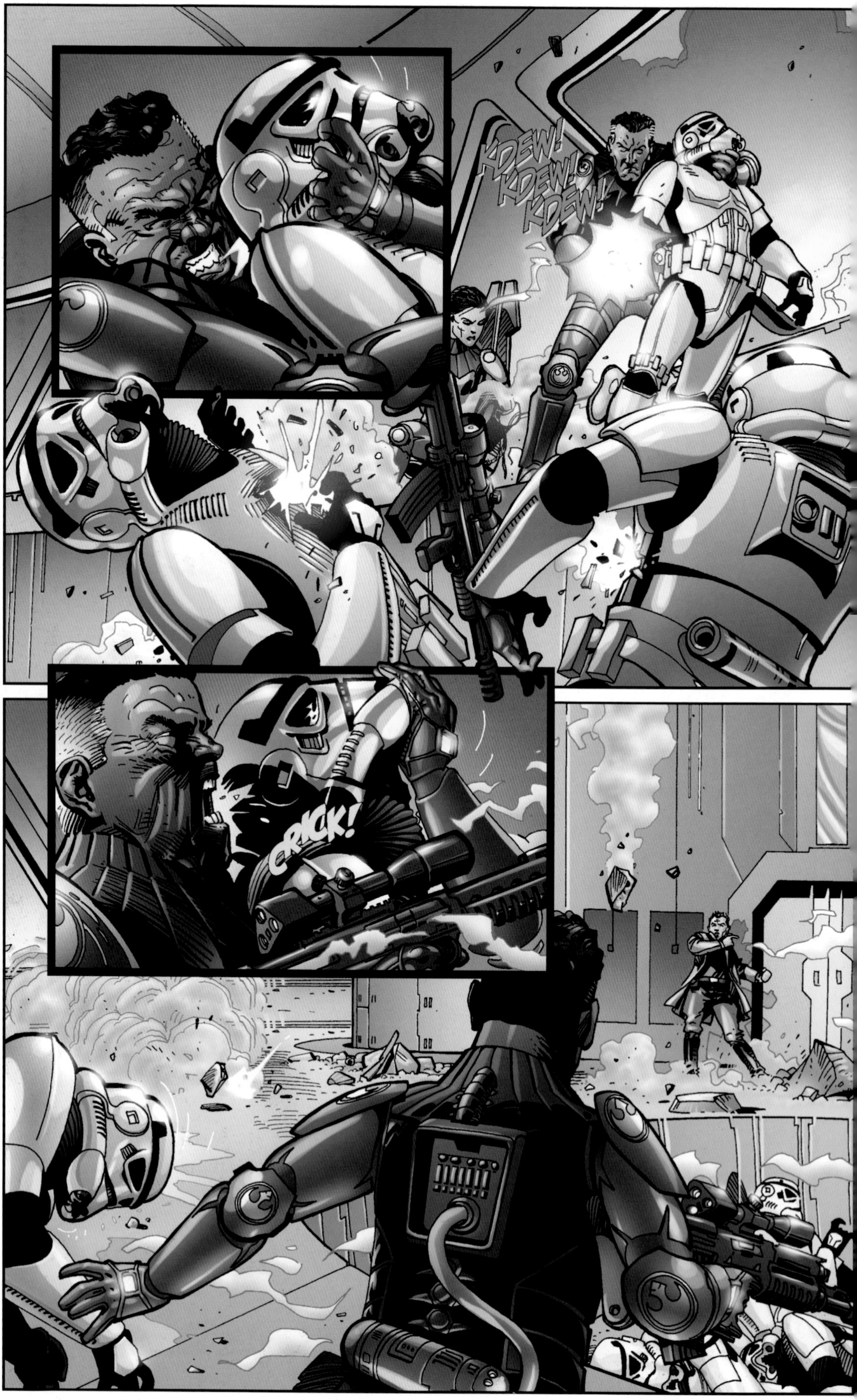

KDEW!
KDEW!
KDEW!
CRICK!

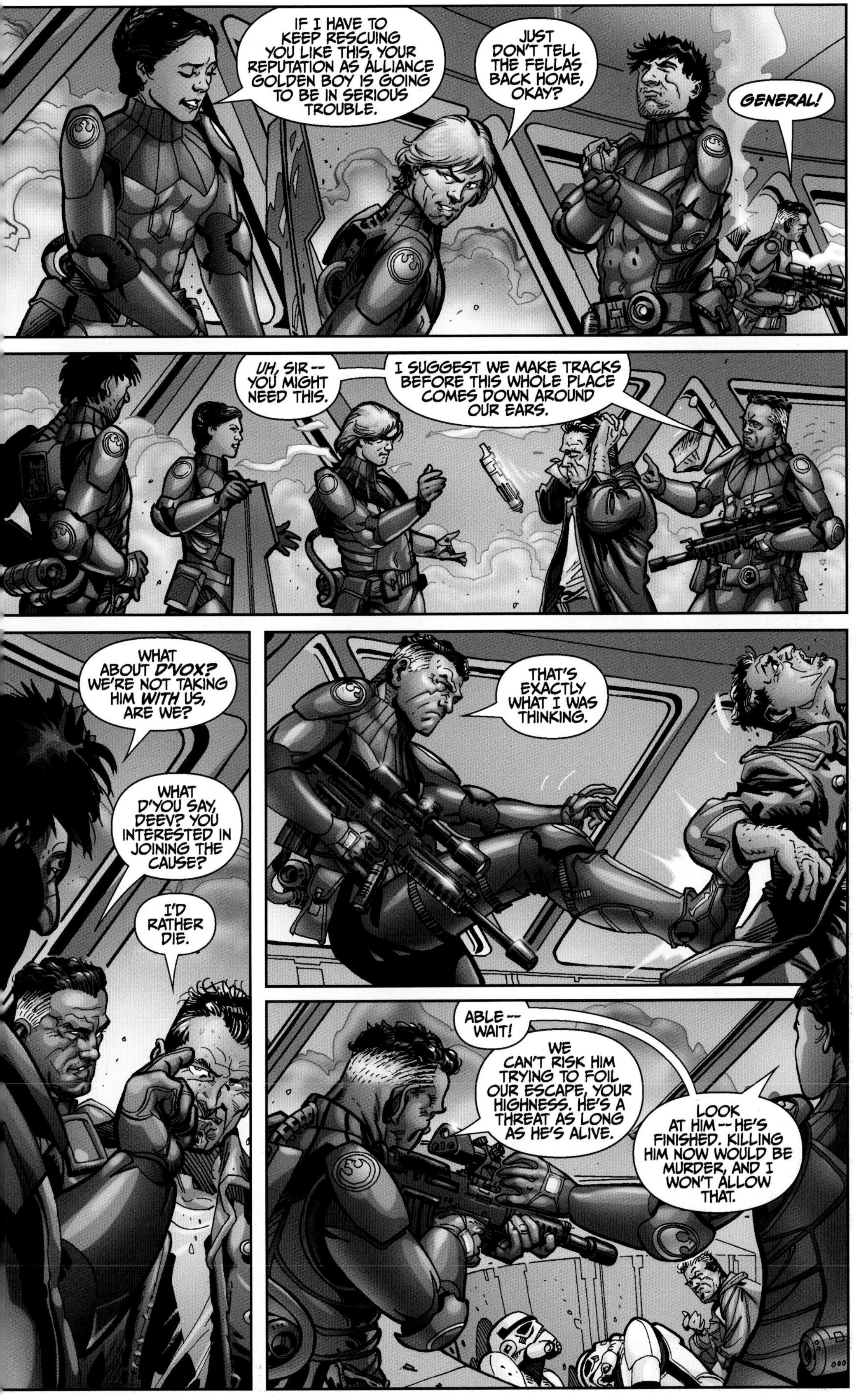

IF I HAVE TO KEEP RESCUING YOU LIKE THIS, YOUR REPUTATION AS ALLIANCE GOLDEN BOY IS GOING TO BE IN SERIOUS TROUBLE.
JUST DON'T TELL THE FELLAS BACK HOME, OKAY?
GENERAL!
UH, SIR-- YOU MIGHT NEED THIS.
I SUGGEST WE MAKE TRACKS BEFORE THIS WHOLE PLACE COMES DOWN AROUND OUR EARS.
WHAT ABOUT D'VOX? WE'RE NOT TAKING HIM WITH US, ARE WE?
WHAT D'YOU SAY, DEEV? YOU INTERESTED IN JOINING THE CAUSE?
I'D RATHER DIE.
THAT'S EXACTLY WHAT I WAS THINKING.
ABLE-- WAIT!
WE CAN'T RISK HIM TRYING TO FOIL OUR ESCAPE, YOUR HIGHNESS. HE'S A THREAT AS LONG AS HE'S ALIVE.
LOOK AT HIM--HE'S FINISHED. KILLING HIM NOW WOULD BE MURDER, AND I WON'T ALLOW THAT.

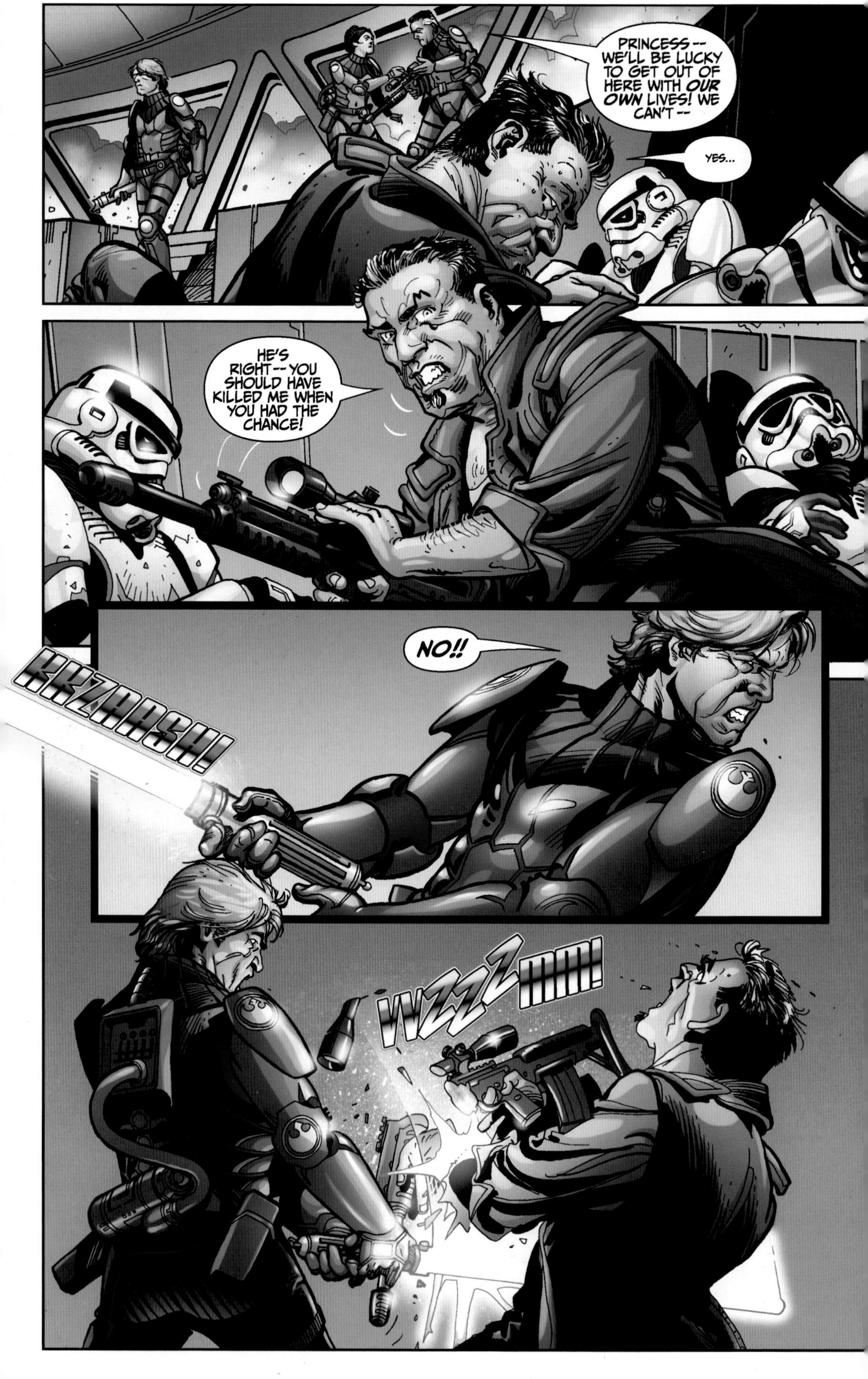
PRINCESS -- WE'LL BE LUCKY TO GET OUT OF HERE WITH OUR OWN LIVES! WE CAN'T --
YES...
HE'S RIGHT -- YOU SHOULD HAVE KILLED ME WHEN YOU HAD THE CHANCE!
NO!!
KKZAASH!
VVZZZMM!

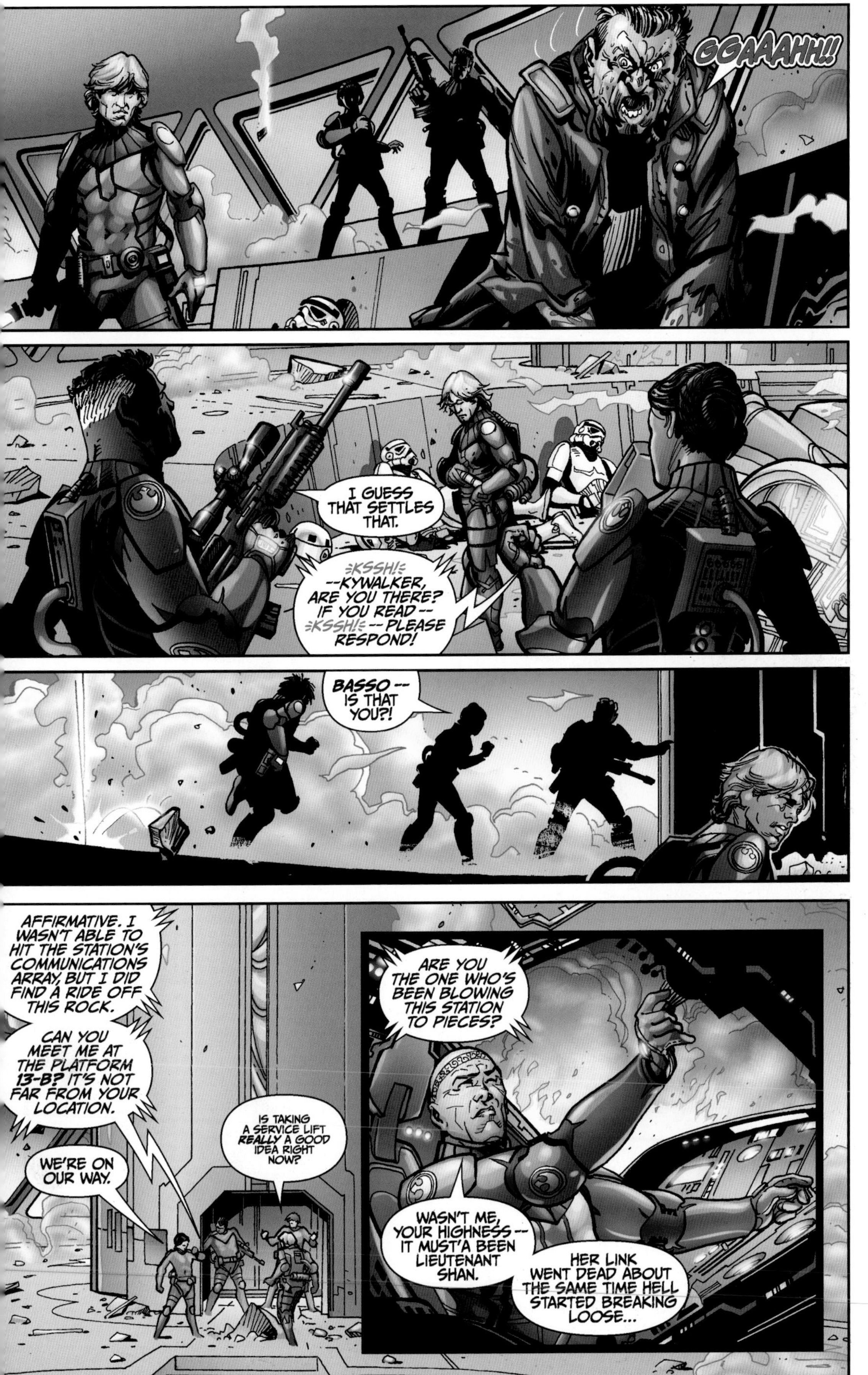

GGAAAHH!!
I GUESS THAT SETTLES THAT.
≷KSSH!≶ --KYWALKER, ARE YOU THERE? IF YOU READ -- ≷KSSH!≶ --PLEASE RESPOND!
BASSO -- IS THAT YOU?!
AFFIRMATIVE. I WASN'T ABLE TO HIT THE STATION'S COMMUNICATIONS ARRAY, BUT I DID FIND A RIDE OFF THIS ROCK.
CAN YOU MEET ME AT THE PLATFORM 13-B? IT'S NOT FAR FROM YOUR LOCATION.
WE'RE ON OUR WAY.
IS TAKING A SERVICE LIFT REALLY A GOOD IDEA RIGHT NOW?
ARE YOU THE ONE WHO'S BEEN BLOWING THIS STATION TO PIECES?
WASN'T ME, YOUR HIGHNESS -- IT MUST'A BEEN LIEUTENANT SHAN.
HER LINK WENT DEAD ABOUT THE SAME TIME HELL STARTED BREAKING LOOSE...

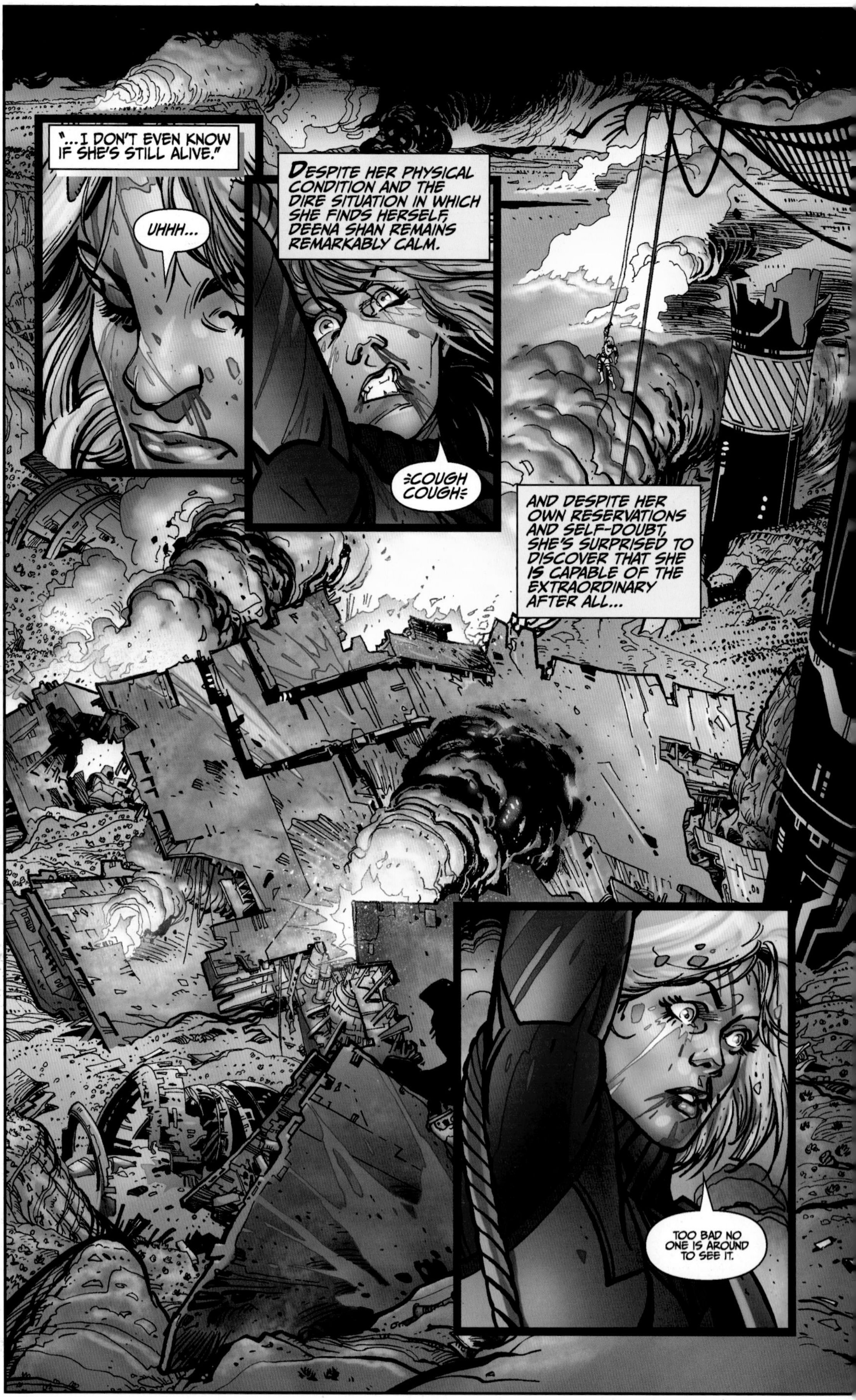
"...I DON'T EVEN KNOW IF SHE'S STILL ALIVE."
UHHH...
DESPITE HER PHYSICAL CONDITION AND THE DIRE SITUATION IN WHICH SHE FINDS HERSELF, DEENA SHAN REMAINS REMARKABLY CALM.
COUGH COUGH
AND DESPITE HER OWN RESERVATIONS AND SELF-DOUBT, SHE'S SURPRISED TO DISCOVER THAT SHE IS CAPABLE OF THE EXTRAORDINARY AFTER ALL...
TOO BAD NO ONE IS AROUND TO SEE IT.

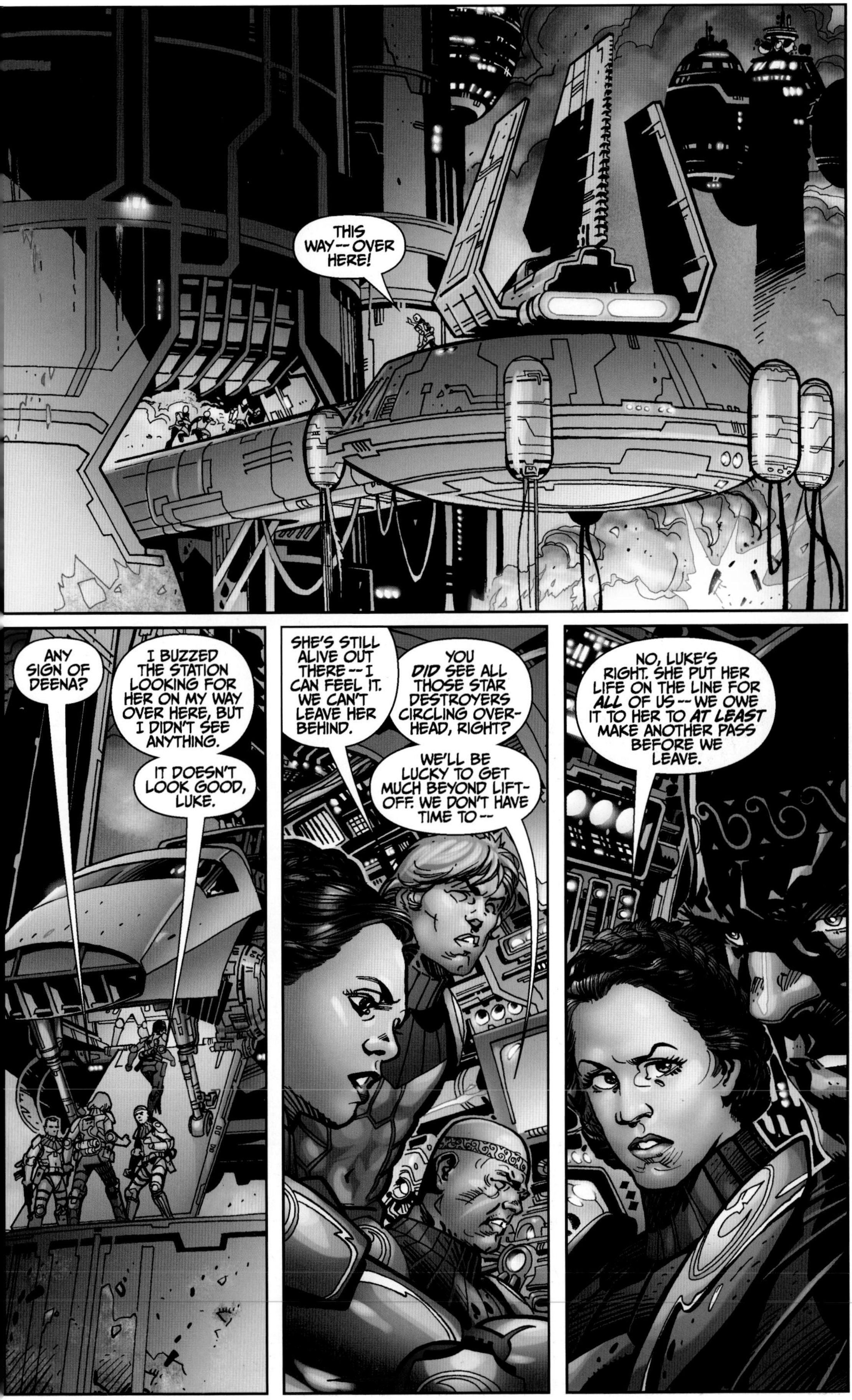
THIS WAY--OVER HERE!
ANY SIGN OF DEENA?
I BUZZED THE STATION LOOKING FOR HER ON MY WAY OVER HERE, BUT I DIDN'T SEE ANYTHING.
IT DOESN'T LOOK GOOD, LUKE.
SHE'S STILL ALIVE OUT THERE--I CAN FEEL IT. WE CAN'T LEAVE HER BEHIND.
YOU *DID* SEE ALL THOSE STAR DESTROYERS CIRCLING OVER-HEAD, RIGHT?
WE'LL BE LUCKY TO GET MUCH BEYOND LIFT-OFF. WE DON'T HAVE TIME TO--
NO, LUKE'S RIGHT. SHE PUT HER LIFE ON THE LINE FOR *ALL* OF US--WE OWE IT TO HER TO *AT LEAST* MAKE ANOTHER PASS BEFORE WE LEAVE.

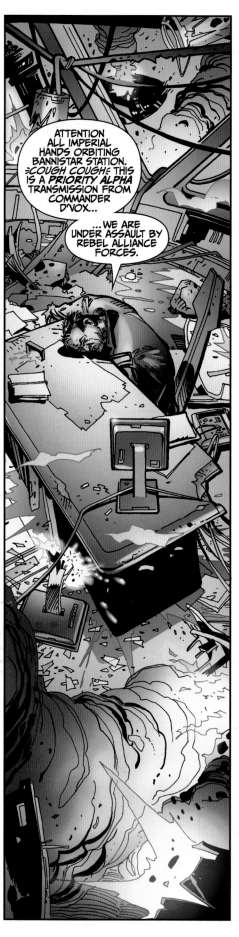

ATTENTION ALL IMPERIAL HANDS ORBITING BANNISTAR STATION. ≋COUGH COUGH≋ THIS IS A *PRIORITY ALPHA* TRANSMISSION FROM COMMANDER D'VOX...

...WE ARE UNDER ASSAULT BY REBEL ALLIANCE FORCES.

THE ORCHESTRATORS OF THIS STRIKE ARE FLEEING IN A STOLEN LAMBDA-CLASS SHUTTLE.

SCRAMBLE ALL AVAILABLE FIGHTERS IMMEDIATELY AND *SHOOT TO DESTROY.*

SKYWALKER, IF YOU SOMEHOW SURVIVE THIS NIGHT, I PROMISE YOU--- I SWEAR I WILL *FIND YOU.*

TO MY LAST DAY, I WILL HUNT YOU DOWN...

"...AND I'LL MAKE YOU *SUFFER* FOR THIS!"

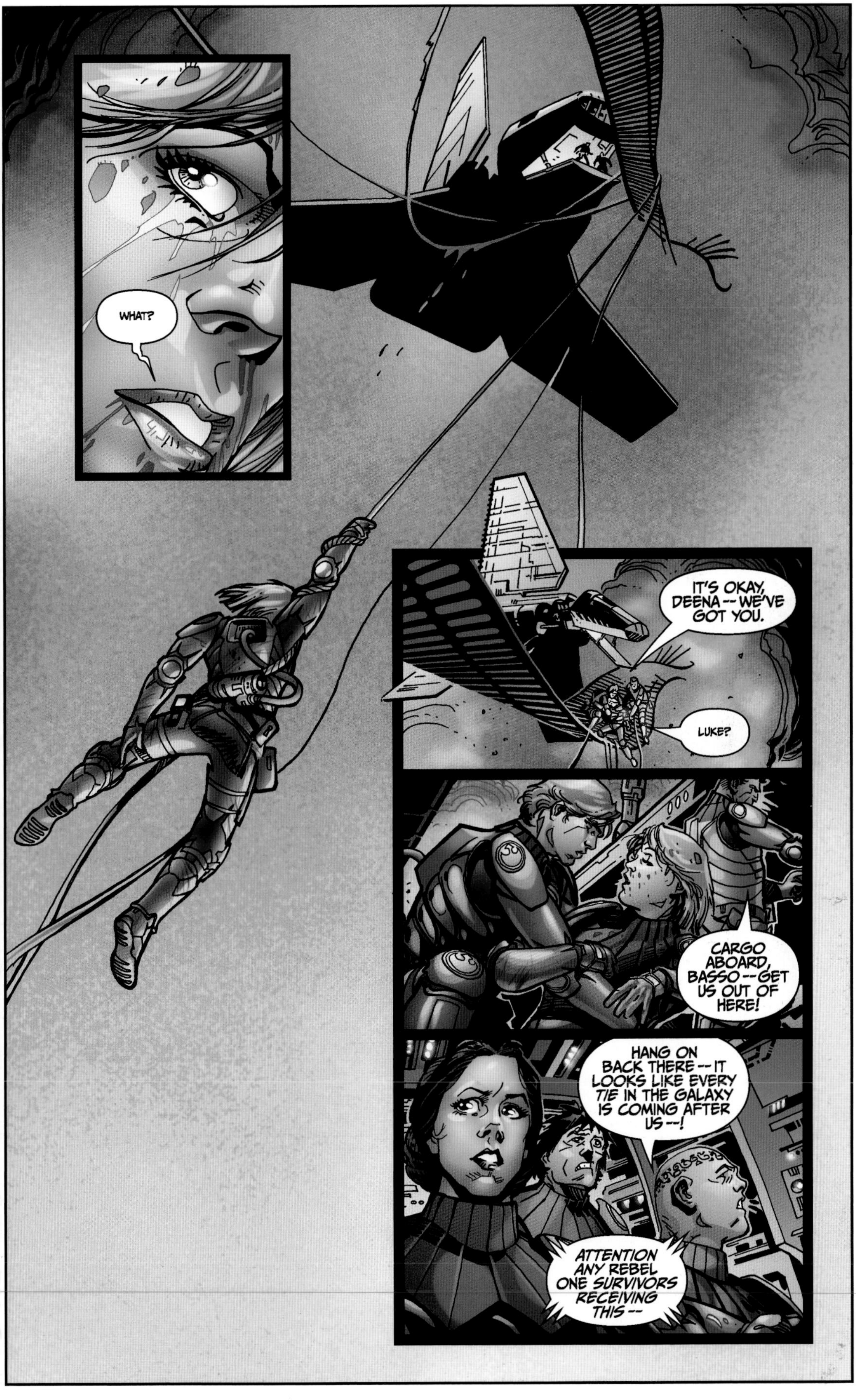
WHAT?
IT'S OKAY, DEENA -- WE'VE GOT YOU.
LUKE?
CARGO ABOARD, BASSO -- GET US OUT OF HERE!
HANG ON BACK THERE -- IT LOOKS LIKE EVERY *TIE* IN THE GALAXY IS COMING AFTER US --!
ATTENTION ANY REBEL ONE SURVIVORS RECEIVING THIS --

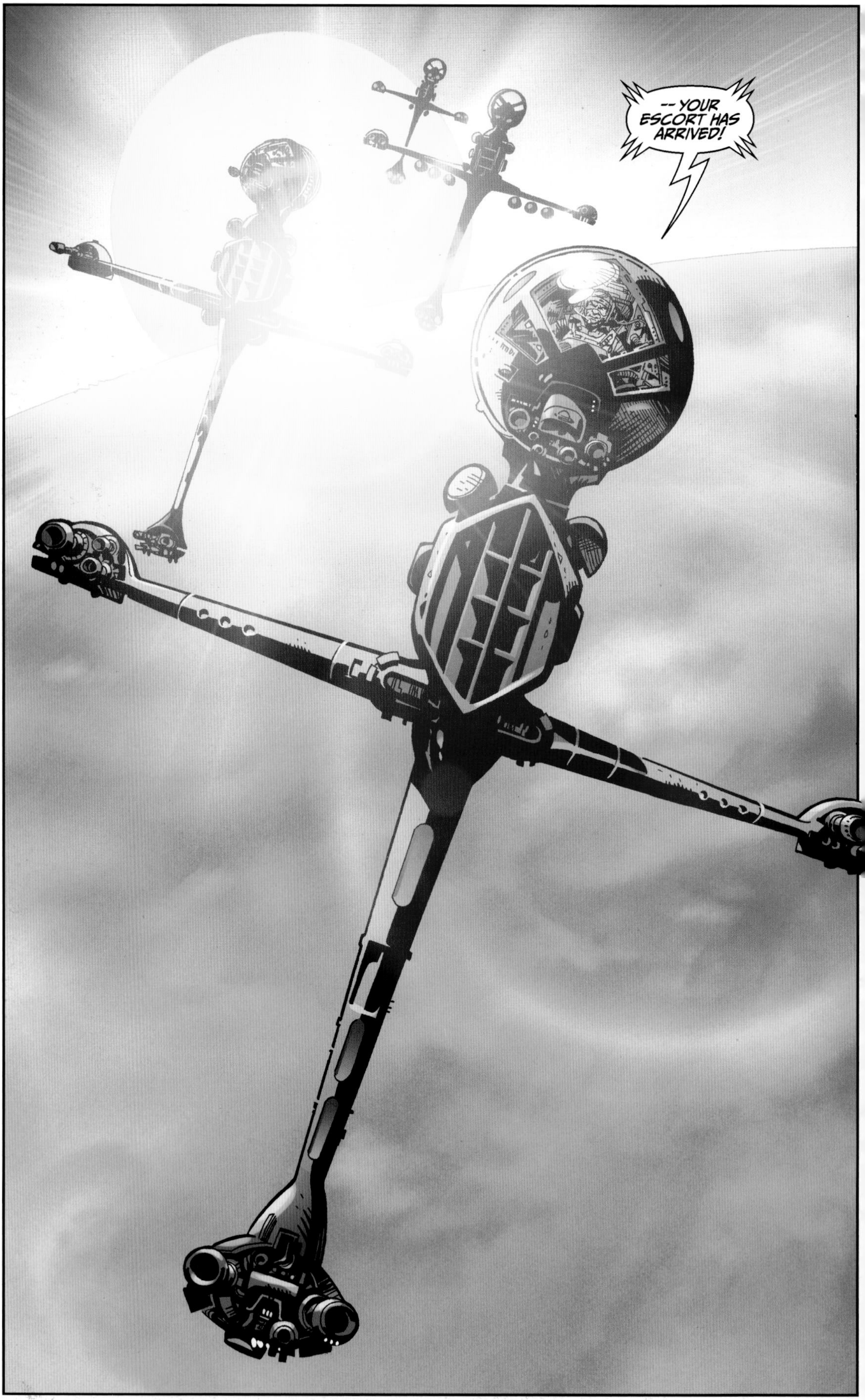
-- YOUR ESCORT HAS ARRIVED!

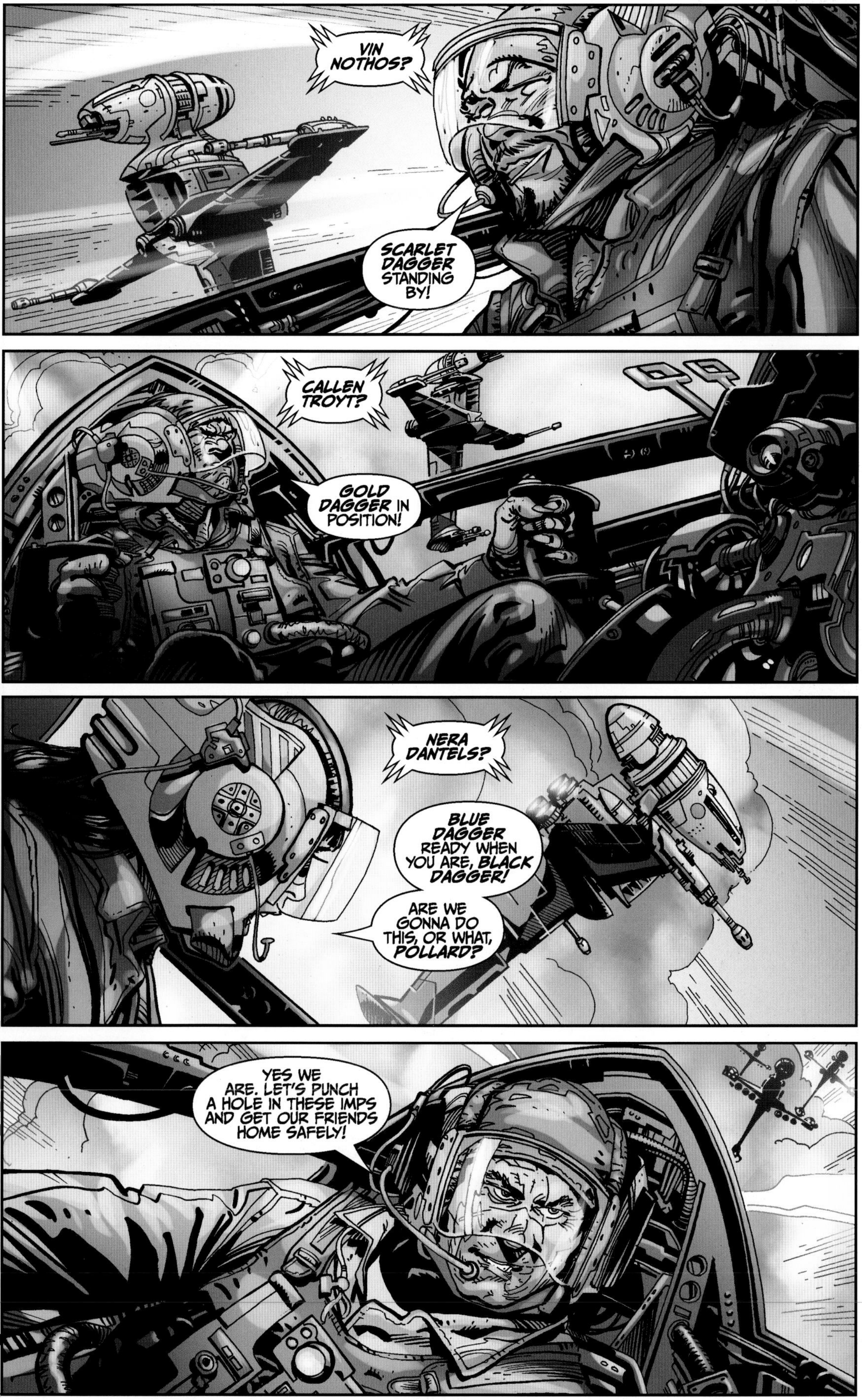
VIN NOTHOS?
SCARLET DAGGER STANDING BY!
CALLEN TROYT?
GOLD DAGGER IN POSITION!
NERA DANTELS?
BLUE DAGGER READY WHEN YOU ARE, BLACK DAGGER!
ARE WE GONNA DO THIS, OR WHAT, POLLARD?
YES WE ARE. LET'S PUNCH A HOLE IN THESE IMPS AND GET OUR FRIENDS HOME SAFELY!

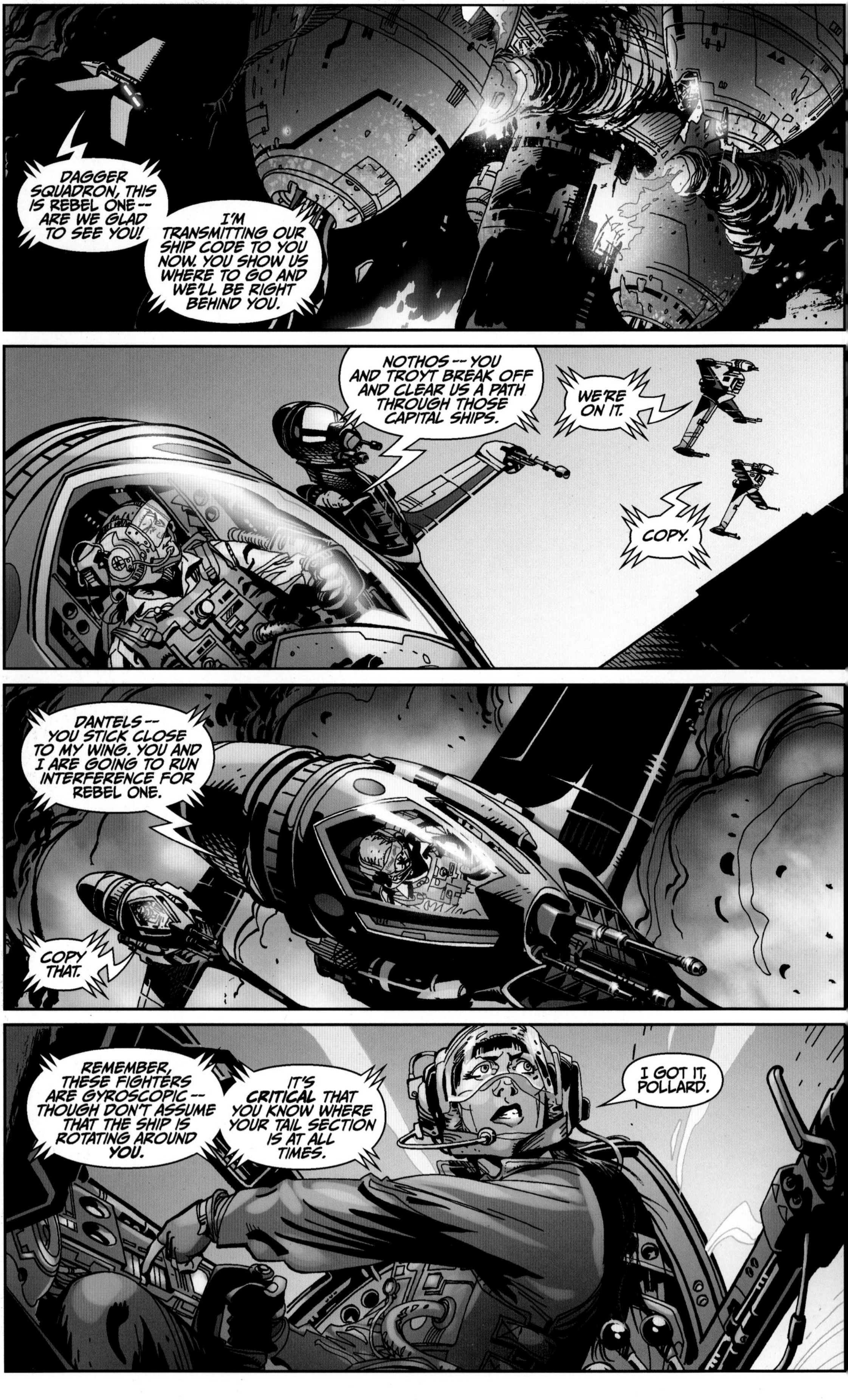
DAGGER SQUADRON, THIS IS REBEL ONE -- ARE WE GLAD TO SEE YOU!
I'M TRANSMITTING OUR SHIP CODE TO YOU NOW. YOU SHOW US WHERE TO GO AND WE'LL BE RIGHT BEHIND YOU.
NOTHOS -- YOU AND TROYT BREAK OFF AND CLEAR US A PATH THROUGH THOSE CAPITAL SHIPS.
WE'RE ON IT.
COPY.
DANTELS -- YOU STICK CLOSE TO MY WING. YOU AND I ARE GOING TO RUN INTERFERENCE FOR REBEL ONE.
COPY THAT.
REMEMBER, THESE FIGHTERS ARE GYROSCOPIC -- THOUGH DON'T ASSUME THAT THE SHIP IS ROTATING AROUND YOU.
IT'S CRITICAL THAT YOU KNOW WHERE YOUR TAIL SECTION IS AT ALL TIMES.
I GOT IT, POLLARD.

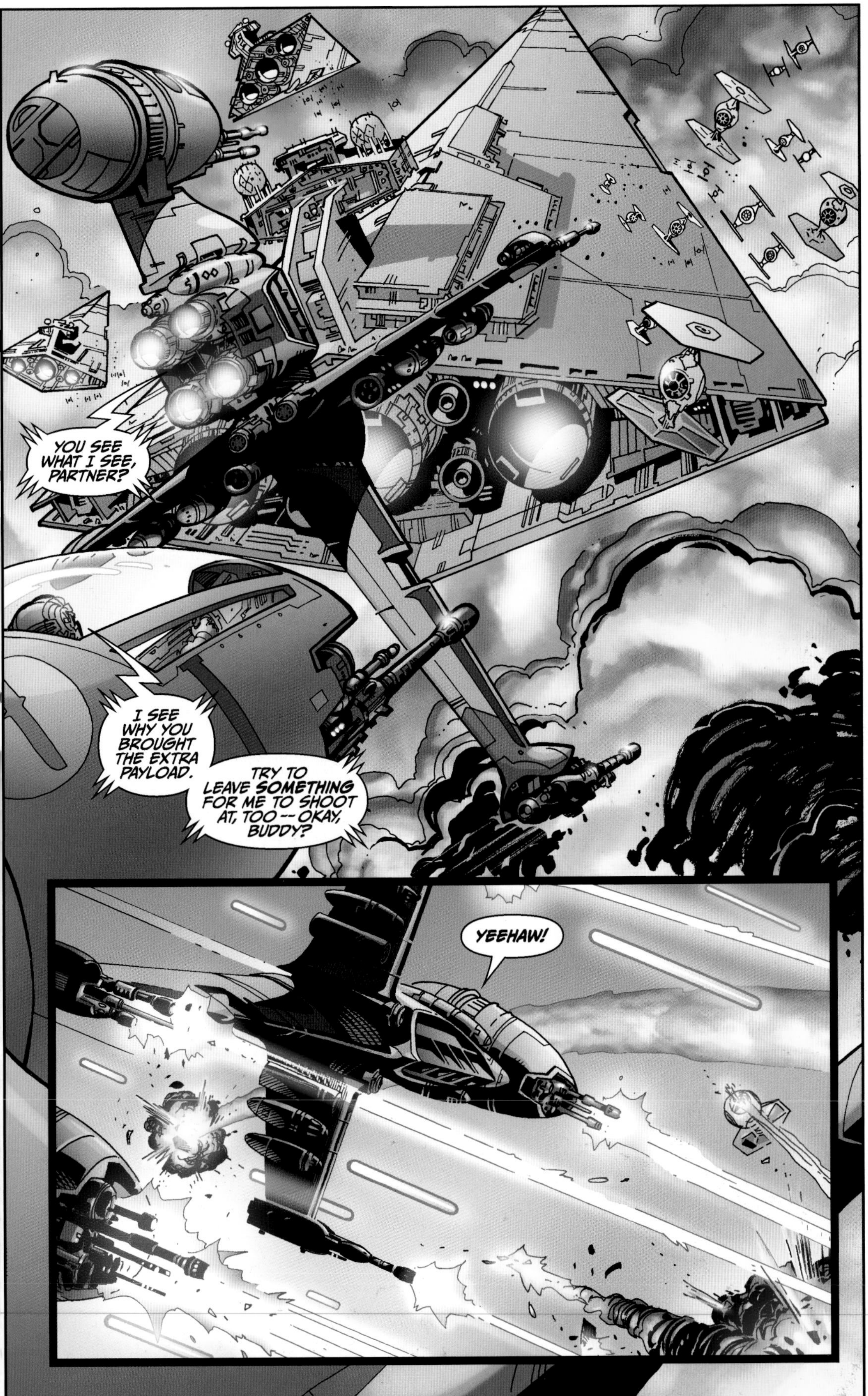
YOU SEE WHAT I SEE, PARTNER?
I SEE WHY YOU BROUGHT THE EXTRA PAYLOAD.
TRY TO LEAVE **SOMETHING** FOR ME TO SHOOT AT, TOO -- OKAY, BUDDY?
YEEHAW!

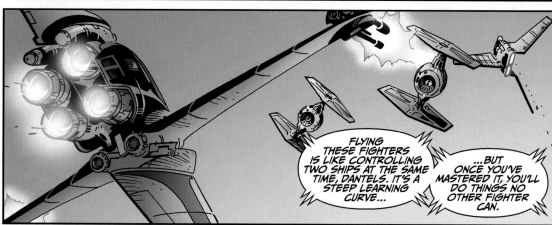

FLYING THESE FIGHTERS IS LIKE CONTROLLING TWO SHIPS AT THE SAME TIME, DANTELS. IT'S A STEEP LEARNING CURVE...

...BUT ONCE YOU'VE MASTERED IT, YOU'LL DO THINGS NO OTHER FIGHTER CAN.

POLLARD -- CUT THE CHATTER! I GOT IT!

THIS IS GOLD DAGGER -- WE'VE PUNCHED THAT HOLE YOU ORDERED.

IT'S FILLING IN FAST, THOUGH. IF WE'RE GOING TO BLOW THIS PLACE, THERE'S NO TIME LIKE THE PRESENT.

COPY THAT, GOLD DAGGER. ALL SHIPS PREPARE TO JUMP TO HYPERSPACE ON MY MARK...

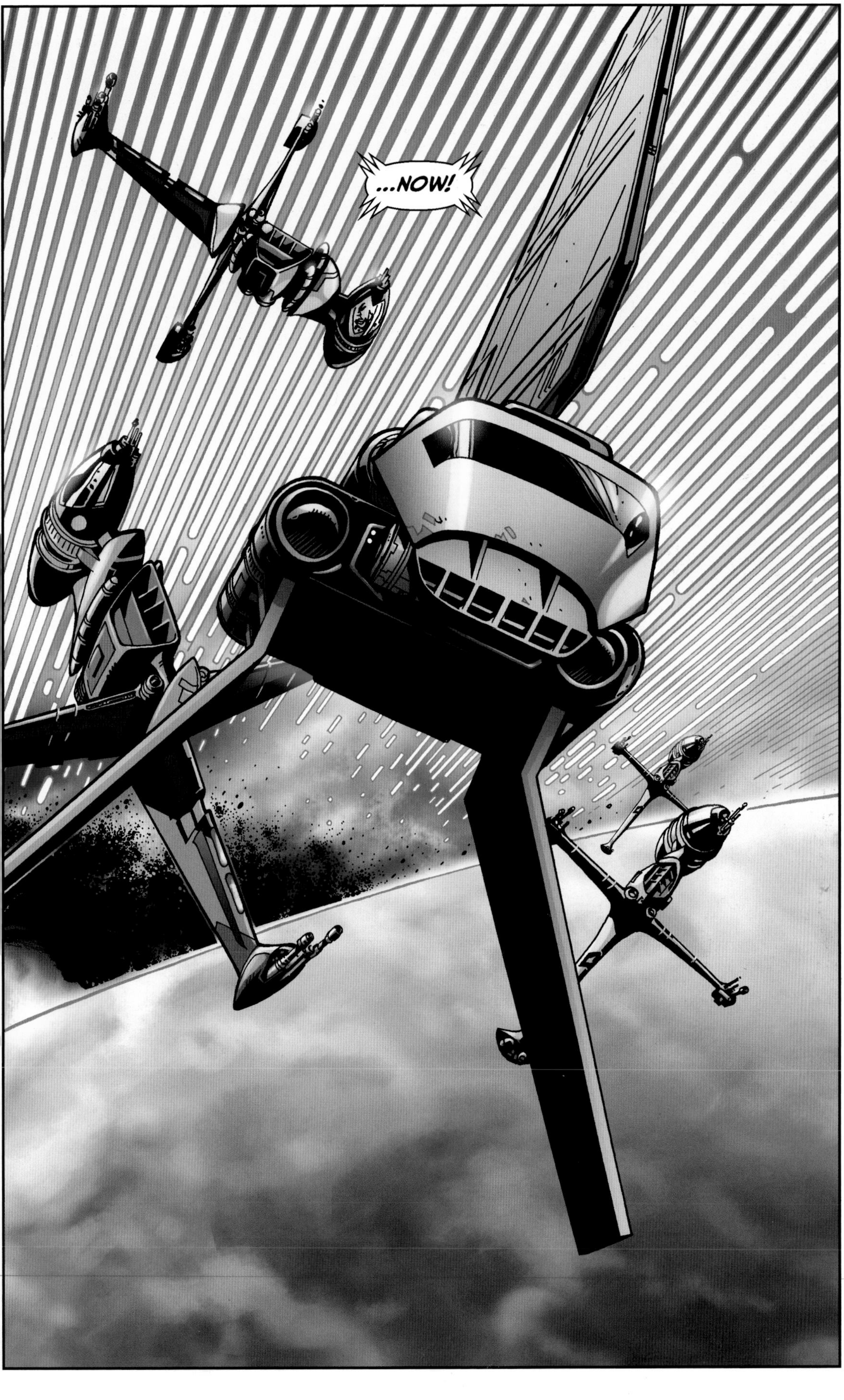
...NOW!

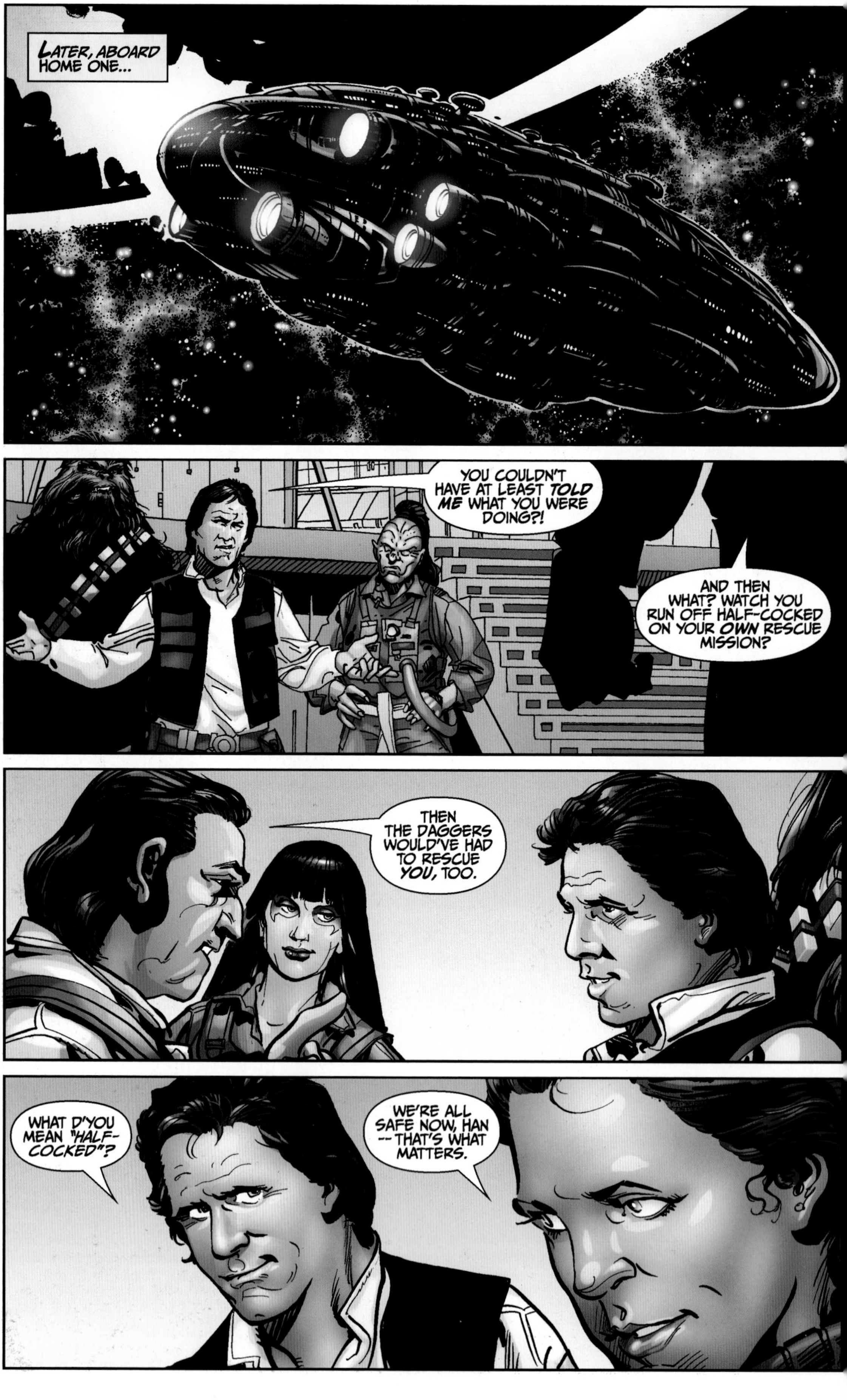
LATER, ABOARD HOME ONE...
YOU COULDN'T HAVE AT LEAST TOLD ME WHAT YOU WERE DOING?!
AND THEN WHAT? WATCH YOU RUN OFF HALF-COCKED ON YOUR OWN RESCUE MISSION?
THEN THE DAGGERS WOULD'VE HAD TO RESCUE YOU, TOO.
WHAT D'YOU MEAN "HALF-COCKED"?
WE'RE ALL SAFE NOW, HAN -- THAT'S WHAT MATTERS.

YES, SAFE FOR NOW...BUT I FIND THE INFORMATION RETRIEVED BY LIEUTENANT SHAN TO BE VERY TROUBLING.

IF THE EMPIRE IS PREPARING A STRIKE AGAINST OUR ALLIES IN THE ANSION SYSTEM -- WE CANNOT ALLOW THAT TO HAPPEN.

THERE ISN'T MUCH *WE* CAN DO ABOUT IT, ADMIRAL.

YOU SAID YOURSELF THAT THIS FLEET ISN'T EXACTLY IN FIGHTING SHAPE.

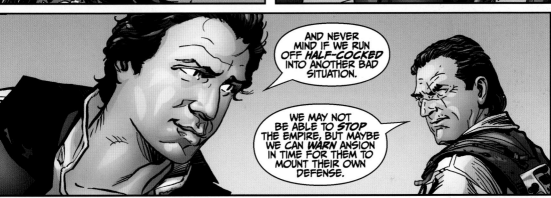

AND NEVER MIND IF WE RUN OFF *HALF-COCKED* INTO ANOTHER BAD SITUATION.

WE MAY NOT BE ABLE TO *STOP* THE EMPIRE, BUT MAYBE WE CAN *WARN* ANSION IN TIME FOR THEM TO MOUNT THEIR OWN DEFENSE.

MY DAGGERS PROVED THEMSELVES TODAY.

WE'RE *PERFECT* FOR SOMETHING LIKE THIS AND WE CAN BE AT ANSION IN LESS THAN A DAY'S TIME...

...JUST GIVE US THE ORDER AND WE'RE GONE.

YES, PERHAPS YOU'RE RIGHT, *POLLARD*. THE EMPIRE EXPECTS TO CATCH ANSION UNAWARE, BUT IF THE SYSTEM'S MILITIAS *KNEW* WHAT WAS COMING...

HAVE SKYWALKER AND ANTILLES PREPARE -- HMM...

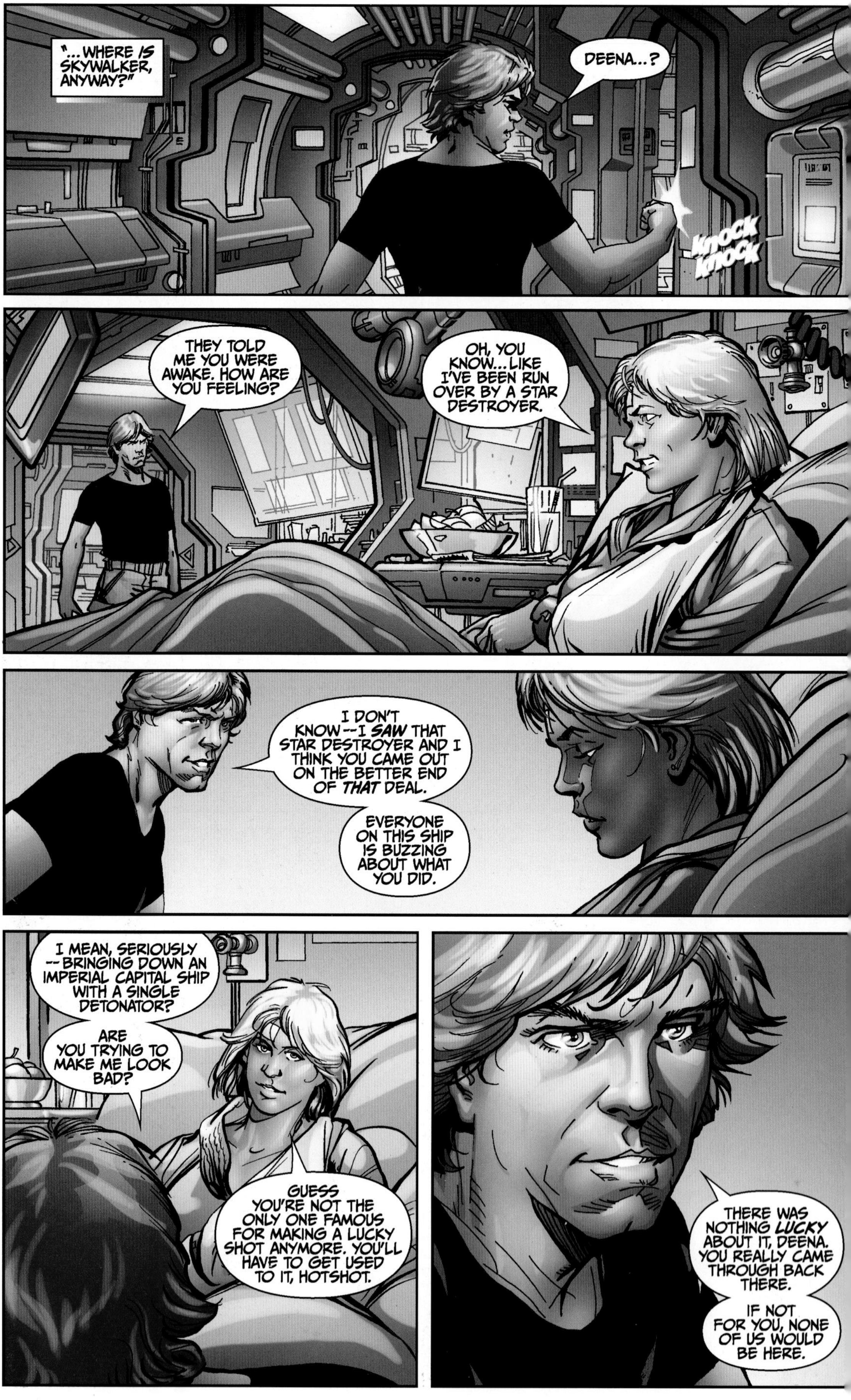
"...WHERE IS SKYWALKER, ANYWAY?"
DEENA...?
KNOCK KNOCK
THEY TOLD ME YOU WERE AWAKE. HOW ARE YOU FEELING?
OH, YOU KNOW...LIKE I'VE BEEN RUN OVER BY A STAR DESTROYER.
I DON'T KNOW--I SAW THAT STAR DESTROYER AND I THINK YOU CAME OUT ON THE BETTER END OF THAT DEAL.
EVERYONE ON THIS SHIP IS BUZZING ABOUT WHAT YOU DID.
I MEAN, SERIOUSLY --BRINGING DOWN AN IMPERIAL CAPITAL SHIP WITH A SINGLE DETONATOR?
ARE YOU TRYING TO MAKE ME LOOK BAD?
GUESS YOU'RE NOT THE ONLY ONE FAMOUS FOR MAKING A LUCKY SHOT ANYMORE. YOU'LL HAVE TO GET USED TO IT, HOTSHOT.
THERE WAS NOTHING LUCKY ABOUT IT, DEENA. YOU REALLY CAME THROUGH BACK THERE.
IF NOT FOR YOU, NONE OF US WOULD BE HERE.

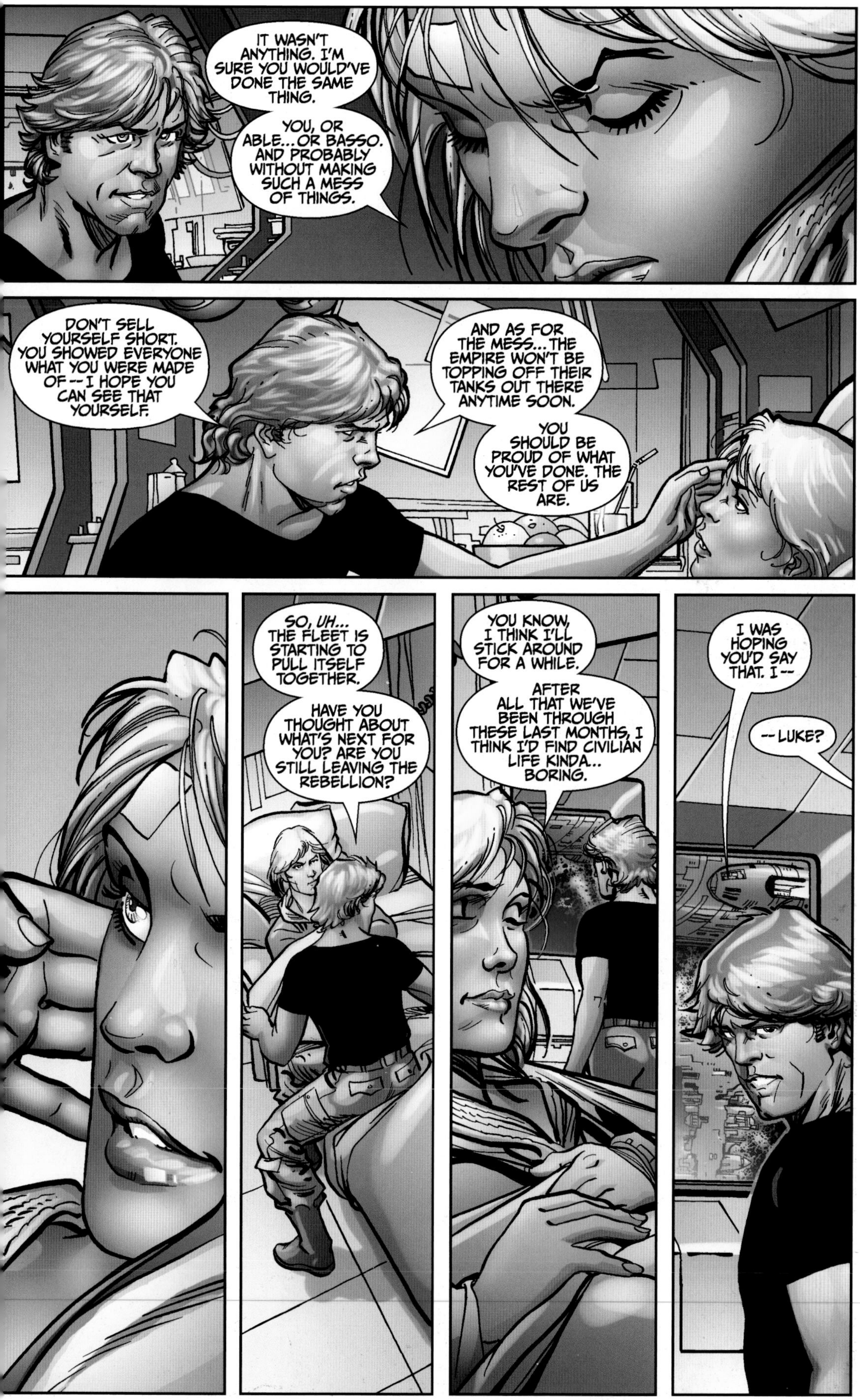
IT WASN'T ANYTHING. I'M SURE YOU WOULD'VE DONE THE SAME THING.
YOU, OR ABLE...OR BASSO. AND PROBABLY WITHOUT MAKING SUCH A MESS OF THINGS.
DON'T SELL YOURSELF SHORT. YOU SHOWED EVERYONE WHAT YOU WERE MADE OF -- I HOPE YOU CAN SEE THAT YOURSELF.
AND AS FOR THE MESS...THE EMPIRE WON'T BE TOPPING OFF THEIR TANKS OUT THERE ANYTIME SOON.
YOU SHOULD BE PROUD OF WHAT YOU'VE DONE. THE REST OF US ARE.
SO, *UH*... THE FLEET IS STARTING TO PULL ITSELF TOGETHER.
HAVE YOU THOUGHT ABOUT WHAT'S NEXT FOR YOU? ARE YOU STILL LEAVING THE REBELLION?
YOU KNOW, I THINK I'LL STICK AROUND FOR A WHILE.
AFTER ALL THAT WE'VE BEEN THROUGH THESE LAST MONTHS, I THINK I'D FIND CIVILIAN LIFE KINDA... BORING.
I WAS HOPING YOU'D SAY THAT. I --
-- LUKE?

I'M SORRY TO INTERRUPT -- ADMIRAL ACKBAR'S LOOKING FOR YOU. CAN YOU COME WITH ME TO THE BRIDGE?

HI, DEENA. HOW ARE YOU FEELING?

OH, YOU KNOW...

THIS SOUNDS IMPORTANT. ARE YOU --?

DUTY CALLS. I'M FINE -- THANKS FOR COMING TO SEE ME.

BUT, HEY -- YOU TWO?

TRY TO HOLD OFF ON TACKLING ANY MORE IMPOSSIBLE MISSIONS UNTIL I'M HEALED UP, OKAY?

I THINK WE CAN DO THAT.

WHEN DEENA SHAN JOINED THE REBELLION, HER EXPECTATIONS WERE MODEST.

SHE ONLY WANTED TO SAVE THE GALAXY.

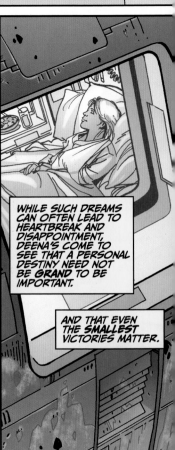

WHILE SUCH DREAMS CAN OFTEN LEAD TO HEARTBREAK AND DISAPPOINTMENT, DEENA'S COME TO SEE THAT A PERSONAL DESTINY NEED NOT BE GRAND TO BE IMPORTANT.

AND THAT EVEN THE SMALLEST VICTORIES MATTER.

STAR WARS GRAPHIC NOVEL TIMELINE (IN YEARS)

Tales of the Jedi—5,000–3,986 BSW4
Knights of the Old Republic—3,964–3,963 BSW4
Jedi vs. Sith—1,000 BSW4
Jedi Council: Acts of War—33 BSW4
Prelude to Rebellion—33 BSW4
Darth Maul—33 BSW4
Episode I: The Phantom Menace—32 BSW4
Outlander—32 BSW4
Emissaries to Malastare—32 BSW4
Jango Fett: Open Seasons—32 BSW4
Twilight—31 BSW4
Bounty Hunters—31 BSW4
The Hunt for Aurra Sing—30 BSW4
Darkness—30 BSW4
The Stark Hyperspace War—30 BSW4
Rite of Passage—28 BSW4
Jango Fett—27 BSW4
Zam Wesell—27 BSW4
Honor and Duty—24 BSW4
Episode II: Attack of the Clones—22 BSW4
Clone Wars—22–19 BSW4
Clone Wars Adventures—22–19 BSW4
General Grievous—22–19 BSW4
Episode III: Revenge of the Sith—19 BSW4
Dark Times—19 BSW4
Droids—5.5 BSW4
Boba Fett: Enemy of the Empire—3 BSW4
Underworld—1 BSW4
Episode IV: A New Hope—SW4
Classic Star Wars—0–3 ASW4
A Long Time Ago . . . —0–4 ASW4
Empire—0 ASW4
Rebellion—0 ASW4
Vader's Quest—0 ASW4
Boba Fett: Man with a Mission—0 ASW4
Jabba the Hutt: The Art of the Deal—1 ASW4
The Force Unleashed—2 ASW4
Splinter of the Mind's Eye—2 ASW4
Episode V: The Empire Strikes Back—3 ASW4
Shadows of the Empire—3.5 ASW4
Episode VI: Return of the Jedi—4 ASW4
X-Wing Rogue Squadron—4–5 ASW4
Mara Jade: By the Emperor's Hand—4 ASW4
Heir to the Empire—9 ASW4
Dark Force Rising—9 ASW4
The Last Command—9 ASW4
Dark Empire—10 ASW4
Boba Fett: Death, Lies, and Treachery—10 ASW4
Crimson Empire—11 ASW4
Jedi Academy: Leviathan—12 ASW4
Union—19 ASW4
Chewbacca—25 ASW4
Legacy—130–137 ASW4

Old Republic Era
25,000 – 1000 years before
Star Wars: A New Hope

Rise of the Empire Era
1000 – 0 years before
Star Wars: A New Hope

Rebellion Era
0 – 5 years after
Star Wars: A New Hope

New Republic Era
5 – 25 years after
Star Wars: A New Hope

New Jedi Order Era
25+ years after
Star Wars: A New Hope

Legacy Era
130+ years after
Star Wars: A New Hope

Infinities
Does not apply to timeline

Sergio Aragonés Stomps Star Wars
Star Wars Tales
Star Wars Infinities
Tag and Bink
Star Wars Visionaries

SW4 = before *Episode IV: A New Hope*. ASW4 = after *Episode IV: A New Hope*.

STAR WARS®
CLONE WARS

Experience all the excitement and drama of the Clone Wars! Look for these trade paperbacks at a comics shop or bookstore near you!

Volume 1: The Defense of Kamino
ISBN 978-1-56971-962-6
$14.95

Volume 2: Victories and Sacrifices
ISBN 978-1-56971-969-5
$14.95

Volume 3: Last Stand on Jabiim
ISBN 978-1-59307-006-9
$14.95

Volume 4: Light and Dark
ISBN 978-1-59307-195-0
$16.95

Volume 5: The Best Blades
ISBN 978-1-59307-273-5
$14.95

Volume 6: On the Fields of Battle
ISBN 978-1-59307-352-7
$17.95

Volume 7: When They Were Brothers
ISBN 978-1-59307-396-1
$17.95

Volume 8: The Last Siege, The Final Truth
ISBN 978-1-59307-482-1
$17.95

Volume 9: Endgame
ISBN 978-1-59307-553-8
$17.95

To find a comics shop in your area, call 1-888-266-4226

DARK HORSE BOOKS

For more information or to order direct:
• On the web: darkhorse.com
• E-mail: mailorder@darkhorse.com
• Phone: 1-800-862-0052
Mon.-Fri. 9 A.M. to 5 P.M. Pacific Time
*Prices and availability subject to change without notice.
STAR WARS © 2008 Lucasfilm Ltd. & ™ (BL8004)